**Walther's Pastorale**

that is

# American Lutheran Pastoral Theology

by Dr. C. F. W. Walther

*translated and abridged by John M. Drickamer
from the Fifth Edition, 1906.*

LUTHERAN NEWS, INC.
New Haven, Missouri

WALTHER'S PASTORALE
American Lutheran Pastoral Theology

Copyright 1995 © Lutheran News, Inc. All rights reserved. No portion of this book may be reproduced in any form, except for quotations in reviews, articles and speeches, without permission from the publisher.

Library of Congress Card 94-74311
Lutheran News, Inc.
3277 Boeuf Lutheran Rd
New Haven, MO 63068
Published 1995
Printed in the United States of America,
Morris Publishing, Kearney, NE
ISBN 0-9644799-0-7

## *Table of Contents*

1. The Definition of Pastoral Theology .................................................. 8
2. The Acquisition of Pastoral Theology ............................................... 11
3. The Sources of Pastoral Theology .................................................... 13
4. The Regular Call to the Pastoral Office ............................................ 16
5. The Valid, Legitimate Call to the Pastoral Office ............................. 21
6. The Conditions of a Call .................................................................... 31
7. The External Arrangements of a Call ................................................ 40
8. The Examination and Ordination of a Candidate ............................. 44
9. The First Sermon by the Pastor ......................................................... 51
10. The First Visitation by the Pastor .................................................... 55
11. The Requirements of Public Preaching ........................................... 60
12. The Administration of Holy Baptism .............................................. 86
13. The Persons to Be Baptized ............................................................. 92
14. The Liturgical Customs of Baptism ............................................... 100
15. The Communicants: Announcement ............................................. 107
16. The Communicants: Private Absolution ....................................... 120
17. The Administration of Holy Communion ..................................... 130
18. The Persons to Be Communed ...................................................... 146
19. The Wedding and Marriage ........................................................... 152
20. The Persons to Be Married: Civil Laws ........................................ 155
21. The Persons to Be Married: Forbidden Degrees ........................... 157
22. The Persons to be Married: Previous Marriages .......................... 160
23. The Public Announcement of a Wedding ..................................... 169
24. The Wedding Ceremony ................................................................ 171
25. The Case of Adultery and Divorce ................................................ 174
26. The Case of Desertion and Divorce .............................................. 177
27. The Institution of Confirmation .................................................... 185
28. The Confirmation Instruction ........................................................ 188
29. The Pastoral Care of the Youth ..................................................... 191
30. The Private Pastoral Care of Souls ............................................... 195
31. The Pastoral Care of the Sick ........................................................ 199
32a. The First Visit to the Patient ....................................................... 203
32b. The Condition of the Patient ....................................................... 204

## Table of Contents

32c. The Primary Need of the Patient .................................. 206
32d. The Approach to the Patient .......................................... 207
32e. The Critically Ill Patient................................................ 210
33. The Patient to Be Communed ....................................... 212
34. The Pastoral Care of the Troubled ................................ 214
35. Welfare of the Congregation's Needy ........................... 218
36. The Pastoral Care of the Dying .................................... 223
37. The Christian Funeral and Burial ................................ 226
38. The Members of Another Parish ................................. 231
39. The Administration of Christian Discipline ............... 234
40. The Order of Fraternal Discipline ............................... 238
41. The Case of Public Repentance .................................. 244
42. The Case of Excommunication .................................. 247
43. The Readmission of the Excommunicated ................. 252
44. The Congregation's Officers ....................................... 254
45. The Congregational Meetings .................................... 257
46. The Admission of New Members .............................. 261
47. The Constitution of the Congregation ...................... 264
48. The Personal Life of the Pastor ................................. 266
49. The Pastor's Synodical Membership ......................... 270
50. The Decision About a Call ......................................... 274

# Author's Foreword

The present writing is in essence a reprint of a longer series of articles which already appeared from 1865 to 1871 under the title, "Materialen zur Pastoraltheologie" ["Materials for Pastoral Theology"] in volumes eleven to seventeen of *Lehre und Wehre*, a theological and church-news monthly magazine. In order not to make the book too large and expensive, the author has permitted himself to expand it only in some places with additions that seemed necessary.

The reader may excuse the name *Pastoraltheologie* [Pastoral Theology] by the intention to give a full book title to the building blocks now presented in book form. The predicate, *Amerikanisch-Lutherische* [American Lutheran], needs no excuse since, in selecting the pastoral-theological materials, the needs of an American Lutheran pastor set the standard.

May the Lord of the Church add His blessing to this small contribution to the correct administration of the holy preaching office. The author hopes all the more for this blessing since he has not only presented what is his own but has much more gathered pastoral-theological material scattered in works of learned theologians.

St. Louis, Missouri, December 1872
C. F. W. Walther

# Translator's Preface

Dr. C. F. W. Walther's *Amerikanisch-Lutherische Pastoraltheologie*, widely known as his *Pastorale*, has never been available to pastors who did not read German. This translation aims to remedy that situation. A few words are in order about the way in which the translation and abridgement have been done.

The translation of Walther's words is more idiomatic than literal, but the translator believes that it is accurate in substance and meaning. To aid the modern reader, long sentences and paragraphs have been divided. Material that Walther quotes from other sources has been treated more literally.

Walther's words have been abridged in two ways. Some sentences and paragraphs have been omitted as not directly relevant. Many sentences have been shortened by dropping smaller German words unnecessary to the meaning. Otherwise the book would be full of words such as "indeed" and "nevertheless," which are superfluous in current American style but which were used almost as a sort of verbal punctuation in German in Walther's day. No ellipses have been used in dealing with Walther's words. Omissions from quotations are indicated by ellipses.

Material quoted from Luther has been translated directly from the German. No attempt has been made to locate the sources in any English edition. The references are those given by Walther, with volume and column numbers in the Walch, the Erlangen, or another edition. When Walther does not specify one edition, it is probable that the Walch edition is meant. The titles of Luther's individual writings have been translated into English to help the reader locate them in an English edition.

Quotations fom the Book of Concord have been translated directly from the German. No reference is given to a modern edition of the Book of Concord.

For quotations from other works, Walther's references have been given in the form he used. Only experts will refer to those works anyway. Hopefully they can find their way on the basis of Walther's abbreviations.

Words in parentheses are Walther's. Some footnotes by Walther have been put into the text as paragraphs in brackets, either translated or summarized as indicated. All other words or comments in brackets are the translator's.

The content of Walther's *Pastorale* will be uncomfortable for those who have compromised with the modern world or with Reformed teachings in areas such as admission to Holy Communion or the role of women in the church. But Walther's Bible-based principles are still valid and fully applicable today, for they are not from Walther, nor from Luther, but from God's Word, the Bible. Those who want to change the principles of Lutheran pastoral theology must argue—not with Walther, nor with Luther—but with the Triune God, Whose Word establishes those principles for all times and ages.

A note of caution is in order from this translator, who is a pastor, to all the pastors and students who read this book. Do not read the book at all if you want to feel comfortable or take it easy in the ministry! Read it only if you want to be faithful and diligent in the holy preaching office!

> Lake County, Oregon
> John M. Drickamer

# 1

# The Definition of Pastoral Theology

Pastoral theology is the God-given (*theosdotos*) practical ability of the soul, acquired (*acquisitus*) through certain auxiliary means, by virtue of which a minister of the church is enabled to carry out all his functions as such in a valid (*rato*) and legitimate (*legitime*) way, to the glory of God, for the salvation of his listeners and himself.

**Comment 1.**
Pastoral theology, like theology in general, can be considered in terms of doctrine, and a kind of book also bears that name. But in those cases it is pastoral theology only in a relative sense, only in a certain relationship, when it is taught or written. Before that can happen it must already be present in a person's soul.

In order to clarify a matter, it is necessary to know what it is essentially and originally (*principaliter*), properly and absolutely, apart from everything relative and non-essential. So we start with the definition of pastoral theology found in the older, orthodox teachers of our church, as its nature is considered subjectively or concretely, as it exists in a subject of concrete person, who has the right to be called a theologian. So we do not call it a doctrine or a book. It is that only by metonymy (the figure of speech in which the effect bears the name of the cause or the container bears the name of the contents). Instead, we call it an ability.

**Comment 2.**
When we call pastoral theology an ability, that means that it is not merely a body of knowledge but rather a disposition or condition of the soul, a preparation to deal with the object. It should indicate at the outset that "equipment" (*exartisis*) and "sufficiency" (*hikanotes*) which the apostle requires of a minister of the church

# The Definition of Pastoral Theology

(2 Tim. 3:17; 2 Cor. 3:5).

When we call pastoral theology a practical ability, that means that it is not a theoretical ability, not a science that has knowledge as its final goal. It is practical in general because its purpose, as that of all theology, consists in leading the sinner to salvation through faith. It is practical also in a narrower sense because its specific object consists in the work or official functions of a pastor, the churchly ministry (*ministerium ecclesiasticum*). It means, according to the apostolic requirement, that through God's Word a man of God be "furnished unto all good works" that his office involves, namely "for doctrine, for reproof, for correction, for instruction in righteousness" (2 Tim. 3:16-17.)

The late Dr. Rudelbach says in a published lecture: "You remember that, with the older [theologians] we designate theology as a practical ability; we cannot give up this designation; it is the living center of our treatment. Theology is practical through and through, practical in roots, means, and relations. But we are still

**Fig. 1: C.F.W. Walther receives his doctoral diploma, 1878.**
Courtesy of Concordia Historical Institute.

justified in calling those disciplines (catechetics, homiletics, liturgics) practical in the narrower sense . . . because they mainly represent the Word in the direct application . . . This now connects . . . doctrine and life and carries the results of the former into the latter. It does not first make it alive (it must be alive in itself if it is of the right nature) but rather shows its living power." ("Ueber den Begriff der Theologie und den der neutestamentlichen Isagogik," in the *Zeitschrift* of Rudelbach and Guerike, 1848, first quarter, pp. 27-28).

When we call pastoral theology a God-given practical ability, that means that it is a supernatural ability to be attained not through human power and diligence but only through the work of the Holy Spirit. It presupposes justifying faith, and only one who stands in grace, only a regenerate person, can have it as the apostle explicitly says (2 Cor. 2:16; 3:5-6). John Gerhard writes; "True theology consists more in attitude (*in affectu*) than in knowledge" (*Methodus studii th.*, Jena, 1654, pp. 14-17).

When we call pastoral theology an ability acquired through certain auxiliary means, that means that it is not that extraordinary theological ability which the apostles and prophets received through direct illumination, but rather that which is indirectly wrought by the Holy Spirit. That is what the apostle has in mind when he writes; "Give attendance to reading, . . . . Meditate upon these things; give thyself wholly to them; that thy profiting may appear to all. Take heed to thyself, and unto the doctrine; continue in them: for in doing this thou shalt both save thyself, and them that hear thee" (1 Tim. 4:13-16).

Ludwig Hartmann writes: "What Tertullian once correctly said about Christians: Christians are made, not born (*Christiani non nascuntur, sed fiunt*), is true also with respect to faithful ministers and teachers of the church, who need a long preparation and much study if they want to be qualified when they enter this very exalted office. For mere personal respectability or seriousness and holiness of life are not sufficient here; rather theological knowledge is also required" (*Pastorale ev.*, Nuremberg, 1697, p. 237).

The apostle says that the general and specific purpose ascribed to pastoral theology in the definition is correct when he writes: "Whatsoever ye do, do all to the glory of God" (1 Cor. 10:31); and "For in doing this thou shalt both save thyself, and them that hear thee" (1 Tim. 4:16).

# 2

# The Acquisition of Pastoral Theology

In order to acquire theological ability in general and pastoral theological ability in particular, the three parts are specifically required which are included in Luther's well-known axiom: *Oratio, meditatio, tentatio faciunt theologum* ["Prayer, study, temptation make a theologian"].

**Comment 1.**
Luther writes: "I want to indicate to you the right way to study theology, which I have practiced myself; . . . . And that is the way which the holy King David (it was certainly followed also by all patriarchs and prophets) teaches in Psalm 119; there you will find three rules, richly presented throughout the Psalm, and that is: *oratio, meditatio, tentatio.—*

"First you should know that holy Scripture is such a book that it turns the wisdom of all other books into foolishness, for none but this alone teaches eternal life. So you should absolutely despair of your mind and understanding, for you will not get it that way, . . . . Rather kneel down in your chamber and, in proper humility and seriousness, ask God to give you the Holy Spirit through His dear Son. He will illuminate, direct, and give you understanding; . . . .

"Second, you should meditate, that is, not just in the heart but rather also outwardly, always push and pursue the spoken Word and the literal words of the book. Read them and read them again, with diligent guard against getting tired of it or thinking that, after one or two times, you have read, heard, said enough and understand everything thoroughly; for no special theologian will ever come out of that; . . . .

"Third there is *tentatio*, temptation [*Anfechtung*], that is the touchstone. That will teach you not only to know and understand but also to experience how correct, how truthful, how sweet, how dear, how powerful, how comforting God's Word is, wisdom above all wisdom . . . . For as soon as God's Word arises through you, the devil will visit you and make you a real doctor and teach you through temptation. For I myself (to mix myself like mouse dung in with the pepper) owe a great deal to my Papists for attacking, pressuring, and troubling me, that is, for making me a fairly good theologian, to which I had otherwise not attained" (Erlangen, LXIII, 403-406). [Both the Latin word *tentatio* and the German word *Anfechtung* mean "attack, assault."]

With reference to this saying of Luther, Rudelbach writes: You know the great saying of Luther: *Oratio, meditatio, tentatio faciunt theologum.* This saying contains our whole theological method. Nothing is to be added to it, and nothing is to be taken away, as in the case with every thought sealed by the Spirit of God" (op. cit., p. 10).

## Comment 2.

As for the second rule, that meditation or study is necessary to acquire theological ability, Luther writes in his Foreword to Spangenberg's 1542 *Postille*: "Therefore it is said: watch, study, *attende lectioni* (give attendance to reading, 1 Tim. 4:13). Truly, you cannot read Scripture too much; and what you read, you cannot understand too well; and what you understand, you cannot teach too well; and what you teach, you cannot live too well. *Experto crede Ruperto* (believe one who has experienced it). It is the devil, it is the world, it is our flesh that rage and struggle against us. So, dear Lords and Brethren, Pastors and Preachers, pray, read, study, be diligent! Truly, at this wicked, scandalous time, it is not the time to laze around, to snore and sleep. Use your gift, which has been entrusted to you, and reveal the mystery of Christ" (Erlangen, LXIII, 370-372).

# 3

# The Sources of Pastoral Theology

Among the human writings which, after Holy Scripture itself, serve the necessary *meditatio* [study] are to be named above all Luther's collected works, in which pastoral theological material is scattered everywhere, and then, in addition to complete pastoral theological texts, those writings which deal with individual parts of the subject or contribute to it, as well as works of casuistry by our orthodox theologians.

**Comment 1.**
The most important study for acquiring pastoral aptitude and fitness is and remains holy Scripture, especially the pastoral epistles of the Apostle Paul. In his preface to 1 Timothy, Luther writes correctly: "St. Paul writes this epistle as a model for all bishops [pastors], as to what they should teach and how they should govern Christendom in all estates so that it should not be necessary to govern Christians by human opinion." But it would be contrary to Scripture to despise all human writings and to want to draw everything directly from Scripture (see 1 Cor. 12:7 ff.; 14:32).

**Comment 2.**
As to the importance of studying Luther's writings, we present the following testimonies. Melanchthon evaluates this way: "Dr. Pomeranus [Bugenhagen] is a grammatician, who searches through the words of the text. I am a dialectician and consider the order, the context, the individual members, the consequences. Dr. Jonas is an orator and understands how to present matters with oratorical charm. Luther—is all [of these] and none of us can compare to him" (N. Selnecker, *Recit. de autorit. Lutheri et Phil.*, p. 323).

The Wuertemberg theologian Brenz writes: "Luther alone lives in his writings. In comparison to him we are all like a dead letter"

(Loescher, *Unschuldige Nachrichten*, 1718, p. 320).

The Brunswick theologian Urbanus Rhegius writes: "Luther is such and so great a theologian that no age has had a similar one . . . . We, indeed, all write and push Scripture, but compared to Luther we are schoolboys; this judgement does not flow from love; rather love [flows] from the judgement" (*op. cit.*).

Not only do all enlightened teachers of our church write this way about Luther's writings, but the most respected teachers of other fellowships do not judge otherwise. So among others, Calvin writes: "I ask you to take this to heart: first, what a great man Luther is and by what great gifts he is distinguished, with what courage, with what constancy, with what ability, with what urgent power he has striven so far to overthrow the kingdom of Antichrist and at the same time to spread the teaching of salvation. I am accustomed to say often: even if he called me a devil, I would still show him so much honor as to call him an excellent servant of God" (*Epp.*, ed. Beza, ep. 57).

After applying Is. 57:1 to Luther in his commentary on Isaiah, Calvin continues; "I believe that I must primarily cite this (example) both because it has recently occurred and because it should be more illuminating in such an excellent herald of the Gospel and prophet of God" (*Opp.*, tom. 3, p. 363).

Beza, known among the Reformed as a yet more vehement opponent of Lutheran doctrine than Calvin himself, must still confess in his vehement writing against Brenz: "Luther was a truly admirable man, and anyone who does not perceive the Spirit of God in him does not perceive anything" (*Tract. adv. Brent.*, fol. 190).

John Bunyan (d. 1688), the well-known English Baptist, author of *Pilgrim's Progress*, tells in his autobiography that he first came to firm faith through reading Luther. Then he adds; "It seems to me that I must say openly that I have to set this book of Luther's, the explanation of the Epistle to the Galatians, above all books (except for Holy Scripture) that I have ever seen because it is so glorious and comforting for a wounded conscience" (see *The Most Tender Heart of the Love of Christ*, appendix, p. 84).

The founder of Methodism, John Wesley, confessed that he was first converted at an assembly of the Moravians in Aldersgate Street in London when he heard the reading of Luther's preface to Paul's Epistle to the Romans!

When Erasmus was offered a bishopric in 1520 if he would take

## The Sources of Pastoral Theology

up his pen against Luther, for the authority of the Pope, he answered at that time: "Luther is too great for me to write against him. Luther is too great for me to understand him. Yes, Luther is so great that I learn more and benefit more from reading one little page of Luther than from all [the writings of] Thomas [Aquinas]" (Gerhard, *Conf. Cath.*, fol. 59).

Melanchthon writes in his preface to the third part of the Wittenberg edition of Luther's Latin works: "I remember that Erasmus of Rotterdam used to say: There is no abler and better interpreter among all those whose writings we have since the apostles" (Walch, XIV, 539).

The famous Papist scholar Andreas Masius (d. 1573), co-editor of the Antwerp *Biblia Regia*, stated openly in the cloister vineyard, in a company of Papists and Lutherans: "There is more thorough theology on one page of Luther's than sometimes in a whole book of a church father" (Osiander, *Centur. 16. hist.*, p. 837).

It does not serve our purpose to cite more testimonies of that nature for the incomparable value of Luther's writings from people of almost all confessions, from all periods since Luther wrote, although large volumes could be filled with them. Luther's writings are an almost inexhaustible source for all branches of theology. We recall the saying of the very learned Altorf professor, Dr. Christoph Sonntag (d. 1717): *"Quo proprior Luthero, eo melior theologus"* ["The closer to Luther, the better the theologian"] (*Vitae theologor. Altorphinor., descript. a Zeltnero*, p. 453).

[In several following pages, Walther explains the value of other pastoral theological texts, which are not available in English. He praises especially *Pastorale Lutheri* by Conrad Porta as well as books by John Ludwig Hartmann, Solomon Deyling, and others. He recommends books on casuistry by orthodox theologians, careful studies of actual, specific cases (see *Lehre und Wehre*, IV, 345-349). Walther finally advises students to read biographies of faithful pastors from the past.]

# 4

## The Regular Call to the Pastoral Office

Article XIV of the Augsburg Confession teaches according to God's Word (Rom. 10:15; Jer. 23:21; James 3:1; Heb. 5:4-5; see the beginning of almost all of Paul's epistles): "No one should teach or preach publicly in the church or administer the Sacraments without a regular call." After the ability for the office has been acquired, the first requirement for God-pleasing and blessed conduct of the office is that the preacher be regularly called to it and be certain of it.

**Comment 1.**
About the necessity of the call for the God-pleasing conduct of the office, Luther writes: "To a good work there belongs a certain, divine call, and not one's own devotion, which is called one's own notions. It gets bitter to those who do have a certain call from God to begin something and carry it out even though God is by them and with them. So what should the senseless fools do who want to go to it without a call and seek only their own honor and glory! For it cannot be any other way than that one who undertakes something without God's call is seeking his own honor. For he is his own god, teaching himself what to do, and does not need God and His Word for it...." (Glosses on the Intended Imperial Edict; Walch, XVI, 2061).

Luther writes: "But now it is highly necessary that one knows things very well as everyone should be certain of his call because of the poisonous, devilish, fanatical spirits [*Schwarmgeister*] who are so skilled at exalting themselves beyond measure, that they have been called from heaven above and are driven by the Spirit, and deceive many people with such babbling although it is nothing but a stinking lie. That is why we certainly need to be sure of our call so that each can boast with John the Baptist and openly say

# The Regular Call to the Pastoral Office

(Luke 3:2) the Word of the Lord came to me so that I now preach, baptize, and administer the Sacrament as I have been ordered and called . . . that I should do it. . . .

"Therefore one should not consider the call a minor matter. It is not enough, even if one already has the pure and unalloyed Word of God and upright doctrine; rather one must also be certain of the call that it is correct. For whoever breaks in uncalled, on his own, certainly comes for nothing else than that he wants to choke and kill (John 10:10). . . .

"So even those who have a correct, certain, divine, and holy call must also in addition have the certain, correct, and pure doctrine; must endure much hard, manifold battle; and can still hardly stand against so much and unceasing deceit of the devil and tyranny of the world. What should he then be able to do who is not at all certain of his call and whose doctrine is also false and impure!

"So this is our comfort that we are in the preaching office, that we indeed have a holy and heavenly office, have been called to it in a correct and orderly way, of which we can also boast against the gates of hell. But it is truly a very atrocious and horrible thing if the conscience speaks this way: Oh, Lord God, what have you done? You have done this and that without call and command! Then such a horror and sorrow of heart begins in the conscience that such an uncalled preacher could easily wish that he had never in his life heard and read what he had taught. For disobedience makes all works evil, no matter how good they may otherwise be in themselves, so that even the greatest and best works become the greatest and worst sins.

"So you can now well see how useful and highly necessary this boast of our office is. When I was previously a young theologian and new doctor, it did not seem very nice to me that St. Paul made such a boast and noise about his call in all his epistles. But I did not at all understand what a special meaning and cause he had for it. . . . For at that time I also did not yet know what a great thing the preaching office was. At that time I also did not yet know either the doctrine of faith or what a correct conscience would be. . ." (Large Commentary on Galatians, on Gal. 1:1-2; Walch, VIII, 1578-82).

In the same book Luther writes: "One must always watch out diligently for such fanatics [*Schwaermer*] and sectarians who are so adept that they think, if they have heard only a sermon or two or read a book or two, that they are already ready to be teachers above all teachers and students, even though no one has ordered, called, or sent them. And such unlearned handworkers may also be so foolhardy as to frivolously take on and assume such a great, high, heavy, and dangerous office without considering that they have never yet in their lives been under a real spiritual assault [*Anfechtung*], never yet seriously felt in their hearts terror before God's wrath and judgment, but much less tasted his grace" (On Gal. 1:6; Walch, VIII, 1637).

Luther writes: "If the devil can deceive the teachers whom God Himself has called, ordered, and consecrated, so that they teach falsely and persecute the truth; how should he then teach anything good and not much rather pure devilish lies through those whom he himself, without and against God's command, drives and has consecrated? I have often said and say it still: I would not give up my doctorate for the world, for I would finally have to lose heart and despair in the great and serious matter that lies upon me if I had begun it as a sneak without call and command. But now God and all the world must bear me witness that I have begun it publicly in my office as doctor and preacher and have brought it so far with God's grace and help.

"Some admittedly claim that St. Paul in 1 Cor. 14 gave everyone the freedom to preach in the congregation, even to bark against the regular preacher, where Paul says (v. 30): 'If any thing be revealed to another that sitteth by, let the first hold his peace.' So the sneaks think that they have the authority and the right, into whatever church they come, to judge the preacher and to preach otherwise. But that is a big, big error. The sneaks do not consider the text correctly and take from it, indeed, brew into it, what they want.

"At this place St. Paul speaks of the prophets who should teach there and not of the people who are listening there. But prophets are teachers who have the preaching office in the church. Why else would one be called a prophet? So let the sneak first prove that he is a prophet or teacher in the church to which he comes and who has commanded him to such an office there; then one should hear him according to St. Paul's doctrine. But if he does not prove it, then let him run away to the devil, who has sent and commanded him to steal another's preaching office in a church to which he does not even belong as a listener or a pupil, much less as a prophet and teacher" (1531 Letter to Eberhard von der Tannen, About the

# The Regular Call to the Pastoral Office

Sneaks and Corner Preachers; Walch, XX, 2080f. See the whole letter).

Martin Chemnitz writes: "It is also beneficial to consider why so much depends on a minister of the church having a correct call. It is not to be thought that this happens on the basis of a human institution or only for the sake of order. Much rather it has the most important causes, and the consideration of them teaches a great deal.

"1. Because the office of the Word is the office of God Himself, which He Himself wants to exercise in His church through regular means and instruments (Luke 1:70; Heb. 1:1; 2 Cor. 5:20). So it is absolutely necessary, if you want to be a faithful shepherd of the church, that you are absolutely certain that God wants to make use of your services and that you are such an instrument of His. For then you can also apply to yourself those statements of Scriptures: Is. 59:21; 2 Cor. 13:3; Luke 10:16; John 1:25).

"2. So that the office may be administered correctly and for the edification of the church, many spiritual gifts are necessary, but primarily divine government and protection. But he who has a legitimate call can call on God with a peaceful conscience and certainly expect to be heard, according to the promises of 2 Cor. 3:2; 1 Tim. 4:14.

"3. The primary nerve of the office is that God wants to be present in the office with His Spirit and grace and wants to be effective through it. Now he who has been legitimately called to the office and administers it in an orderly way, can believe with certainty that those promises apply also to him: Is. 49:2; 51:16; Luke 1:76; 1 Tim. 4:16; 1 Cor. 15:58; 1 Cor. 16:9; 2 Cor. 2:12; John 10:3.

"4. The certainty of a divine call is useful for this that the ministers of the church conduct their office with that much greater diligence, faithfulness, and cheerfulness in the fear of the Lord and are not easily frightened away. Indeed, this doctrine of the call awakens true respect and obedience toward the office also in the listeners" (*Locc. theol.*, Part III, 1. de eccl., s. 4, fol. 120).

**Comment 2.**

Luther speaks in various places about how important the regular call is, not only for the preachers themselves but also for the congregation. He writes: "It is useful and necessary for the people that they be warded and deterred away from the sectarian spirits and can make this distinction between preachers: This is our preacher whom God has given us . . . That one snuck in or pushed himself in without command and to despise the former, and no one knows who he is or how much he is to be trusted. So we want to hear and remain with the former, whom God has given us. . .

"Anyone who wants to may insult and despise me because of my person, but because of my office you should respect me and lift me up, as dear as Christ and your salvation and blessedness are to you. For you are not my pastor or preacher, but rather God has installed me so that you receive the Gospel from me and come in the kingdom of God through my office" (Commentary on 1 Cor. 15, preached in 1534; on 1 Cor. 15:8-10; Walch, VIII, 1198-1200).

It cannot be expressed how important it is for the listeners to be certain of the divine call of their preacher. If the listeners are convinced of it, they will be satisfied at heart to have even a preacher with lesser gifts if only he is faithful. They will not leave their church and run after someone more highly gifted. They will rather in simplicity hold to this: Our preacher is the one whom God has given us, through whom God wants to lead us to heaven. Under his shepherding God will not let us lack anything that is necessary for our salvation.

At another place Luther writes: "So it is most necessary for the people to be certain of our call so that they really know that our doctrine is God's own Word. That is why we also boast so gloriously of it, and it is not vain and frivolous but rather totally holy boast and pride, boasted of only to spite the devil and the world. But with respect to God, it is a correct and truthful humility" (On Gal. 1:1; Walch, VIII, 1582).

# 5

# The Valid, Legitimate Call to the Pastoral Office

In the question of the call to a specific pastoral office, two matters come into consideration: 1. whether it is valid (*ratus*), and 2. whether it is legitimate (*legitimus, rectus*). It is valid if it is extended by those who have the right and authority from God to do so. It is legitimate if it has been arrived at in a correct way.

**Comment 1.**
The validity of a call depends on those who extend it having the right and the authority from God to do so. That lies in the nature of the matter and needs no proof. But that it is every Christian local congregation that has this right and this authority can be seen in the following writings:

"Reason and cause from Scripture that a Christian Assembly [*Versammlung*] or Congregation [*Gemeinde*] Has the Right and the Authority to Judge All Doctrine and to Call, Install, and Depose Teachers," by Dr. M. Luther, 1523 (Walch, X, 1794ff.; Erlangen, XXII, 140ff.).

"Letter About How Ministers of the Church Should Be Chosen and Installed, to the Council and Congregation of the City of Prague," by M. Luther (Walch, X, 1808ff.).

"Who Has Power, Authority, and Right to Call Preachers, by Tilemann Heshusius (St. Louis: L. Volkening, 1862, 8.).

A collection of testimonies for this doctrine from the Lutheran confessions and from the private writings of the orthodox teachers of our church's: "The Voice of our Churc in the Question of Church and Ministry" (Erlangen, 1852; second edition, 1865), Part II, Thesis 6, Section A. We refer here only to the following testimonies.

The Smalcald Articles say: "Where (*ubicunque*, wherever) the church is, there is the command to preach the Gospel. Therefore the churches must retain the authority to promote, elect, and ordain ministers of the church. And such authority is a gift, which has been given to the church by God and cannot be received from any human authority of the church, as St. Paul testifies in Eph. 4[:8], when he says: 'He ascended up on high, . . . and gave gifts unto men.' Here belong the statements of Christ that the keys are given to the whole church and not to some special persons, as the text says: 'Where two or three are gathered together in My name, there am I in the midst of them' [Matt. 18:20]. Finally, this is also confirmed by the statement of Peter: 'Ye are . . . a royal priesthood' [1 Pet. 2:9]. These words apply to the church, which because it alone has the priesthood, must also have the authority to elect and ordain ministers of the church."

Luther writes: "Where there is a holy Christian church, there must be all Sacraments, Christ Himself, and His Holy Spirit. Should we now be a holy Christian church and have the greatest and most necessary things, such as God's Word, Christ, Spirit, faith, prayer, Baptism, the Sacrament, keys, the [pastoral] office, etc., and should not have also the most minor things, namely the authority and right to call some persons to the office, to administer to us the Word, Baptism, the Sacrament, forgiveness [Absolution] (which are already there), and to serve in those things? What kind of a church would that be? Where would Christ's Word be where He says, Matt. 18:20: 'Where two or three, etc.'? And again, v. 19, 'If two of you shall agree on earth as touching any thing that they shall ask, it shall be done for them of My Father Which is in heaven'? If two or three have such authority, how much more a whole church?" ("Writing on Corner Masses and the Consecration of Priests," 1533; Walch, XIX, 1565).

After having proven in his letter to the council and congregation at Prague that every Christian originally has all rights and authorities of the priesthood, Luther continues: "But we have said all of this about the common rights and authority of all Christians. For since all Christians should have all things in common, . . . it is not proper for one who wants to promote himself, to appropriate for himself alone that which belongs to all of us. . . . But the right of the commonality requires that one, or as many as the congregation wants, be chosen and accepted to carry out these functions publicly instead of and in the name of all those who have just the same right, so that a horrible disorder does not occur among the people of God, and the church, in which everything should be

## The Valid, Legitimate Call to the Pastoral Office

done decently and in good order, as the apostle has taught (1 Cor. 14:40), does not become a Babylon" (Walch, X, 1857).

Luther writes: "That is the call of a public office among Christians. But if one would come into a group of non-Christians (heathens), there one might do as the apostles and not wait for a call. For they do not have the office of preaching there. And one may say: Here are non-Christians. I want to preach and instruct them in Christianity, and if a group comes together, chooses and calls me to be their bishop, then I will have a call" (On Ex. 3:1, III, 1079).

Luther writes: "Here (Matt. 18:19-20) we hear that even two or three, gathered in Christ's name, have all the authority of St. Peter and all the apostles. For the Lord Himself is there as he also says in John 14:23. So it has also happened that one person who believes in Christ has withstood a whole group, a Paphnutius at the Council of Nicea, and as the prophets withstood the kings of Israel, the priests, and all the people. In short, God will not be bound to the number, greatness, majesty, authority, and personality of people but rather will be only with those who love and hold His Word, even if they are only stable boys. What does He care about high, great, powerful lords? He alone is the greatest, highest, and most powerful. We have here the Lord Himself above all angels and creatures, Who says: They should all have the authority, the keys, and the office, even two simple Christians, gathered in His name" ("Against the Papacy at Rome, Established by the Devil," 1545; Walch, VII, 1346ff.).

So even if there are here no high, distinguished persons, royal officials, consistorial councils, etc., but only workers and farmers participating in the call, that does not rob it of its power and validity. Luther writes this comfort to the Bohemians, against the temptation of thinking that their small group cannot issue a valid divine call: "But if such a doubt tries to trouble and confuse you, that you would think that you are not a church or people of God, then here is my answer to that: one cannot recognize the church by outward manners; one recognizes it only by the Word of God" (Walch, X. 1870f.).

**Comment 2.**

For the call to the preaching office to be not only valid but also legitimate, it is necessary that the one called has not sought the office by pushing in, sneaking in through devious ways, convincing people, using the favor of one party, or bribery, but that he has accepted the call which has been extended to him, without his own participation, on the urging of others, out of obedience to God and the love for the neighbor.

Luther writes: "Now there are two kinds of calls to the preaching office. One comes from God without means. The other comes through people and yet also from God. One should not believe the first unless it is proven with miraculous signs.... Indeed, even if you show us signs, we still want to take a look first at what your doctrine is, whether it agrees with the Word of God. For false prophets can also do signs, as Moses said to the Jews (Deut. 13:1-4).

"The other comes through people and yet also from God, namely through means. And that is a call of love, as when one is chosen from the group to be bishop or preacher when it is seen that he has the Word of God and can also communicate it to others through his teaching and preaching.... If you are learned and understand God's Word well, if you also believe that you want to present it to others uprightly and beneficially, wait! If God wants it, He will surely find you.... Do not set any purpose, time, or place for Him. For He will drive you where you do not want to go, and you will not end up where you would like to be. If you were wiser and more clever than Solomon and Daniel, you should still flee, as from hell, from speaking even one word that you would like to be furthered or called to something. Believe me, no one will do any good by preaching unless he is furthered and pushed to preach and teach without his will and desire. For we have only one Teacher, our Lord Jesus Christ, Who alone teaches and produces fruit through His servants, whom He has called for it. But whoever teaches without a call does not teach without harming both himself and his listeners, for Christ is not with him" (Walch, XI, 2549, 2555).

They are not legitimately called who come first without a call and artfully bring it about that they are called afterwards. In a comment on Ex. 3:1, Luther writes about the sneaks: "Yes, they can certainly get behind people, sneak in, and wash long enough that they are afterwards chosen and called. One can soon talk people into doing it. But they are thieves, murderers, and wolves (John 10:1)" (Walch, III, 1077).

Carlstadt had a call like that. Luther writes about him: "But

## The Valid, Legitimate Call to the Pastoral Office

if he claims... that he was chosen by them to be their pastor and so has been outwardly called, then I answer; it does not matter to me that they called him afterwards. I am speaking about the first entrance.... How easily one has convinced a people! That is not being called. That is starting a sect and an uproar and despising authority" ("Against the Heavenly Prophets"; Walch, XX, 230).

But there can be cases in which offering oneself is not contrary to conscience and does not call into question the legitimacy of the call. According to 1 Tim. 3:1 and Is. 6:8, it may rather be the sign of a true divine call. Let us hear our Reformer [Luther] on this point also. He writes: "But one should also not reject those who form the attitude from a godly, good intention, that they are not considering their profit and pleasure, not their praise, not a good, soft life, but are pursuing only this that they would like to teach and preach God's Word. But they are rare birds. Indeed, one should praise such men, as St. Paul says in 1 Tim. 3:1: 'This is a true saying. If a man desire the office of a bishop, he desireth a good work.' But that is why he quickly adds in vv. 2ff. and says: 'A

**Fig. 2: Walther at the age of 32. Drawn by Gustav Pfau in 1843.**
Courtesy of Concordia Historical Institute.

bishop then must be blameless, the husband of one wife, vigilant, sober, . . .' and all that follows there. All that pertains to a bishop. Now one who desires that desires a precious work [Luther's translation of 'good work' in 1 Tim. 3:1]. For such an office calls for one who can despise honor, life, and all goods; for it is a service of the truth that has previously proclaimed and said in Matt. 10:22: 'and ye shall be hated of all men for My name's sake.' Since those who are drawn to it with force, without their own will, can hardly endure that, one hopes in vain that one will endure it who pursues it on his own, or one who pursues such an office without being moved inwardly by a special grace" (On Ps. 8:3; Walch, IV, 769f.).

## Comment 3.

What should they do whose call is valid but not legitimate? Our theologians answer that they should not leave the call but that repentance and faithfulness are necessary in the office. Naturally that presupposes that the one so called has the absolutely necessary aptitude to conduct the office. Luther writes: "Here the question is: whether it is permitted to offer oneself for a call? The answer is this: if it happens out of a carnal thought and intention, that is, from ambition or greed, then it is not at all fitting. Just the same, if one has come into the preaching office in this way, and is afterwards converted so that he becomes a different man, then it is good for him to remain in it" (Walch, VII, 116f.). [Walther also refers to Walch, X, 1825f.]

## Comment 4.

Here in America many congregations have the custom of calling the preachers only temporarily. But a congregation is not justified in extending such a call, and a preacher is not authorized to accept such a call. It is an abuse. It fights against the divinity of a correct call to a preaching office in the church, which is clearly testified to in God's Word (Acts 20:28; Eph. 4:11; 1 Cor. 12:28; Ps. 68:12; Is. 41:27).

For if God is really the One Who calls preachers, the congregations are only the instruments for separating the persons for the work to which the Lord has called them (Acts 13:1). The preacher stands in God's service and office, and no creature can dismiss God's servant from God's office unless it can be proven that God Himself has dismissed him from office (Jer. 15:19; see Hos. 4:6),

## The Valid, Legitimate Call to the Pastoral Office

in which case the congregation is not really dismissing the preacher but is only carrying out God's clear dismissal. If the congregation does it otherwise, then the instrument is making itself the mistress of the office (Matt. 23:8; see 2 Tim. 4:2-3) and is interfering in God's government.

The preacher who gives the congregation the right to call him in this way and to dismiss him arbitrarily, is making himself a hireling and servant of men. Such a call is not what God has ordained for the holy preaching office but something quite different that has nothing to do with it. It is not an indirect call from God through the church but rather a human contract. It is not a lifelong call but a temporary function outside of the divine ordinance, a human ordinance made against God's ordinance, or rather an atrocious disorder. So it is null and void, without any validity. One called in this way is not to be considered a minister of Christ or the church.

Such a call fights against the relationship in which congregation and preacher stand with each other according to God's Word. For it fights against the respect and obedience which the listeners should show toward those who administer the divine office according to God's Word (Luke 10:16; 1 Tim. 5:17; 1 Thess. 5:12-13; 1 Cor. 16:15-16; Heb. 13:17). For if the listeners really had that alleged authority, it would stand completely in their power to withdraw that respect and obedience.

Every kind of temporary call is against the faithfulness and constancy until death which God requires of preachers (1 Pet. 5:1-4; 1 Tim. 4:16; 1 Cor. 4:1ff.). It is against the accounting which the preacher will have to give as a watchman over their souls (Heb. 13:17). Finally a temporary call is against the practice which the Lord commanded and which the apostles followed. It is against the practice of the church at all times in which corruption in doctrine, life, order, and discipline had not entered.

It needs no proof that, when that kind of call exists, the church could never be properly provided for, have correct discipline practiced, be grounded in faith and godly living, or be extended. Such a call opens the gate and the door for all disorder, confusion, and harm by the gainsayers and by the men-pleasing, men-fearing belly-servants [see Rom. 16:17-18].

When the people at Zwickau had dismissed one of their preachers, Conrad Cordatus, because of his rebuking sermons,

Luther wrote to Valentin Hausmann in 1532: "You can well consider for yourself: when a young man has studied all his life, devoured his father's goods, and suffered all misfortune to be a pastor at Zwickau, ... that they should be the lords and the pastor should be the servant who would have to sit on the scales [be uncertain] every day. ... We are unwilling to do or permit that unless they want to confess that they are not Christians. We should and will suffer it from heathens, but Christ Himself does not want to suffer it from Christians. But if those at Zwickau, or you yourself, my dear lord and friend, do not want to nourish your brother, you can certainly let it go. Christ is somewhat richer than the world though He may seem to be poor. It says: *Esurientes implevit* ("He hath filled the hungry" [see Luke 1:53]; we will leave it at that, and those at Zwickau may pursue it further" (Walch, XXI, 357; Erlangen, LIV, 219).

Ludwig Hartmann writes: "We are God's servants, and the office is God's, to which we are called by God, through people. So this holy work must be handled in a holy manner, but not according to human arbitrariness. People can hire someone to herd sheep or cows, and then, if the service no longer pleases them, dismiss him at the determined time ... if they wish. But to treat a shepherd of souls in that way is within the authority of no human being. Nor can the minister of the Word himself accept the holy office in this way if he does not want to be a hireling. Those who were called in this way would certainly not carry out the office diligently and faithfully. Rather they would become flatterers and say that pleased the people, or they would have to expect every hour to be dismissed from the service" (*Pastorale evang.*, p. 104).

[Footnote: Those preachers are by no means guilty of conducting the office on a temporary basis who, without giving up the office to which they have a regular, legitimate call, and with the approval of their congregation, serve another one for a time on a loan basis.]

But as little as a conscientious preacher can accept a temporary call, so little can he let himself be bound to remain with one congregation, under all circumstances, until his death. Dr. Joh. Nikolaus Misler, professor at Giessen (d. 1683), writes: "To sell himself to one local congregation for his whole life overthrows the whole doctrine of the Gospel about the legitimate calling of preachers and denies God the authority to transfer His ministers, as seems good to Him, to work elsewhere in His vineyard. This

## The Valid, Legitimate Call to the Pastoral Office

undertaking lacks any basis in God's Word and his Christian church. At the same time it takes away from a preacher all authority to get out of an ungodly yoke, even for the most important and righteous reasons or even for the sake of conscience, so that the preacher would retain no freedom to contradict or, with Lot, to leave Sodom at God's command, even if the civil authority at the place would be overthrown or would degenerate into a godless and tyrannical one, or if atrocious abuses, heresies, and idolatries would be commanded. But one can promise to serve a congregation as long as one can remain with it in good conscience and to administer his office according to the proper freedom of the Holy Spirit" (*Opus novum quastt. practico-theol.*, fol. 491).

**Comment 5.**

It is not only sinful and dangerous to usurp an office without a valid and legitimate call; it is also sinful and dangerous to decline a valid and legitimate call because of human considerations (Jer. 1:4-8; Ex. 4:10-14). That is also not justified by a feeling of one's own inability or unworthiness, for "Who is sufficient for these things?" (2 Cor. 2:16 [Luther's translation: "Who is fit for it?"].

[In a footnote, Walther notes that the following quotations can also comfort those who are already in the ministry and are under temptation from thoughts about their own inability or unworthiness.]

Luther writes: "For if the people want to force and urge me, and I can do, or even if I cannot do, what is required of me, I will do it to the best of my ability. There He [God] is driving me through people, and so God's command also stands there, which the Holy Spirit also calls to me and says, 'Thou shalt love thy neighbor as thyself' (Lev. 19:18). No human being should live for himself alone but should also serve the neighbor . . . If the same commandment grabs me and is held before me, no resistance would help unless I would resist so long that I came under God's wrath because of it. Now this call is through human beings, but it is also confirmed by God. So I remember and serve God in it . . . " (Commentary on Some Chapters of Exodus, 1524-1526; Walch, III, 1076ff.; Erlangen, XXXV, 58ff.).

About God calling Moses who wanted to withdraw from the call because of his stuttering, Luther writes: "If God were as smart as we are, He would certainly have begun everything better than otherwise happened. For here He takes for this difficult, high work one who cannot speak well, as Moses himself confessed. But God says to him: Go and carry it out. That is the same as if He told a blind man that he should see well, a lame man that he should run well, a mute man that he should speak well. Could God not find someone else to use for this work?

"But it is written so that we may learn God's attitude. What counts in the eyes of the world, He does not regard. He rejects and discards what others grab for. He throws away what others love and exalt. And what the devil does not want, that He accepts. He gives Moses a correct answer and says: You are a clever and a fine fellow. That is nettling, as if He meant to say: Do you think that I do not know that you stutter, as if I did not hear it?—

"So it seems to us, for we always want to outdo God in His works, as if we were the very first to see these faults, shortcomings, and frailties, but God did not see them. What does it matter, God says, so what if you are deaf, blind, or mute? If I say and command something to you, can I not give you sight, hearing, and speech? Who is talking to me? It is not some shoemaker but rather the One Who gives eyes and sight to the blind, ears and hearing to the deaf, and can make the inarticulate eloquent, but silences the great babblers. And you who cannot speak want to set the goal and standard for Me, Who has chosen you, because you cannot speak! If you could speak well, you would yet get too proud for yourself. But if you now see that I am the One Who does it, and not you, then I will use a stutterer like you for this work. For if one were as capable as Gabriel and all angels, and God did not call him, he would still not accomplish anything.... Again, if one is not a good speaker, and God calls him, he will carry it out, no matter how he is, so that the world may see that we are not pushing it, but God Himself is doing it...." (Walch, III, 1129-32; Erlangen, XXXV, 102-104).

Luther writes: "It is also nothing if someone wants to object that he is unsuited because of his weak faith, frail life, or cold devotion. They should look at their call and office, indeed, at God's Word that has called them. If they are impure or unsuited, the office and the call or the Word is still pure and suitable enough. And if they certainly believe that they have been called, then they are also suitable enough themselves through such faith.... I want to go and take care of my office. What is that other than so much as: I want to obey God and serve my neighbor?" (1528 Letter to Lazarus Spengler; Walch, X, 2780-82; Erlangen, LIV, 32-33.)

# 6

## The Conditions of a Call

A Lutheran candidate can, in good conscience, accept as valid and legitimate the call to be the pastor of a congregation only if the congregation states: 1. that it wants to be served as an orthodox, Evangelical Lutheran congregation; 2. that it therefore confesses the Scriptures of the Old and New Testaments to be God's Word; and 3. that it publicly confesses the symbolical writings of the Evangelical Lutheran Church (specifically Luther's Small Catechism and the Unaltered Augsburg Confession) to be its confession and wants to know that the office is conducted accordingly in it; as well as that it wants: 4. to conform to the confessional ceremonies of the orthodox Lutheran church; 5. to introduce pure church and school books; 6. to announce in advance for the holy Supper; and finally, 7. in general to give free course to the Word of God (whether it is presented publicly or individually) in doctrine, admonition, comfort, and rebuke, and to subordinate itself to it.

**Comment 1.**
It is not right for the one called to let the calling congregation wait very long to learn that he has received the call document. The recipient should report its arrival to the concerned congregation right away, even if he cannot yet definitely decide about accepting the call. From time to time he should let the congregation know the status of the call matter if it is necessary for him to delay his decision.

**Comment 2.**
It can happen, without harm to the conscience, that an orthodox pastor preach God's Word to a congregation with a false confession or a mixed confession, but not that he become its pastor and

administer the holy Supper to its members. For the orthodox pastor would thereby not only enter into the fellowship of those with a false confession but would also be approving of the false confession through the Sacrament (2 Cor. 6:14 ff.; 1 Cor. 1:10; Rom. 16:17; 2 John 10-11; Rom. 4:11).

That holds true not only for those congregations which as a whole have a false confession but also for those congregations which accept the orthodox name but in which those with a declared false confession have the right of membership. In his 1533 "Admonition to Frankfurt," Luther writes about the case of a preacher who administers the Sacrament to those who state that they do not believe in its mystery: "And in sum, to have done with this matter, it is a horror for me to hear that in one and the same church, at one and the same altar, both parties take and receive one and the same Sacrament while one part believes that it is receiving only bread and wine and the other part believes that it is receiving the true body and blood of Christ. And I often doubt whether it is to be believed that a preacher and pastor [*Seelsorger*] could be so hardened and wicked as to be quiet about it and let both parties go, each with its own idea, that they receive one and the same Sacrament, each according to its faith, etc.

"But if there is one [such preacher], he must have a heart that is harder than stone, steel, and diamond. He must admittedly be an apostle of wrath. For Turks and Jews are much better, who deny our Sacrament and openly confess that. For we thereby remain undeceived by them and fall into no idolatry. But these fellows would have to be the real high archdemons, who would give me only bread and wine and would let me consider it the body and blood of Christ and so would let me be miserably deceived. That would be too hot and too hard. God will let them have it in short order. So whoever has such preachers, or perceives this of them, let him be warned against them as against the devil incarnate himself" (Erlangen, XXVI, 304; Walch, XVII, 2446).

Here Luther certainly has only Zwinglian-minded preachers in view, for it seems impossible that anyone who really believed in the presence of the body and blood of Christ in the holy Supper would enter into such a sacrilegious union. But if it happened that preachers with the correct confession of Christ's body and blood administered it and let a number of their communicants consider it to be mere bread and wine, the atrocity would be only that much

The Conditions of a Call

greater.

**Comment 3.**
The essence of an orthodox congregation is not in its name but in its confession of pure doctrine. After God has, at this late stage in world history, restored the pure doctrine of His Word to His church through His chosen instrument, Luther; and after the enemies of this doctrine have laid the name "Lutherans" upon those who confess it, and the name "Lutheran Church" upon their fellowship, and so have made these the distinctive names of the orthodox; then the orthodox should not be ashamed of the Lutheran name any more that believing Jews should have been ashamed of the Israelite name (John 1:47), or orthodox Christians of the Athanasian name, although Israel and Athanasius are names of human beings just as is the name Luther.

It is perverse to appeal to Luther's protest against the use of his name ("Faithful Admonition to All Christians to Guard Against Uproar and Uprising," 1522; Walch, X, 420f.; Erlangen, XXII, 55). Which Lutheran would not subscribe, from his heart, to this protest if the name were to indicate that one believed in Luther instead of believing in Christ and so adhered to a sectarian doctrine?

[Footnote: In "Against the Blind Condemnation of the Seventeen Articles," 1524, Luther writes: "So we have such a disgraceful and shameful name before the world as admittedly no one has had in a thousand years. Whoever they can call Lutheran or Evangelical, they believe they have called him more than ten times devilish, and he must then also deserve more than one hell" (Erlangen, XXIV, 77f.; Walch, XXI, 130).]

But if we are called Lutheran because we believe what Luther taught according to God's Word, and if we can clearly and fully confess our faith only by calling ourselves Lutherans, then we would be ashamed of the truth we have learned if we were ashamed of the Lutheran name. As Luther protested against the enemies' calling Christians by his name, he warns in another place, with reference to 2 Tim. 1:8, that rejecting his name would be denying the divine truth if the question: Are you a Lutheran? means nothing other than: Do you believe what Luther taught? ("Of Both Kinds in the Sacrament, etc." 1522; Erlangen, XXVIII, 316f.; Walch, XX, 136f. [Luther says here: "Let the person go; but you must confess the doctrine"]).

So already in 1524, Luther prophesied: "Although I do not like it that the doctrine and the people are called Lutheran, and must suffer it that they so abuse God's Word with my name, they will still have to let Luther, the Lutheran doctrine, and the Lutheran people come to honor. And they and their doctrine will succumb and perish even though it would offend all the world and anger all devils. . . . For we know Whose Word it is that we preach" ("A Christian Letter of Comfort to the Miltenbergers"; Erlangen, XLI, 127f.; Walch, V, 1858f.).

But it cannot be denied that conditions could occur under which the Lutheran name may not be allowed to be a *sine qua non* of serving a congregation with Word and Sacrament. [Footnote: This would especially be the case if a preacher of a congregation of a false confession, for example, Papistic, Reformed, Union-Evangelical, Methodist, etc., would come to the [correct] knowledge.] [Walther quotes Luther giving such advice to the Regensburg City council in 1534 (Erlangen, LV, 57f.).]

**Comment 4.**

Already in the early church those who wanted to be baptized and accepted into the Christian congregation, had to declare publicly that the Apostles' Creed was their own confession, over against the false teachers and sects which had arisen. So if a congregation wants to be considered orthodox now, it is even more necessary for it to declare that the confession of the orthodox church of this time is its own. Since it cannot be expected that all members know each of the symbolical writings of the Lutheran church, it is enough that a congregation confess Luther's Catechism and the Unaltered Augsburg Confession.

The one called owes it to the congregation to be bound to God's Word and the churchly confession, as a guarantee that he will not preach his own wisdom but the pure Christian doctrine. This obligation is a great advantage for the one called in the conduct of his office, for he can appeal to it against the attacks of false spirits that arise in the congregation and so can nip in the bud many unnecessary and harmful disputes.

**Comment 5.**

According to Article VII of the Augsburg Confession and Article X of the Formula of Concord, it would be thoroughly unevangelical

## The Conditions of a Call

and un-Lutheran if a candidate wanted to accept the call of a congregation only on the condition that it accept all the ceremonies and institutions that had ever been customary in the Lutheran Church. That would be Papistic, Anti-Christian.

[Footnote: Our orthodox theologians number among the adiaphora customary in our Evangelical-Lutheran Church: pictures, holidays, organ music, chanting, the liturgy; at Baptism: applying the water three times, Baptism by lay people in emergencies, the sign of the cross, the Baptismal gown, the renunciation of the devil, the exorcism, the sponsors confessing the faith, etc.; at the administration of the holy Supper: unleavened bread in the form of wafers, the distribution of the bread without breaking it, placing the elements into the mouth, kneeling at the reception, the private Communion of the sick, etc.; with respect to the preaching office: vestments, private confession, etc.; Latin songs; the bowing of the head when the name of Jesus is spoken; the system of pericopes; candles and the crucifix on the altar; the division of the Ten Commandments with three in the first table and seven in the second table; the beginning of the Our Father with word order *Vater unser* and saying *Erloese uns vom Uebel* in the Seventh Petition, etc.].

[In the Our Father, Luther retained the traditional word order, *Vater unser*, "Father ours," which had become archaic already in his day but had been hallowed by long usage. Bowing the head when the name Jesus is spoken is a sign of worshipping Jesus, a confession that Jesus is true God and true Man in one Person. It is a confession against the Nestorian tendency of the Reformed to separate the Son of God from Jesus, claiming to worship God the Son without worshipping Jesus.]

But a case can occur in which the institution or removal of an adiaphoron would indirectly deny the truth. We have an example in the history of the Apostle Paul. He circumcised Timothy for the sake of the weak, when it was still a free adiaphoron (Acts 16:3). But he would absolutely not let himself be moved by the false teachers to circumcise Titus as if it were something necessary. He did that, he wrote to the Galatians, "that the truth of the Gospel might continue with you" (Gal. 2:3-5).

If the enemies of pure doctrine insist, as something necessary, that the orthodox either remove or institute a free adiaphoron, it is not a matter of the adiaphoron alone but of the truth of the

Gospel, especially the doctrine of Christian freedom, which the enemies are attacking and which they are tempting the orthodox actually to deny. Anyone who yields to them in that case is not using his freedom but surrendering his freedom.

When Carlstadt insisted on doing away with the elevation of the host as something necessary, Luther wrote: "Although I intended to do away with the elevation, I will not do it now for a while in spite of and against the fanatical spirit [*Schwaermergeist*] because he wants to forbid it and declare it a sin and deprive us the freedom. For before I would yield a hair-breadth or an eye-wink [the least space or the least time] to the spiritually murderous spirit, to give up our freedom (as St. Paul teaches in Gal. 5:1), I would sooner become yet tomorrow such a strict monk and hold firmly to all the cloistered life as I once did. Christian freedom is no joke here. We want to hold it as purely and wholly as our faith. It cost our dear, faithful Savior and Lord Jesus Christ too much. It is also all too necessary for us. We cannot give it up without losing our salvation" ("Against the Heavenly Prophets"; Walch XX, 255; Erlangen, XXIX, 194f.). [Luther means that giving up Christian freedom would be returning to works righteousness and losing the Gospel, the teaching of salvation by grace alone through faith alone.]

Because Carlstadt also wanted to make it a sin to call the holy Supper a Sacrament, Luther writes in the same writing: "Dear fellow, do not let it be a small thing to you to forbid what God does not forbid; to break Christian freedom, which cost Christ His blood; to encumber consciences with sin where none is. . . . So listen, my brother, we should surrender body and life for Christian freedom, as for every doctrine of faith, and do everything that is forbidden contrary to it, and omit everything that is commanded contrary to it, as St. Paul teaches in Gal. 5:1. . . .So you see that there is not a minor danger in these minor things if one wants to make them matters of conscience. Just the same, if you are forbidden to eat meat on a fish-day, you must eat it. If you are commanded to eat it on a meat day, then you must not eat it. If you are forbidden to marry, you must marry or at least show that you want to do it, and so on. Wherever someone wants to make command, prohibition, sin, good works, conscience, and danger where God wants to have freedom and neither commands nor forbids anything, you must hold to this freedom and always do the opposite until you have preserved freedom" (Walch, XX, 278; Erlangen, XXIV, 214f.).

On this point, compare Article X of the Formula of Concord. As far as the confessional ceremonies are concerned, they may not be enumerated for all cases, according to what has just been said. Something that is a confessional ceremony at one time and one place may not be one at another time and another place. If the confession of doctrine and the preservation of Christian freedom are not endangered, the use or non-use of any adiaphoron is free for every church, as long as there is no offense against love and the good order and edification of the church are not disturbed. Ceremonies which the Evangelical Lutheran Church and its preachers cannot give up at the present time without weakening the confession of pure doctrine include: the omission of the breaking of the bread in the holy Supper as well as the use of the Apostles' Creed and the renunciation of the devil at holy Baptism. If a congregation did not want to conform to the Evangelical Lutheran Church in these matters, a Lutheran candidate would not accept its call with a clear conscience.

[Calvinists opposed the renunciation of the devil at infant Baptism because they denied that the child could ever have been under the devil's sway if he was one of the elect. The Reformed opposed the creed at Baptism because they denied that the Holy Spirit worked through Baptism to bring people to faith. The Reformed insisted on breaking the bread in the holy Supper because they saw it as a total symbolical action, not as a means of grace in which the body and blood of Christ are distributed as the pledges of forgiveness and salvation. Giving in to the Reformed on these matters would have been agreeing with their reasons and so confessing their doctrine.]

## Comment 6.

No further discussion is needed that one cannot in good conscience accept the call of a congregation that does not state that it wants to introduce pure church and school books. A preacher who would look on calmly and permit his congregation to sing out of song books and its children to be instructed out of school books which contained the poison of false doctrine would certainly not be a pastor [*Seelsorger*] but a murderer of souls [*Seelenmoerder*]. If the congregation does not yet have completely pure books of this nature, it would be enough under certain circumstances to demonstrate what was false in them and to warn against it. But it should declare itself ready to replace them with pure books as soon as possible.

## Comment 7.

In Article XXV of the Augsburg Confession, our church declares: "We retain the custom of not administering the Sacrament to those who have not previously been examined and absolved." In the Article about the Mass in the Apology, it says: "The Sacrament is administered to those who request it, but in such a way that they are first examined and absolved."

It would be contrary to conscience to accept a call to a congregation that did not agree to personal announcement for the holy Supper. That is incontrovertible because, according to God's Word, the preachers are supposed to be not only teachers but are also shepherds, bishops (overseers), and watchmen over souls and so have to be careful that no one receives the holy Supper to his judgement. Especially where the holy Sacraments are concerned, they are not mere distributors but stewards of them (1 Cor. 4:1) and so are responsible for their misuse as far as it depends on them. Finally, according to Christ's explicit, earnest command and faithful warning (Matt. 7:6), they are not to give that which is holy to dogs nor cast their pearls before swine. There will be opportunity to speak about this matter in greater detail when we discuss the correct procedure of the preacher in private confession and absolution.

## Comment 8.

That the congregation join any synod should not be made a condition of accepting the call. But the one called should also not agree to the condition of not joining a synod. The former would be contrary to the freedom of the congregation. The latter would be contrary to the freedom of the one called. [In the nineteenth century, some immigrants shied away from synods because they feared that a synod would lord it over the local church as had the consistories in Germany.]

## Comment 9.

A number of persons who still lack the correct knowledge and yet want a call a Lutheran pastor could and should first be

## The Conditions of a Call

presented with something like the following as the minimum requirements:

"We, the undersigned Lutherans in and around _____, hereby declare the following:

"1. We are willing to form an Evangelical Lutheran congregation, to which only those can and should belong who want to be Lutherans.

"2. We are resolved to call a preacher who will preach God's Word to us pure and unalloyed, as it is contained in holy Scripture and presented in the public confessional writings of the Evangelical Lutheran Church, summed up in Dr. Martin Luther's Small Catechism (and in the Unaltered Augsburg Confession), who will administer the holy Sacraments according to Christ's institution, and who will faithfully conduct his whole office according to God's Word.

"3. We do not want to hire our preacher for one or two years as a servant of men but rather to issue him a regular call as a minister of Christ, as the Bible prescribes; so we want to recognize him as our preacher as long as he teaches correctly, lives without scandal, and faithfully administers his office. But we reserve to ourselves the authority to depose him if he becomes a false teacher, lives scandalously, or is maliciously unfaithful to his office.

"4. We are ready to be instructed from God's Word and to accept the necessary Christian correction from it. We do not want to hinder our preacher from proceeding as God's Word prescribes in all aspects of his office.

"5. We are willing to announce to the pastor in advance every time we are resolved to go to the holy Supper and to announce to him personally at least once a year.

"6. We want only correct books to be used in our church and school and are willing to exchange any incorrect books that may be in use for correct books as soon as possible."

# 7

## The External Arrangements of a Call

It is good for the matter of the salary to be clarified and for the demands which the congregation will make upon the services of the one newly called to be determined before the call is accepted. But here the one newly called must avoid burdening himself with the appearance of greed and of being a hireling. In order to avoid possible tensions later, it is advisable for the one called to be given a written diploma of vocation signed by the representatives of the congregation in its name and by its authority, in which the promise of the necessary support is expressed and the main requirements made of him are specified (1 Cor. 16:3).

**Comment 1.**
Friedrich Balduin writes about pay for preachers in his commentary on St. Paul's epistles: "It is permitted for the ministers of the Word to request salary for their work from the congregation which they serve, as St. Paul teaches in our text (1 Cor. 9:1-14) with six reasons. Among the pious there is none any more who should doubt that unless one wanted to kill the ministers of the Word by hunger and so at the same time suspend the preaching office itself. For they cannot get their support in any other way; indeed, it is disgraceful if the teachers of the church must also in addition be busy working with their hands, about which one may consult the explicit passage in Sirach 39ff. The support of the ministers of the Word is to be requested of the congregations which they serve. Here it is indeed proper that one have public boxes (*aeraria*), in which congregational receipts may be gathered and from which that which is necessary for the support of the office may be taken; at the same time propriety suggests that the listeners also be privately generous toward their teachers; for 'who planteth a vineyard, and eateth not of the fruit thereof?' (1 Cor. 9:7). And

## The External Arrangements of a Call

'Let him that is taught in the Word communicate unto him that teacheth in all good things' (Gal. 6:6), especially since the times are gradually becoming more difficult, and there is no hope that an increase of the support may be achieved from the public boxes.

"One may also not suppose that gifts given to such ministers of the Word are alms or that the people are committing bribery; it is rather the due recompense for the work and a matter of necessity if the preaching office is to be preserved. For if the preachers suffer want, then the preaching office itself must suffer harm. Although nothing definite can be determined about the

**Fig. 3: This is the most widely recognized painting of Walther. It is currently on display at Concordia Seminary, St. Louis, MO.**
Courtesy of Concordia Historical Institute.

amount of the salary of a minister of the church, both extremes must still be avoided: on the one side, that what is necessary not be withdrawn from them; but on the other side also that not too much is demanded by the minister of the church. For they must consider that the salary is given to them not for luxury but for need. ... But that the extent of the need not be limited too narrowly, it is to be known that not only the minister of the Word but also his family is to be nourished, and indeed, in such a way that they have enough in sickness and after death of the husband and father" (*Commentar. in omnes epp. S. Pauli*, p. 404).

Shortly before that, Balduin answered the objection that Christ says, "Freely ye have received, freely give" (Matt. 10:8): "In Matthew the Savior is not speaking about preaching but about the gift of miracles, as the directly preceding words show: 'Heal the sick, etc.' For God did not want the miracles to be bought with money, which the Prophet Elisha could therefore not tolerate in his servant Gehazi (2 Kings 5:20ff.). But one must not suppose that the acceptance of a salary is a selling of the Gospel, as the Anabaptists object. For the salary is not given for the doctrine, with which all the treasures of the world are not to be compared, but for the work of the minister of the church which he rightly and properly receives for his needs since he cannot procure his living for himself and his family in any other way" (*Ibid.*, p. 401).

[Footnote: Luther explains the passage differently and certainly more thoroughly when he writes: "And it is commanded that we should teach, comfort, and absolve all who accept, believe, and receive such goods from us, all without cost, according to the saying in Matt. 10:8. But as the Christians enjoy the preaching office without cost, so they should also nourish the ministers without cost, support and protect them, as St. Paul says in Gal. 6:6 and 1 Tim. 5:17. And Christ Himself says in Matt. 10:10: 'The workman is worthy of his meat.' Again the Lord says in Isaiah 49:22-23 that the princes and kings will give gifts to the church. But these gifts are not payments, buying or selling. For we need daily support, food and drink, but the absolution is not being paid for by that. For who could pay for it? What are a hundred or a thousand guldens for this immeasurable, great gift of the forgiveness of sins? ... But since such a great, boundless gift cannot otherwise be distributed than through human beings who need nourishment and food, one must indeed nourish and support them. But that is no payment for the gift but rather for their effort and work" (On Gen. 23:3-4; Walch, I, 2432f.).].

**Comment 2.**
As desirable as it is that the salary and benefits of the one newly called be fixed right away, so that he will also know right away how to set up his household, he should still not insist on a fixed sum but only request that the congregation state that it will give him what is necessary (Gal. 6:6; 1 Cor. 9:7-15; Luke 10:4-8). He should not insist on additional gifts but may accept them when they are offered [a footnote mentions Baptisms, weddings, funerals, etc.]. But he should absolutely not accept anything for visiting the sick so that he can otherwise hardly escape accusations for visiting the well-to-do too often.

In any case, the one newly called would do best to let the matter of salary be arranged by brothers in office, the visitor [circuit counsellor], or others in general. Above all he should never forget that it is not people but the Lord, Whose minister he is, Who cares for his poor life and that of his family, and that the less his reward is in the world the more beautiful the crown that is laid by him if he keeps faith to the end.

We recall here the beautiful words of Luther: "Look at the pastors here and there in the villages, how so many of them absolutely have to languish because of hunger and thirst and often do not have enough to buy a shirt for their little children.... There is no earnestness, no diligence, no heart for godliness there, for no one is caring about it in a serious and heartfelt way.... 'Let the elders who rule well be counted worthy of double honor' (1 Tim. 5:17). Indeed, they truly are worthy of double honor. But where is that? Answer: with God; for in the world they are considered worthy of sword, gallows, hell, and anything that could be even worse. What do we care about that? We who serve the unthankful world have the promise and hope of the kingdom of heaven, and the recompense and payment for this our misery will be so great that we will also criticize ourselves for ever having let tears or sighs fall. Why, we will say, did we not suffer something yet harder? If only I had believed that there would be such great glory in eternal life! For otherwise I would not have shied away if I should have suffered yet so much more (On Gen. 39:5-6; Walch, II, 1812f.; Erlangen Latin, IX, 235).

# 8

# The Examination and Ordination of a Candidate

Neither the examination which one who has been called to the preaching office passes before an appointed commission outside of the calling congregation, nor the ordination which he receives from appointed persons outside of the congregation, are what make the call valid. But both procedures are among the most beneficial ordinances of the church and have—especially the latter—among other things the important purpose of publicly confirming that the call is recognized by the whole church as legitimate and divine. Anyone who unnecessarily omits one or the other is acting schismatically and making it known that he is one of those whom congregations with itching ears heap up for themselves (2 Tim. 4:3).

**Comment 1.**
When the Apostle [Paul] says of the deacons: "And let these first be proved; then let them use the office of a deacon, being found blameless" (1 Tim. 3:10), that obviously holds true to an even greater extent for the elders to whom the office of the Word is to be entrusted: "And the things that thou hast heard of me among many witnesses, the same commit thou to faithful men, who shall be able to teach others also" (2 Tim. 2:2).

We should let Ludwig Hartmann speak about that. He writes: "Before ordination, an examination or exploration of the ordinand is required, and, indeed, it is necessary for it to precede the ordination for the sake of the dignity of the office and the salvation of the congregation (2 Tim. 2:2). For he is not permitted to be appointed as a teacher who has not yet learned himself what he should teach others. Nor should one 'suddenly' (frivolously, inconsiderately, without further ado) apply the laying on of hands to anyone (1 Tim. 5:22). What happens when wicked, uninstructed, or unsuitable men are ordained is that they are confirmed in their

## The Examination and Ordination of a Candidate

ignorance and godlessness, their audacity in wanting to fly without feathers to such a high peak is approved, and the congregation is poorly cared for by such useless workers.

"Such an examination is carried out by a careful questioning which is sufficiently organized according to God's Word. Through it there should be discovered whether the person to be ordained or called is orthodox with respect to the faith as well as being suitable for the holy office also 1. with respect to the necessary education and knowledge; 2. with respect to the grace to explain Scripture and the gifts for the office which serve for edification; and 3. with respect to godliness and holiness of life.

"To make the matter clearer, I want to express the same with the words of the blessed Tarnov" (professor of theology at Rostock, died in 1633), "who says, among other things: 'What we say should be required of ability and will. With the word "ability" we include three things:

"'1. The *synesis* or the knowledge of all Christian doctrine contained in the catechism and in the *Locis communibus* or *theologicis* and the foundations or main testimonies of Scripture, on which the main points [of doctrine] are based; for he who does not understand what he is saying or how he is basing it is not qualified to teach others, according to the testimony of the Apostle (1 Tim. 1:7).

"'2. The *dynamis hermeneutike* or the gift and ability to teach others (2 Tim. 2:2), which the one who is to be called should have to the degree not only that he certainly holds to the Word and can teach it but also that he is powerful to exhort with sound doctrine and to refute those who contradict (Titus 1:9), that is, to present the true doctrine of the faith, to institute the improvement of morals in righteousness, the refutation of false doctrines, and the rebuking of vices (according to the purposes of Scripture in 2 Tim. 3:16), and also to lift up with comfort those who are visited with temptations and troubles (Rom. 15:4).

"'3. An *anepileptos kai anegkletos bios* (1 Tim. 3:2; Titus 1:6), that is, a blameless and irreproachable life, which is free of crimes and shameful deeds, which are not to be tolerated in a servant of the Word, and is adorned with all virtues which are necessary for him to present himself as a Christian (Gal. 5:6; 2 Pet. 1:5-7) and to edify others.

"'With the word "will" we include two things:

"'1. The desire to serve the church (1 Tim. 3:1), and, indeed, not one that has been forced or extorted by necessity, but one that is voluntary and proceeds from zeal to further the glory of God and the salvation of people, not for the sake of [financial] gain nor from the lust to dominate others (1 Pet. 5:2-3).

"'2. Constancy in the faithful administration of office that has once been received, and in all it parts (1 Cor. 4:2), to which pertain diligence in awakening and increasing the gift of God through the correct means (2 Tim. 1:6, which is also presented in other passages such as 1 Tim. 4:12-13) and patience in labors and troubles, which is most highly necessary for a pastor as a good warrior (2 Tim. 2:1)'" (*Pastoral. ev.*, Lib. I, c. 8, p. 130s.).

To the question: "Is he to be considered sufficiently equipped with the gifts necessary for the office who has learned something of the Latin language and can recite from memory sermons drawn from the writings of others?" the Danish theologian Brochmand answers; "By no means. For, first, the whole Word of God should be thoroughly known to a true servant of the divine Word (Mal. 2:7; Matt. 13:52; 2 Tim. 1:13; 3:14-15, 17).

"Second, a servant of the divine Word should be so familiar with holy Scripture that he understands how to apply the same wisely to his listeners with respect to time, place, and various circumstances according to that statement of Paul in 2 Tim. 2:15: 'Study to shew thyself approved unto God, a workman that needeth not to be ashamed, rightly dividing the Word of truth.'

"Third, he who is to be considered worthy of the holy office must have made such progress in God's Word that he can give account of that which he teaches when that is required of him and that he can stop the mouths of those who contradict, as Paul reminds in Titus 1:9."

To the question: "Can those who, in the examination, are found not to be equipped with the knowledge of the articles of faith and of the holy Scripture which is necessary and sufficient for the holy office, nevertheless be ordained and admitted to the holy office, but with the condition that they make the sacred promise to be diligent and careful in learning?" the same [Brochmand] answers: "Not at all. For first, Paul does not permit someone to be entrusted with the holy office who is not qualified to teach and powerful to stop the mouths of those who contradict the truth (1 Tim. 3:2; Titus 1:9).

"Second, the Spirit of God explicitly reminds that one who could

## The Examination and Ordination of a Candidate

lay hands on an insufficiently qualified person would be making himself a participant in the sins of another (1 Tim. 5:22).

"Third, experience testifies only too abundantly that those who are admitted to the holy office without education remain in their uneducated condition even if they have promised diligence in learning.

"Fourth, how could we answer God if many of the listeners would be lost before the pastor learned what he should impress upon others (Ezek. 33:1ff.)" (*System. univers. th.*, Loc. 30, c. 3, Tom. II, fol. 372, 375).

From that it is to be seen how un-Biblical, how unscrupulous and soul-killing a thing is the so-called licensing system which is still practiced here in some synods. According to that system, those whom one does not dare to ordain to the office because they have not been proven or because they lack the fitness for the office, are given only a so-called license, on the basis of which they should work in a congregation on probation.

**Comment 2.**

Ordination with the laying on of hands is not a divine institution but only an apostolic, ecclesiastical institution. That needs no proof since Scripture mentions the custom but is silent about any divine institution of it. An argument *a silentio* [from silence] is certainly valid when it is a matter of divine institution as is seen from the polemics against the Roman Church and its alleged sacraments and doctrines which are traced back to tradition.

Ordination is an adiaphoron and does not make the call and the office but only confirms them. That has always been the doctrine of all orthodox teachers of our church. One may compare the testimonies cited in "The Voice of Our Church in the Question of Church and Ministry," second edition (Erlangen: Deichert, 1865), Part II, Thesis 6B. At the same time it is proven that that was the teaching of the ancient church since it also, like the Lutheran Church, rejected absolute ordination, ordination without a call.

But the benefit and relative necessity of ordination are also found in the presentations of our theologians cited in that book. Here we cite only the words of an earnest champion of Lutheran orthodoxy, Johann Fecht, professor of theology at Rostock (d. 1716): "Ordination is an ecclesiastical custom which should be highly esteemed because of its purposes, of which it has primarily three.

For, first, it is a public testimony that the candidate has been found fit and worthy for the souls of men to be entrusted to him. Second, this custom makes the candidate himself publicly certain that he has been legitimately called and that the church is therefore obligated to the holy office. Third, the whole congregation prays over him that his gifts, necessary for the church, may be increased, and that he may be granted the courage to serve God steadfastly and to care for the salvation of souls.

"The question about what is to be held about the necessity of this custom is to be decided on this basis. For here two extremes are to be avoided. First, that one does not, with the Papists, invent an absolute necessity according to which this custom impresses a character upon the person that turns him from a worldly into a spiritual person, from a layman into a cleric, so that he is able to carry out holy functions, especially to consecrate the Sacraments. Therefore they also ordain people who have not been called so that the same can immediately enter their offices if they are called. Second, that one does not, with the Calvinists, consider it unimportant, as if nothing depended on it. For if we do not even consider a marriage a truly Christian marriage which has not been consecrated by public blessing, how much less the holy office?

"Two rules follow from this. First, that one called, if necessity demand it or if he cannot be ordained right away because of some hindrance, can carry out the office of preaching as well as administering the Sacraments, and that in such a case the congregation should be instructed that these things do not depend on ordination as a means of impressing a holy character without which the minister cannot carry out the holy functions. Second, that except for a case of necessity one not ordained, although he has been called, should not carry out these functions without further ado, not because they would not be valid once they had been carried out, but rather because one should not give others a cause for offense as if one did not need the prayers of others in such a holy and important matter and can fall into the office as animals fall upon their fodder" (*Instructio pastoralis,* Cap. 5, Section 1, 2; p. 47s.).

Chr. Tim. Seidel reminds: "At most places it is usually connected with the function of the ordination that the holy Supper is administered to the candidate immediately afterwards in order to remind the candidate thereby that in his congregation he is to know nothing but Christ the Crucified, that he is to proclaim Him

## The Examination and Ordination of a Candidate

in his teaching and life, and that he should remain in union with Christ not only for his own person but should also present Him to the congregation entrusted to him" (*Pastoraltheologie*, ed. F. E. Rambach (Leipzig, 1769), p. 37).

So that the one to be ordained may concentrate his thinking only on the important, holy function, he does not, as a rule, preach on the day of his ordination.

### Comment 3.

Where possible, the ordination should always take place in the congregation which the ordainand is entering. If that cannot be done, it is all the more important that the one ordained be publicly installed in his congregation. While ordination is not usually repeated at transfers [when another call is accepted], the installation is repeated as often as the preacher enters a new office.

### Comment 4.

In the Evangelical Lutheran Church, the one entering office is obligated to the symbolical books at ordination and installation. Friedrich Eberhard Rambach adds to Seidel's *Pastoraltheologie*: "This custom of our church has recently been disapproved and so also criticized because of misunderstanding. So the following should be noted: First, we do not consider the symbolical books to be the basis of faith, which is holy Scripture alone, but only to be the norm of our confession of the faith, and by a written statement that one will teach according to this confession we require only the assurance that our church is getting ministers and shepherds, and not foxes and wolves, in its teachers. No one is absolutely forced to do it, and if he has reservations about such subscription, he can stay away and find another way of living. But if he has once declared this [subscription] and later departs from it, he cannot maintain the character of an honorable man unless he resigns and lays down his office.

"Second, our symbolical books are no instrument of curiosity and interference in the consciences of other people; rather they were composed because of necessity. The Augsburg Confession had to be composed on the command of Charles V, under some apparent danger. The Smalcald Articles were set up because of the need to present them to the council which the Pope had called for Mantua. Luther's two catechisms were forced upon him by the horrible ignorance of the people and the irresponsible negligence of the Roman clergy. And we can also say that of the Formula of Concord, which is often insulted by unwashed tongues, which, however, precisely thereby betray their ignorance and frivolity.... Freedom of conscience admittedly does not permit that anyone should be forced into the true religion; but it also does not require that everyone be permitted the freedom to spread harmful doctrines and to cause confusion in the church" (*op. cit.,* p. 38).

But it would be just as devoid of conscience if a candidate would let himself be obligated to the confessions of the church only in order to get into the office, without having read them, having tested them according to God's Word, and having become convinced of the truth of their content *in rebus* and *phrasibus* [in subject matter and in phrasing].

**Comment 5.**

After ordination, the one who has entered the office should join an orthodox synod at the next opportunity. If he did not do that when he had the opportunity, he would thereby betray a sinful, independentistic, schismatic spirit, contrary to Eph. 4:3; 1 Cor. 1:10-13; 11:18-19; Prov. 18:1. Compare the writing, "The Proper Form of an Evangelical Lutheran Local Congregation Independent of the State" (St. Louis [Concordia Publishing House], 1863), pp. 212-217.

It is admittedly even worse that standing alone in a separatistic way if a preacher, who either does not want to join any of the existing synods for impure reasons or cannot find acceptance in any of them because of his unworthiness or unfitness, seeks to form a synod of his own out of ambiguous characters or out of men just as unfit as he is, and even to exalt himself to be its head, and in this way to escape the reproach of separatism.

# 9

## The First Sermon by the Pastor

A great deal depends on a correct beginning for the administration of the office. The initial or inaugural sermon must primarily say two things to the congregation: 1. what it is to expect from the one it has chosen; and 2. what he expects from it; and all that without flattery or worldly *captatio benevolentiae* [capturing good will], in Christian seriousness and holy truthfulness, but in evangelically winsome friendliness and heartfelt, sincere humility. It is most fitting for the sermon to begin with a prayer for God's help and blessing for the one entering the office himself and to close with a fervent prayer for the congregation so that all ages and estates and all official functions are specifically presented to God.

**Comment 1.**

It would clearly be misguided to preach only on the pericope in the inaugural sermon without referring to the new relationship into which the preacher is entering with the congregation. The congregation wants and expects the preacher to express himself about that relationship and would leave the church disappointed and dissatisfied if he did not do so. He would be missing an opportunity to make an especially blessed gesture and to lay a good basis for his future effectiveness.

Christoph Tim. Seidel writes: "The final goal of the inaugural sermon is that the new preacher present himself to his congregation and begin his teaching office. So in the inaugural sermon the following should be observed:

"First, a main point should be chosen that would fit sufficiently well with the purpose.

"Second, in the application one should relate how he has come to the call; one should assure the congregation of his constant faithfulness, love, and concern; one should request with moving words that they love him in return and trust him; one should finally close the sermon with a prayer for the whole congregation and call upon God for His help in a blessed conduct of the office.

"Third, it would not be wise, in the inaugural sermon, to speak of many innovations and changes which one intends to make. That is the most certain way to awaken mistrust in the minds against oneself.

"Fourth, one should guard against all promises to which he is not obligated by his office. The listeners will note those very exactly, and if they cannot be fulfilled, one faces a constant reproach.

"Fifth, one should guard against overly sharp expressions and threats. For these would embitter and alienate their minds from the entering teacher as much as assurances of fatherly love and concern would incline them toward him.

"Sixth, one should guard against praising his own person. That would certainly make him despised" (*Pastoraltheologie*, ed. F. E. Rambach (Leipzig, 1769), pp. 46f.).

Adam Struensee writes: "Inaugural sermons have the special purpose that a newly entering preacher gain access to his congregation and awaken his listeners to love and trust his person and to obey the truths which are to be presented to them, so that through his ministry they are enlivened to hurry with him toward a blessed eternity and that teacher and listeners may be together in unceasing joy before the throne of God.

"In the application, the preacher can remember the special providence of God through which he has been led to the congregation as a teacher; present to his mind and the minds of his congregation the importance of the teaching office and the severe responsibility connected with it; and request the prayers of his congregation that he may conduct it according to God's mind; let it be known with all seriousness that he will be concerned to please God rather than men; briefly touch on what he wants for his congregation and how he wishes from his heart that all hindrances to edification may be removed out of the way and that the saving truths may have a powerful effect on their souls for their eternal salvation.

"In the whole inaugural sermon, a great demonstration of love should shine forth through all words, expressions, and gestures, which is connected with sadness about the godless, abhorrence of hypocrisy, kindness toward the troubled and penitent, and sincerity

## The First Sermon by the Pastor

toward the blessed" (*Anweisung zum erbaulichen Predigen* (Halle, 1756), pp. 414ff.).

It would also be of blessing for the new preacher to refer to the confession of the orthodox Lutheran Church, to which he has been formally bound by this call and ordination, which is also the confession of his personal faith, and with which he intends to remain in doctrine and practice no matter what may happen.

**Comment 2.**

It would be most fitting for the new preacher, if possible, to make that Sunday's pericope the basis for his first sermon. If that does not work out, the following texts are some that would be suitable, having been used repeatedly by godly preachers for this purpose: Rom. 1:16-17; 15:29-33, 1 Cor. 1:21-25; 2:1-5; 4:1-2; 2 Cor. 1:24; 4:5-6; 5:17-21; 1 Thess. 2:13; Acts 26:22-29; John 17:20-21.

When the blessed Professor J. A. Dietelmair entered the office of deacon in Nuremberg in 1744 on the Nineteenth Sunday after Trinity, his theme for the Gospel for that Sunday [Matt. 9:1-8] was: "The Knowledge of Salvation in the Forgiveness of Sins as the Proper Goal of the Office of the Messenger of Peace."

When the pious Siegmund Basch entered his office as Senior Court Preacher in Hildburghausen in 1751 on Exaudi Sunday, his theme on the basis of the Gospel pericope [John 15:26-16:4] was: "The Testimony of Jesus the Most Prominent Work of His Servants."

When the excellent theologian J. Melch. Goeze, who was scorned by the brilliant but bitter enemy of the Gospel, Lessing, entered his office in Magdeburg in 1750 on the First Sunday after Trinity, his theme based on the Epistle for that Sunday [1 John 4:16-21] was: "The Proclamation of Divine Love the Most Pleasant Business of an Evangelical Preacher."

(In the introduction he says, among other things: "There are two points which an Evangelical preacher must especially consider in the presentation of the divine Word: he must preach Law and Gospel. He must preach both in the correct order. He must connect both correctly but also know how to divide them properly at the right time. I know that I am also obligated to preach the Law and to present wrath and curse to the godless so that he may be warned about his godless life. I will not neglect this duty. Should I be advised to be hypocritical so that I would seek to be pleasing to people and would so cover my hands with blood, which the Lord, the righteous Judge, would demand from me on that day? Lord, let that be far from me!... But all the while I will observe this part of my official work with inward agony of soul. But I will proclaim the Gospel of peace with joy... For it is and remains the most pleasant occupation of an Evangelical teacher to praise for souls the love of God.")

When J. Ph. Fresenius entered his office as Senior Minister at Frankfurt am Main on Invocavit Sunday, 1749, he presented "the Evangelical Nature of the Preaching Office" on the basis of the free text 2 Cor. 5:19-21, and indeed, 1. its Evangelical basis—the reconciliation of God with people; 2. its Evangelical goal—the reconciliation of people with God; and 3. the Evangelical means which this office employs to reach its goals—the preaching of reconciliation. In the introduction he proceeds on the basis of Is. 40:2.

Finally, when Spener entered his office as provost in Berlin on the Second Sunday after Trinity in 1691, he first presented the teaching of salvation on the basis of the Gospel for the Sunday [Luke 14:16-24] according to: 1. its cause, 2. its nature, and 3. the persons who receive it. Then he showed: 1. what he asked of his listeners: namely a. that they recognize him as one sent by God; b. that they obey not him but the One in Whose name he was coming to them; and c. that they pray for him; and 2. what the listeners should look to him to provide: namely a. that he proclaim to them the whole counsel of God for their salvation; and b. that he strive to be an example to them; and c. that he would pray for them. He took this introduction from Ps. 34:9.

**Comment 3.**

Seidel makes the not unnecessary remark that the new preacher should do as much as he can to alleviate for the congregation the burdens connected with his arrival, specifically as it relates to travel and transportation costs, the preparation of the parsonage, and the like.

# 10

## The First Visitation by the Pastor

If the new preacher has entered his office, then it is his duty to use the first weeks or months, in part, to visit all families and individuals who belong to his parish, in order to get to know them personally (Acts 20:20: "publicly and from house to house," *demosia kai kat' oikous;* 1 Thess. 2:11; John 10:3; Ezek. 34:16; 1 Tim. 5:1-3; Eph 4:11 ("pastors")). He should first of all visit the sick (Matt. 25:36; James 5:14) and those who cannot attend public worship because of age or infirmity, but he must not overlook anyone at all. He should turn his attention to everyone and let it be known that he bears in his heart the concern of a pastor for every individual soul and that he considers the poor and those of lesser status no less than the rich and prominent (James 2:1-9). Here he should extend a certain amount of trust even to those who do not make the impression of being zealous Christians (2 Tim. 2:24; 1 Cor. 9:19-23). It would be out of place immediately to start a sharp examination of everyone's spiritual condition. But if a person begins to open up without being asked, the new preacher should meet the expressed needs. If the preacher finds a school there, he should also visit it in the first days of the first week (John 21:15; 1 John 2:13).

**Comment 1.**
Since we will later discuss home visits, we will say here only what Seidel says about the duty of the new pastor in this respect: "In the days following the inaugural sermon, it is the duty of the teacher to get to know his congregation. For that the following will be helpful.

"1. He should visit each house in order and observe the impression that each one makes and the outward circumstances from which he can evaluate their way of life.

"2. He should ask on such visits whether they have Bibles, hymnals, etc.

"3. He should have the schoolmaster call all the children together to inquire about their condition and to give them a moving and enlivening talk.

"4. He should call the male and female servants to meet him at the parsonage at a certain time and admonish them to be concerned about what is best for their souls and offer to do all he can to help them in it.

"5. He should call the herdsmen, who are not often seen, to meet him early in the morning or late in the evening, and instruct them the same way.

"6. Without any delay, he should visit the sick and those who stand in particular spiritual need.

"7. He should especially call those from the congregation who, above others, are suspected of a wicked way of life and speak to them, with the most moving words, about amending their lives.

"8. He should be concerned about the poor and needy and either be generous to them according to his ability or get them some other help.

"9. He should seek to reconcile those who live at enmity and in lawsuits. Because he has not previously known their conditions, and so they cannot suspect him of taking sides, he will find that much more access to their minds.

"10. As quickly as possible, he should seek to take care of those church matters that have been neglected during the vacancy" (*Pastoraltheologie*, ed. F. E. Rambach (Leipzig, 1769), pp. 47f.).

Later Seidel advises that the pastor "call the elders to meet with him and request their advice" (p. 49).

## Comment 2.

The new preacher should not permit, much less encourage, members of the congregation to tell him unfavorable things about other members or to warn him about them. All too often those who at first throng the preacher and make a show of the greatest zeal are the ones who are first struck by the Word and fall away, become hostile to the preacher, and abuse the trust that has been given to them. From the first the preacher should guard against the temptation of wanting to gather around himself an *ecclesiola in ecclesia* (a holy, chosen, smaller group within the group [literally:

## The First Visitation by the Pastor

"a little church within the church"]), as the Pietists used to do, and giving the appearance of considering those who zealously push themselves forward to be the only true Christians and his real congregation (1 Cor. 1:10-13).

Anyone who has not been excommunicated must notice that his pastor considers him, too, to be his dear little sheep. Both impurity and God's work are often so well hidden that the preacher who looks too much at the outward appearance will easily consider as most Christian those who are least Christian, and as dead and unawakened those in whom God has already gloriously begun his work of grace.

**Comment 3.**

It would be a sign of a despicable attitude if the new preacher tried to gain respect in the congregation at the expense of his upright predecessor, criticized his methods, and did not want to

„So, nu laffen Se fich's recht gut fchmecken!"

**Fig. 4: Christian Charity helps the poor. The German Words may be translated: "So now have a good taste of this."**
Courtesy of Concordia Historical Institute.

follow his procedures. Seidel writes: "If one has had a predecessor who was beloved by the congregation, one should indeed try to walk in his footsteps where that can be done with a good conscience. On the other hand, one should note the mistakes of his predecessor and judge from them what he must do to motivate the love of the congregation. That can (and should) happen without considering the person of the predecessor or criticizing him because of his mistakes" (*op. cit.,* p. 49).

If the new preacher finds that there is already a colleague in his congregation, he must with all seriousness and diligence guard against doing anything to gain for himself greater favor and respect in the congregation and to turn hearts away from the colleague and to himself. He should do everything to preserve the unity of the spirit in the bond of peace with his co-worker. Basil writes correctly, "The right hand does not need the left as much as the church needs harmony" [no reference].

If the new preacher is an assistant, he must be that much more diligent not to exalt himself above the one whom he has been appointed to help. He should not make the senior pastor sigh by claiming superior knowledge or by working against him secretly or openly and so making the office more difficult for him. Rather he should make it easier for him. Instead of crippling his effectiveness, he should try to further it. It [working against the other pastor] is so displeasing to God that it will certainly be avenged in time.

**Comment 4.**

It is obvious that the pastor should be concerned about the school right away. Dr. Johannes Fecht, professor of theology at Rostock (d. 1716), writes: "Since the schools are the seminaries (nurseries) of the church, it becomes clear from that that the church would suffer an irreplaceable loss from the decline of the schools. So the pastor must be intent with the greatest concern that schools at places in his pastoral care are entrusted to capable teachers. But where villages are not of the type to be able to support a schoolteacher, he must at least try to find honorable church members to instruct the youth during the winter, to which work he should invite them by compensation for this work from the church treasury, even if it is not much. For without the help of the schools, divine knowledge and godliness cannot be planted in

## The First Visitation by the Pastor

any way. Therefore many preachers, where no schoolmaster could be had, have been driven by their conscience to take this very necessary, very beneficial work upon themselves, namely during the winter.

"But where schools have been set up, the pastor absolutely must visit them. In part, so that he can be shown the nature, the method, and the way faithfully and fruitfully to set up the instruction; in part, so that he can especially fulfill what is lacking in catechetical instruction; in part, so that the youth can be spurred to make greater progress every day. The pastor of the church must not be deterred by dislike for the heavy labor from sitting daily for hours with the little ones in the school. He should also not merely listen to the instruction of the teacher but should himself get involved in the work, praising the diligent [children] and scolding the lazy. For in that way he will lay a firmer foundation for the catechetical instruction which he himself will later undertake in the church.

"He must also daily strive to awaken the uncaring parents, who are often little concerned for their children, even though they may grow up like animals with little knowledge of God. He must show them how they will some day have to give account to God, and how God's curse will be poured out on their whole household, if they here fail to do their duty; and, on the other hand, the blessing [which will be theirs] if they raise their children in the fear of the Lord, to which they are primarily led in the school.

"This part of the pastoral office indeed seems to be of less importance at first glance. But be certain of this that it is most of all from this part that one can distinguish between a true pastor of the church and a hireling, between a real pastor and a pastor in name only. For how can he who does not care about the foundation be seriously concerned about the building itself?" (*Instructio pastoralis*, ed. G. F. Fecht, second edition (1722), pp. 199f.).

### Comment 5

Three hints for the new pastor may be mentioned here. First, he should not travel away in the first half year unless it is most urgently necessary. Second, if he cannot afford to purchase his household needs, he should not incur any more debt than is absolutely necessary, and, if at all possible, he should not borrow what he needs from his own church members. Third, he should right away start a register of souls and a church book if there is none.

# 11

## The Requirements of Public Preaching

The most important of all official functions of every pastor is public preaching. He should devote the greatest diligence to it. The most important requirements of public preaching are: 1. that it contain nothing but God's Word pure and unalloyed (1 Pet. 4:11; Acts 26:22; Rom. 12:7; Jer. 23:28; 2 Tim. 2:15); 2. that God's Word be correctly applied (2 Tim. 3:16-17); 3. that the whole counsel of God be proclaimed to the listeners for their salvation (Acts 20:20, 26-27); 4. that it meet the special needs of the listeners (Luke 12:42; 1 Cor. 3:1-2; Heb. 5:11-6:2); 5. that it be timely (Matt. 16:3); 6. that it be well organized (Luke 1:3); and finally, 7. that it not be too long. Whatever else may be said about the correct way to preach belongs to the discipline of homiletics.

**Comment 1.**
Even if a preacher conducts the liturgy very well or is very gifted at governing the congregation or carrying out private pastoral care, etc., all of that can never replace correct preaching. It is and remains the main means for the blessed administration of the holy office. The Apology of the Augsburg Confession, Article XXIV, Of the Mass, says: "There is nothing that keeps the people in church more than good preaching." In the Article on Confession [it says]: "If you want to keep the church with you, you must be concerned that you have correct teaching and preaching. Thereby you can bring about good will and constant obedience."

**Comment 2.**
In no other way can a pastor incur greater guilt for unfaithfulness in his office—in no other way does his high, holy office work greater damnation for him—than if he does not apply the greatest diligence in study, reading, and prayer to give his

## The Requirements of Public Preaching

congregation the best that he can give every time. [In a footnote, Walther lists testimonies about the necessity of study and preparation, including J. A. Quenstedt's advice that beginning pastors write out their sermons word for word and that even the most experienced pastors still use a detailed outline (*Ethic. pastoral.*, pp. 113f.)].

The horrifying declaration of the prophet applies primarily to the public preaching of the Word: "Cursed be he that doeth the work of the Lord deceitfully" (Jer. 48:10 [Luther's translation: "negligently"]). Woe to the preacher who—from laziness and fear of hard work, or fear of people, or desire to please people, or desire for fame, or because he spends time on other things (whether from passion for other occupations or greed or ambition)—does not plan his sermons according to the text and the needs of his listeners but according to how he can most easily talk for a while without special preparation, shake something out of his sleeve, and take care of this obligation without effort—or according to how he can give the least offense or be the most pleasing and brilliant "pulpit orator!"

Things which the preacher should not allow to deprive him of the time necessary to prepare sermons and fulfill his other official duties include: farming, ranching, gardening, doctoring, music, painting, academic studies, writing, and other hobby horses. That is not even to speak of things which are absolutely incompatible with the office of a preacher, such as: habitual hunting and fishing, going to bars and other public places of amusement, merchandising, political activity, and the like. More about this later when we speak about the life and behavior of the preacher.

### Comment 3.

The first requirement of a sermon is that it contain nothing but God's Word pure and unalloyed.

Luther writes: "A preacher must not pray the Our Father nor seek the forgiveness of sins when he has preached (if he is a correct preacher). Rather he must say and boast with Jeremiah: 'Thou knowest: that which came out of my lips was right before Thee' (Jer. 17:16). Indeed, with St. Paul and all Apostles and Prophets, [he must] say: *Haec dixit Dominus*, God Himself has said that. . . . Here it is not necessary, indeed, not good to ask forgiveness of sins as if there had been incorrect teaching. For it is God's Word, not mine, which God neither can nor should forgive to me but rather confirm, praise, crown, and say, You have taught correctly, ... and the Word is Mine. Whoever cannot boast that of his sermons should just give up preaching; for he is denying the blaspheming God" ("Against Hans Wurst" [1541]; Walch XVII, 1685).

The purity of doctrine includes "rightly dividing the Word of truth" (2 Tim. 2:15), the distinction between Law and Gospel. He is not rightly dividing the Word of truth:

1. Who uses the Gospel to take away the sharpness of the Law or the Law to take away the sweetness of the Gospel:

2. Who teaches in such a way that the [carnally] secure are comforted and those who are terrified at their sins become yet more terrified;

3. Who directs those struck by the Law to prayer for grace instead of to the means of grace;

4. Who presents the Law, with its threats and demands, as if God overlooked weaknesses and were content if the Christian did as much as he could, and presents the Gospel as if it were a comfort only for those already pious;

5. Who tries to move the irregenerate to good works by the demands, threats, and promises of the Law and demands that those who are still unbelievers give up sinning and love God and the neighbor;

6. Who demands a special degree of penitence and comforts only those who have already become new people;

7. Who confuses not being able to believe with not being allowed to believe, and the like.

He is mixing and confusing Law and Gospel. Even if he otherwise correctly divides Law and Gospel and even defines them correctly, his doctrine is false.

In his 1532 "Sermon on the Distinction Between Law and Gospel," Luther writes: "Therefore it is highly necessary that these two words be well and rightly distinguished, for where that is not done, neither Law nor Gospel can be understood, and consciences must perish in blindness and error. For the Law has its goal, how far it should go and what it should do, namely up to Christ, in that it terrifies the impenitent with God's wrath and disfavor. In the same way, the Gospel also has its special office and work, to preach the forgiveness of sins to troubled consciences. So these two cannot be mixed with each other without falsifying doctrine, nor can one be taken for the other. For Law and Gospel are indeed both God's

## The Requirements of Public Preaching

Word, but not the same kind of doctrine...

"So whoever is adept at this art of dividing Law and Gospel, set him above and call him a doctor of holy Scripture. For without the Holy Spirit it is impossible to hit upon this distinction. I experience in myself, and also see daily in others, how difficult it is to separate the doctrine of the Law and the Gospel from one another. The Holy Spirit must be the Master and Teacher here, or no man on earth will be able to understand or teach it. Therefore not Papist, no false Christian, not fanatic [*Schwaermer*] can distinguish these two from one another.... The art is common. It is quickly said, how the Law is a different work and doctrine from the Gospel. But to distinguish *practice* (in application) and to bring the art to effect, that is effort and labor" (Erlangen, XIX, 236ff.).

That is how it happens that many sermons, in spite of all the Christian talk that they contain, are false through and through.

**Comment 4.**

The second requirement of a sermon is that it correctly apply God's Word. Two passages of holy Scripture show us the necessary, correct application: 2 Tim. 3:16-17 and Rom. 15:4. God's Word is to be applied in a five-fold way. To retain the Greek designations with our old [theologians]: not only didascalic (for doctrine), but also elenchtic (for reproof or the refutation of false doctrine), epanorthotic (for correction of sins), paedeutic (for instruction in righteousness), and paracletic (for comfort).

That does not mean that every sermon must be organized according to these five uses but that these five uses, indicated by the Holy Spirit, should be the foundation for every sermon. Joh. Jak. Rambach writes: "Some preachers bind themselves to the well-known five uses in such a way that they consider it a mortal sin if they (one time) do not touch one because they do not consider a sermon complete if it does not have the five uses, if one does not: 1. teach a little; 2. refute the heretics a little; 3. rebuke sin a little; 4. exhort to righteous living a little; 5. comfort a little in it... Sometimes it is fitting, without being forced, that all five uses *sua sponte* (of themselves) flow out of a Gospel [pericope]. But the preacher must always find out what the subject matter, the condition of the listeners, and other conditions require and permit" (*Erlaeuterung ueber die Praecepta homiletica,* second edition

(Giessen, 1746), pp. 204f.).

a. The didascalic use, for doctrine, is the one the holy apostle places before all others. It is the most important of all. It is the foundation of the other four uses. Even if a sermon is so rich in admonitions, rebukes, and comforts, if it is without doctrine, it is still a thin, empty sermon, with admonitions, rebukes, and comforts suspended as in mid-air.

It is inexpressible how much many preachers sin in this respect. The preacher has hardly touched his text and doctrinal topic and already starts to admonish, rebuke, or comfort. His sermon consists of almost nothing but questions and exclamations, blessings and woes, so that the listener can hardly consider anything calmly. Far removed from going to the heart and producing true life, such preaching is much more suited to preach people to death, to kill any hunger for the bread of life, methodically to produce boredom with God's Word. It must be repugnant to every listener to be tastelessly admonished, rebuked, or comforted without first having the doctrinal foundation laid.

It is admittedly easier to do that on the spur of the moment, so that the sermon seems living and powerful, than to present a doctrine clearly and thoroughly. That it is easier may well be the main reason why some preach so little doctrine. They usually pick a theme that presupposes that the listeners already know the subject matter, and so they promise only a practical application of the matter. But in many [preachers] the reason certainly lies in the fact that they cannot present revealed doctrine thoroughly to others because they themselves have no thorough knowledge of it.

Others may preach so little doctrine because of the delusion that detailed doctrinal presentations are too dry, leave listeners cold, and do not serve for awakening, conversion, and true Christianity of the heart. But that is a great error. It is precisely the eternal thoughts of God's heart, counsels, and mysteries of faith, which had been kept secret since the world began but have been made known to us through the Scriptures of the Prophets and Apostles [Rom. 16:25-26], are the heavenly seed which must be sunk deep into the hearts of the listeners, if the fruit of a true repentance, a sincere faith, and an upright, active love is to grow forth in the same. The true growth of a congregation is not possible without sermons rich in thorough doctrine. He who falls short here is not faithful in his

## The Requirements of Public Preaching

office, even if, by zealous admonition, earnest rebuking, and evangelical-sounding comfort, he gives the appearance of being consumed with faithful concern for the souls entrusted to him.

The first use of God's Word is "for doctrine" (2 Tim. 3:16). The first, necessary, indispensable characteristic of a bishop as a preacher is that he be "apt to teach" (1 Tim. 3:2; 2 Tim. 2:24). The first office in the church is that of teaching (Rom. 12:7-8). The most important requirement of a sermon, after that it contain only God's pure Word, is that it be rich in doctrine. The highest model in this respect is St. Paul's Epistle to the Romans, in which the practical application follows only after the doctrinal foundation has been laid in the first eleven chapters.

b. The elenchtic use, to reprove or refute false doctrine, also belongs to the correct application of God's Word. The apostle says that explicitly in 2 Tim. 3:16. We see it in the example of all prophets and apostles and of our Lord Jesus Himself. As often as we see them and the Lord Himself occupied with doctrines, so often we see them add defense, not only against coarse errors (1 Cor. 15:12ff.) but also against more subtle ones (Gal. 5:9); not only in a friendly way (Gal. 4:10-12) but also in a serious, vehement way (Gal. 1:8-9; Phil. 3:2); not only with reference to the false teachings but also with reference to the false teachers, with or without naming them and their sects (1 John 4:1; Gal. 5:10; Matt. 16:6; Rev. 2:15; 2 Tim. 2:17; nominal elenchus! [reproof by name]).

That is required of every preacher: "Holding fast the faithful Word as he hath been taught, that he may be able by sound doctrine both to exhort and to convince the gainsayers. For there are many unruly and vain talkers and deceivers, specially those of the circumcision: whose mouths must be stopped" (Titus 1:9-11; those who insist on works instead of faith, Law instead of Gospel). He who presents pure doctrine but does not refute the contrary false doctrine, does not warn against wolves in sheep's clothing, against false prophets [Matt. 7:15], is not faithful steward of God's mysteries [1 Cor. 4:1], no faithful shepherd of the sheep entrusted to him, no faithful watchman on the walls of Zion. According to God's Word, he is an unfaithful servant, a silent watchdog, a traitor.

It is only too clear how many souls are lost and what harm the church suffers because doctrinal reproof is not practiced. The correct doctrine is often correctly grasped only when the opposite is made clear at the same time. The false teachers try to wrap their error cleverly in the appearance of truth so that simple people are all too easily deceived, in spite of their love for the truth, if they have not been warned in advance. If his sheep fall prey to ravening wolves, while he is their pastor or after he has had to leave them, the preacher will seek in vain to wash his hands in innocence because he has preached the truth if he has not warned against error at the same time, in some circumstances including the name of the errorists.

Luther writes: "Contradict the arrogant spirits. Otherwise your confession is a mask and good for nothing. Whoever holds his doctrine, faith, and confession to be true, correct, and certain, cannot stand in the same stall with others who present or adhere to false doctrine or ever speak kind words to the devil and his flakes. A teacher who is silent about errors and yet wants to be a correct teacher is worse than a manifest fanatic [*Schwaermer*] and is doing more damage by his hypocrisy than a heretic. He is not to be trusted. He is a wolf and a fox, a hireling and a belly-servant, etc., and may despise and surrender doctrine, Word, faith, Sacrament, churches, and schools. Either he is secretly in bed with the enemies; or he is a doubter and windbag and wants to see how it comes out, whether Christ or the devil will be victorious; or he is completely uncertain within himself and is not worthy to be a pupil, much less a teacher, and wants to anger no one, nor speak a word for Christ, nor cause woe to the devil and the world" (Walch, XVII, 1477).

c. Equally necessary is the epanorthotic application of God's Word, to correct sins. We recall here two general rules. The first is from Lukas Osiander's book about preaching: "In the whole presentation, one would do well to guard against being bitter, much less venomous, so that one does not unnecessarily embitter and alienate the listeners' spirits. For rebukes can be earnest and yet without bitterness; untimely toughness in speech recalls a rough, surly, and unkind attitude. But a modest and yet earnest way of speaking overcomes the listener's heart more quickly. For the listener who is not yet incorrigible then perceives that the preacher is being somewhat strict, not from a personal passion, but rather for the sake of his office, and he notices that one intends indeed only his salvation. But if one must necessarily present something in a rougher form, then one must carefully put down in writing,

## The Requirements of Public Preaching

in his arrangement, the words which one expects to be somewhat sensitive, so that he can consider them before he presents them, and also for this reason that then no one can give them a false interpretation by adding or taking something away from them. For the servant of the church can assure in a holy and precious way that neither more nor less, and no other words, than he has written down can go over his lips" (*De ratione concionandi*, p. 71).

A second rule about rebuking sins is given by Luther in his 1527 letter to Hausmann in Zwickau: "It has been told to me, and also indicated by N., what one of your preachers is beginning to do in the pulpit in an inept way, and is attacking the persons of the council in a disorderly way, which pleases the people. And so there shows through again and again the spirit which sees its own glory and following. Therefore it is my friendly request that you would look into that together with the council so that sleep and negligence do not again give us something to do. You indeed know from God's (grace) that such personal rebukes belong nowhere else than in the assembly of Christians. But now you have not yet instituted such an assembly, as we hope will be set up by the visitation. Also, even if the assembly had already been instituted, yet such scolding would not be correct, because St. Paul says: 'Rebuke not an elder, but intreat him as a father' [1 Tim. 5:1]. And Christ in Matt. 18[:15-20] wants one to be admonished individually first. Whatever spirit does not hold this order intends nothing good. But in the public *theatrali concione* (in the assembly where everyone may run together without distinction), where Christian and non-Christian stand next to one another and listen, as happens in the church, one should also rebuke in general all kinds of unbelief and vice and not depict anyone in particular. For it is a common sermon [for everyone] and should remain common and not shame anyone or make him blush in front of others until they are separated and come into the assembly where one admonishes, requests, and rebukes in an orderly way" (Walch, XXI, 167f.).

d. If God's Word is not applied paedeutically, "for instruction in righteousness," the sermon is lacking not something peripheral but something essential. Even most Christians, since they all still have the flesh to a great extent, are of such a nature that even the most glorious and richest doctrinal sermons will go by them without leaving a trace if the preacher does not connect exhortation with the teaching, not only showing the correct use but also encouraging it in the most moving way.

On the other hand, all true Christians are of such a nature that one can accomplish all kinds of things in them through urgent exhortation. So many preachers accomplish so little in bringing Christians to good works or bringing them away from sinful living because they do not exhort but rather demand, command, threaten, and rebuke. They do not suspect what a powerful weapon they have but do not use. Upright Christians, even if burdened with various weaknesses, do not want to reject God's Word. They want to live for Him Who died for them. They no longer want to serve sin, the world, and the devil. They want to be completely renewed according to the image of God. If they hear in the exhorting preacher the voice of their gracious God, they neither can nor want to oppose it.

In the Church Postille, Luther says about the Epistle for the Nineteenth Sunday after Trinity [Eph. 4:22-28]: "That is again an exhortation to the Christians that they may follow through with their faith in good works and new life. For although they have forgiveness of sins through Baptism, yet the old Adam still adheres to their flesh, who always moves in evil inclinations and desires, both worldly and spiritual vices; so that, if they do not withstand and resist such, they will again lose the faith and forgiveness of sins which they have received, and will then become worse than they had been before, will begin to despise and persecute God's Word by which they are rebuked. Indeed, even those who like to hear it and appreciate it and intend to live according to it still daily need such admonition and encouragement. For the old hide of the sinful flesh is so strong and wild, the devil himself is so powerful and wicked where he gains a little room. Where he can set a claw, he gets all the way in until he sinks the person again into the previous, old, damnable life of unbelief, despising and disobeying God.

"That is why the preaching office is necessary in the church, not only for the ignorant whom one should teach, such as the simple and unwise people and the young folks, but rather also for those who know well how they should believe and live, to awaken and admonish them so that they are on guard every day so that they do not become lazy nor bored and tired in the struggle which they must have on earth with the devil, with their own flesh and all vices. Therefore St. Paul also diligently pursues such admonition

## The Requirements of Public Preaching

to his Christians that it even seems as if he were doing too much of it, that he is everywhere drumming it into them so vehemently as if they were so foolish as not to know, or to be unaware and to forget to do it without being ordered and driven. But he knows also that, although the Christians have begun to believe and are in a condition in which the fruit of faith should prove itself, yet everything is not therefore done and accomplished so quickly.

"So it is not valid here to say and think: indeed, it is enough that the doctrine is given; so where the Spirit and faith is, the fruits and good works will follow on their own. For although the Spirit is there and, as Christ says, is willing and also works in them who believe, there stands against that also the flesh. The devil is also not on holiday but wants to bring the weak flesh down again through temptation and provocation, etc. So one must not just let the people go as if one might not admonish nor urge them by God's Word to the good way of life. No, you are not permitted to be negligent and lazy here, for the flesh is already all too lazy to obey the Spirit. Indeed, it is all too strong in resisting the same, as St. Paul says elsewhere (Gal. 5:17): 'For the flesh lusteth against the Spirit, . . . so that ye cannot do the things that ye would.'

"Therefore here, too, God must act like a good householder and ruler who has a lazy servant or maid or officials who are not diligent (even if they are otherwise not wicked or unfaithful). He must not think that he has accomplished it by once or twice commanding them what they are to do if he is not himself always on their backs, pushing them. So with us also it has not come to the point that our flesh and blood go and leap in pure joy and desire for good works and obedience toward God, as the Christian would like to be and as faith shows. Rather, even if he is always pushing and urging him, he can still hardly accomplish it. Then what would happen if one wanted to omit such admonition and urging and yet go along and think (as many secure Christians do): Yes, I myself know very well what I should do; I heard it so often so many years ago and have even taught others! etc. So that I hold that if one would be quiet for a year with preaching and admonishing, we would become more wicked than any heathen" (Erlangen, IX, 306ff.).

Paul shows the nature of exhortation, which is only for Christians, when he writes, "I beseech you therefore, brethren, by the mercies of God" (Rom. 12:1). Luther comments: "He (Paul) does not say: I command you; for he is preaching to those who are already pious Christians, in the new man, through faith, who are not to be forced with commands but rather exhorted so that they willingly do what is to be done with the sinful old man. For whoever does not do it willingly, through friendly exhortation alone, is not Christian. And whoever forces it by laws from the unwilling, is already no Christian preacher by a worldly jailer. A law-driver urges with threats and rebukes; a grace-preacher draws and encourages with demonstrated divine kindness and mercy. For he wants no unwilling works and unhappy service. He wants joyous and happy service to God. He who is not moved and drawn by such a sweet, dear Word of God's mercy, granted and given to us so abundantly in Christ, so that he also does it with love and will, for God's glory and his neighbor's benefit, is nothing, and everything is lost on him" (Church Postille on the Epistle for the First Sunday after Epiphany [Rom. 12:1-5]; Erlangen, VIII, 5f.).

e. From Rom. 15:4 it follows that, as the use of God's Word for doctrine must be the foundation, its use for comfort and hope must be the constant goal of all sermons. The true Christian is not the person floating in undisturbed, blessed calm and joy, as he is sadly! so frequently—with complete falsehood—described in the sermons of inexperienced or fanatical [*schwaermerisch*] preachers. Rather the true Christian must through much inward and outward tribulation enter into the kingdom of God [Acts 14:22]. He finds himself more often in comfortlessness than in serene certainty.

A servant of Christ and shepherd of His sheep is administering his office very poorly if the often burdened and bothered Christian heart that hurries to church does not find the comfort he so much needs and wants. Sermons that are empty of all comfort for the person under cross and affliction are not true evangelical sermons.

They must contain not only comfort in the anxiety about sin and the need of the conscience but also in all kinds of misery in this life. A preacher must not think that every true Christian must be so spiritual, so strong and heavenly minded, that he does not sense earthly trouble and needs no special comfort against it. A preacher must show a fatherly, indeed, a motherly heart toward his listeners (1 Cor. 4:15; 1 Thess. 2:7; see Is. 66:13) and measure the causes of all kinds of sorrow and trouble not as they are in themselves but as they are felt by the Christians entrusted to his care, who are weak or sometimes become weak. He must consider that nothing is more dangerous for the Christian than worldly sorrow and heaviness and that Satan, that spirit of sorrow, continually wants to sink Christians in it. Comfort is the main means for making Christians willing to run zealously the race of sanctification, in all good works; as David says, "I will run the way of Thy commandments, when Thou shalt enlarge [Luther's translation: "comfort"] my heart" (Ps. 119:32).

An evangelical preacher must not be deterred from delivering abundant comfort because he sees so many weaknesses in his Christians. He will cure these weaknesses not through pushing the Law (although he should not fail to present the demands and threats of the Law) but through genuine evangelical comfort. Just consider how Christ dealt with His frail disciples, and how the prophets and apostles dealt with their frail but upright listeners. Sometimes they do grab them harshly, but the primary element in their treatment is friendly speech and comfort. For the whole Gospel is nothing but a joyous message, a great preaching of comfort.

There is no passage of Scripture from which a true evangelical preacher cannot draw rich comfort for believing Christians. [Walther gives examples from Articles II and XI of the Epitome of the Formula of Concord; the former on Phil. 2:13; the latter on predestination.] The writings of Luther and Hieronymus Weller are full of masterpieces of comforting application, from which a preacher can learn how to speak with the wary as those men learned it from the Lord Jesus Himself and from the prophets and apostles, and in living experience. Without one's own experience of comfort in all inward and outward trouble, it is impossible to become a true preacher of comfort (2 Cor. 1:3-7) and to obey God's command: "Comfort ye, comfort ye My people, saith your God. Speak ye comfortably to Jerusalem, and cry unto her, that her warfare is accomplished, that her iniquity is pardoned" (Is. 40:1-2).

The third requirement of preaching is that the whole counsel of God be proclaimed to the listeners for their salvation. That follows from the serious divine command to the preacher: "Thou shalt not add thereto, nor diminish from it" (Deut. 12:32). It follows from the fact that all Scripture is not only inspired by God but also useful for doctrine (2 Tim. 3:16; see Matt. 4:4; Rom. 15:4). We see it in the example of the holy Apostle Paul, who showed that he was "pure from the blood of all men" in that he had "kept back nothing that was profitable" but had declared to them "all the counsel of God," proclaiming "repentance toward God, and faith toward our Lord Jesus Christ" (Acts 20:20-21, 26-27).

Something essential is missing if a preacher presents only Biblical doctrines but not all the Biblical doctrines revealed for our salvation, or if he mentions them all but does not present them fully, in the context of all doctrine, according to their importance for faith and life. A preacher is not a lord over his listener's faith or over the Word but a steward of God's mysteries and a servant of the Word (2 Cor. 1:24; 1 Cor. 4:1, Luke 1:2). Keeping silent about a doctrine of the Word is inexcusably robbing the listeners.

It is to be advised that at the start of the church year, the preacher make a plan to use the pericopes so that, if possible, every fundamental article of the Christian faith finds its place during the year. It is no small reproach to a preacher if an attentive listener has heard him for years without being instructed in important aspects of Christian faith and life. [Walther's examples include: neighborly love, Christian freedom, church discipline, the church, the ministry, the last things, duties of Christians in various states of life, betrothal and marriage, raising children, prayer, home devotions, usury, the inspiration of Scripture, the difference between a church and a sect, temptation, the sin against the Holy Spirit, the election of grace, Christian perfection, etc.] It can happen, by the preacher's fault, that some of his listeners stray into the greatest danger, and the preacher cannot boast with Paul that he is innocent of the blood of all men.

Another shortcoming here is when a preacher does indeed diligently preach that one should believe but does not thereby show how one can attain such faith. This shortcoming, which is now sadly! very frequent everywhere, is already reproved in the 1528 instructions to the visitors: "Now we find in teaching, among other things, primarily this error that, although some preach of the faith through which we are justified, yet there is not enough of showing how one comes to faith, and almost all omit one part of Christian teaching, without which not one can understand what faith is or means. For Christ says in Luke 3:8 and Luke 24:27 [*sic*, see v. 47] that one should preach repentance and forgiveness of sins in His name, But many now speak alone of the forgiveness of sins and say little or nothing of repentance. Forgiveness of sins can also not be understood without repentance. And if one preaches forgiveness of sins without repentance, it follows that the people suppose that they have already received forgiveness of sins and thereby become secure and fearless.

"That is a greater error and sin than all errors that have been before this time, and it is certainly a concern, as Christ says in Matt. 12:45 and Luke 11:26, that the last will be worse than the first. Therefore we have instructed and admonished the pastors that they preach the Gospel completely, as they ought to do, and not one part without the other. For God says in Deut. 4:2, that one should not add to nor subtract from His Word. And the current preachers scold the Pope that he has added much to Scripture, which is sadly! all too true; but these who do not preach repentance tear a large part out of Scripture while they are preaching about eating meat and similar minor matters. Although they are also not to be silenced at the right time for the sake of tyranny, to defend Christian freedom: what is that other than, as Christ says in Matt. 23:24, to strain out a gnat and swallow a camel?

"So we have admonished them that they diligently and frequently admonish the people to repent, to have repentance and sorrow over their sins, and to fear God's judgement; and that they also do not neglect the necessary matter of repentance, for both John [the Baptist] and Christ rebuke the Pharisees more harshly for their hypocrisy of holiness than [they rebuke] common sinners. So the preachers should rebuke the coarse sins in the common man, but where false holiness is, [they should] admonish much more harshly to repentance" (Walch, X, 1912ff.).

A third shortcoming here is when a preacher does indeed preach again and again about repentance and faith but does not preach about the necessity of good works and sanctification, or gives no thorough instruction about good works, Christian virtues, and sanctification. An explicit, clear, and calm description of a truly Christian life and behavior accomplishes more than a constant, threatening, and warning assurance of its necessity.

Luther writes about that: "My Antinomians preach very finely and (as I cannot think otherwise) with true earnestness about the grace of Christ, the forgiveness of sins, and whatever more is to be said about redemption. But they flee this conclusion like the devil, that they should tell people about the Third Article, sanctification, that is, the new life in Christ. For they think that one should not frighten nor trouble the people, but should rather always preach about grace and the forgiveness of sins in Christ, and at the same time they avoid these or similar words: You hear this, you want to be a Christian, and nevertheless you remain an adulterer, whoremonger, full sow, arrogant, greedy, a usurer, jealous, vengeful, wicked, etc. Instead they say: You hear it, you are an adulterer, a whoremonger, a greedy person, or some other kind of sinner—if you only believe, you are saved and must not be afraid of the Law; Christ has fulfilled everything.

"Friend, tell me, is that not *Antecedens concedirt,* and *Consequens negirt* (admitting the premise but denying the conclusion that follows)? Indeed, it means taking Christ away from one and the same person and making Him nothing when he is preached in a most exalted way. And that is all yes and no in the same things. For such a Christ is no one and nothing, who died for such sinners who, after the forgiveness of sins, do not abandon the sins and lead a new life. So they preach Christ with fine Nestorian and Eutychian dialectics, that Christ is something and yet is not that. They are indeed fine Easter preachers and shameful Pentecost preachers. For they preach nothing *de sanctificatione et vivificatione Spiritus Sancti,* (that is) of the sanctification (and vivification) of the Holy Spirit, but rather only of the redemption of Christ. But Christ (Whom they preach highly, as is proper) is Christ or has gained redemption from sins and death for this purpose that the Holy Spirit should make us new people from the old Adam, that we die to sin and live to righteousness, as St. Paul teaches in Rom. 6:2ff., beginning and increasing here on earth and being perfect there.

"For Christ has earned for us not only *gratiam*, grace, but also *donum*, the gift of the Holy Spirit, so that we should have not only the forgiveness of sins but also cessation of sins (John 1:16-17). Now whoever does not cease from sin but remains in the previous sinful life, must have gotten a different Christ from the Antinomians. The true Christ is not there even if all angels cried nothing but Christ! Christ!—and he must be damned with his new Christ" ("On the Councils and the Churches," 1539, Walch XVI, 2741f.).

If one wants to learn how to describe thoroughly a truly Christian life according to its inward basis and its outward representation, then he has, next to holy Scripture itself, a glorious model in the epistle part of Luther's Church Postille.

## The Requirements of Public Preaching

As much as the above is contrary to the preacher's duty to proclaim the whole counsel of God, he is active even more inexcusably, doing even greater harm to his listeners, contrary to this duty, if he preaches more Law and Gospel; if he does not make the Gospel predominate in his sermons; and if he does not make the comfort-rich doctrine of the justification of a poor sinner by grace, through faith in Jesus Christ, without the works of the Law, the golden thread through all his sermons (2 Cor. 3:6; 2 Tim. 4:5; John 15:27).

Luther writes: "In my heart there rules alone that one article, namely faith in Christ; from which, through which, and unto which all my theological thoughts flow back and forth, day and night" (Erlangen Latin, I, 3).

Preaching the whole counsel of God means that every single sermon should contain enough of the whole order of salvation that a person could learn the way of salvation even if he heard only this one sermon. As much as it deadens the desire of the listeners if the preacher always speaks of repentance, faith, and sanctification with the same words, it is still necessary for this order to be the foundation for every sermon. "The same things" (Phil. 3:1) should be presented in the most various ways.

Asked about including the order of salvation, which a listener called his favorite topic, in every sermon, a preacher answered: "I always think that this sermon may be the last one I deliver or the last one someone from my congregation hears, being close to departing. I do not want to miss the last opportunity to call sinners to repentance and to point them to Jesus Christ, so that not one of the souls God has committed to my care can one day accuse me before Christ's judgement seat and say: Once, the last time I heard you preach, I had this quiet question in my heart: What must I do to be saved [see Acts 16:30]? But you did not answer this question for me!"

In no country on earth is this rule more important than in this land of immigration, where many inhabitants lead a truly nomadic life. In these circumstances a preacher often has a soul among his listeners who hears him only once and then goes away, either into the wilderness or into a labyrinth of the most varied sects. How important it is that such souls, when God leads them into the church of an orthodox preacher, hear what is absolutely necessary for their salvation!

## Comment 5.

The fourth requirement of correct preaching is that it correspond to the special needs of the listeners.

The holy apostle does indeed write: "Preach the Word; be instant in season, out of season; reprove, rebuke, exhort, with all longsuffering and doctrine" (2 Tim. 4:2-3). But it would be a gross misunderstanding if one concluded from that that a preacher can do his duty even if he does not consider the time, the opportunity, or the condition of his listeners. The apostle means only that, when it is required for the salvation of souls and the glory of God, a preacher should preach God's Word whether or not people like it, whether or not it seems to them to be the right time. [Walther cites St. Augustine and Abraham Calov.]

If a preacher proclaims God's Word, pure and unalloyed, for doctrine, reproof, correction, comfort, and instruction in righteousness, he can still not wash his hands in innocence if he does not mete it out according to the individual conditions of his congregation. God has instituted a personal, public preaching office so that God's Word may be applied according to the different natures of human beings. Recognizing the special circumstances and special needs of the congregation to which God's Word is to be presented is a major portion of the pastor's sermon preparation. Comparing the text with the needs of his own congregation, with the failings and frailities it suffers, with the dangers it faces, must determine not only the choice of the theme but also the whole way in which it is handled.

The same Word of God contains St. Paul's Epistle to the Romans and the Epistle to the Hebrews. But how different is the choice of subject matter and the manner of presentation in these two epistles. It depends on the needs of those to whom each one is addressed. Everywhere Paul, the great Apostle to the Heathen, proclaims the same counsel for salvation. But how differently he speaks in Athens, the city of philosophers (Acts 17:15-34), than in Jerusalem, and there differently before the people than before the high council (Acts 21-23)!

Concerning the application of God's Word for doctrine, one must decide the substance and the manner [literally: "the what? and the how?"] according to the level of knowledge of the congregation. If they are still largely ignorant, they must be given milk, not meat,

## The Requirements of Public Preaching

and be taught the ABC's. The foundation must be laid in repentance, faith, etc. But those who have been accustomed to it must be given stronger food for their growth and maturity. See Heb. 5:11-6:2; 1 Cor. 3:1-2; Eph. 4:13-14.

Luther writes in his preface to the Epistle to the Romans: "Every doctrine has its measure, time, and age. . . . For as strong wine is death to children, it is a refreshment of life to the aged. So one cannot simply present all kinds of doctrine to everyone" (Walch, X. 2317).

It would be perverse to give an ignorant congregation a subtle discussion of the communication of attributes or the election of grace; or to give an inexperienced congregation an explicit description of high spiritual temptations; or to speak of all matters of Christian freedom, as it can be correctly understood only by firmly established Christians, to a congregation that was either caught in problems of conscience or inclined to carnal liberty. Primarily the basics of Christianity, faith and love, must be taught to such congregations. When a preacher had confused his listeners by

Fig. 5: This picture of Walther is the one most well known. It was printed with I Peter 2:9 in Walther's handwritting below it.
Courtesy of Concordia Historical Institute.

speaking against Papistic abuses of auricular confession before having laid the foundation, Luther said that the man had wanted to throw away the old shoes before he had new ones and had tried to put new wine into old wineskins.

Luther said: "He should first have taught the people nothing but faith and love. This doctrine (of abuses) would have come soon enough after a year, if they first understood Christ well. . . . I preached a good three years in Wittenberg before I brought it to the people, and these fellows want to finish it in an hour" (Walch, XV, 2499f.).

Even in a congregation that has many knowledgeable and experienced Christians, the preacher should never forget that there are also people who need milk. He should give them special consideration. He must guard against reaching too high or presenting the divine truths to the people in unintelligible words. Luther once said: "A curse and malediction on all preachers who reach for high, difficult, and subtle matters in church and want to present them to the people and preach about them, seek their own honor and glory, and want to please one or two ambitious people. When I preach here, I get down as low as I can; do not consider those who have doctors' and masterss' degrees, of whom there are about forty; but consider the many young people, children, and servants, of whom there are hundreds and thousands. I preach to them; I direct myself according to them; they need it. If the others do not want to hear, the door is open!

"So, hear Bernhard, be diligent to preach simply, understandably, purely, and plainly. . . . To sprinkle Greek, Hebrew, Latin into sermons is nothing but arrogance, which is not proper and fitting at this time and place; it only happens that the poor, uneducated laypeople are amazed and praise them. Oh, they say, that is a learned and eloquent man; even though they understand nothing of it nor learn from it" (Erlangen, LIX, 272ff.).

In his preface to his 1527 exposition of Zechariah, Luther [notes how many learned preachers there are and thanks God for them; but he remarks how few there are who are really good at teaching the Catechism to the common people; Luther continues]: "One should consider them to be the best and most useful preachers, the exemplary ones, who can push the Catechism well, that is, can correctly teach the Our Father, the Ten Commandments, and the Creed. They are rare birds. For in them there is not much glory

## The Requirements of Public Preaching

or show; but there is greater benefit. And it is also the most necessary preaching because the whole of Scripture is summarized therein, and there is no Gospel [pericope] on the basis of which one cannot teach it if one only wants to and will undertake to teach the poor, common man" (Erlangen, XLII, 109ff.).

Second, with respect to the refutation of false doctrine, a preacher must consider the special needs of the congregation to which he is preaching. In a congregation that does not yet know the correct doctrine, it can only have a harmful effect to preach much against false doctrines. Such a congregation will either be filled with antipathy toward the preacher as a loveless debater and controversialist because it cannot yet perceive the importance of doctrinal unity, and so it will be frightened away from pure doctrine and filled with sympathy for the false doctrine; or it will thereby be made fanatical and brought to an unreasoning zeal against the sects, and it will place its Christianity and Lutheranism, not in true and living faith, but in zealotry for orthodoxy and the customs of the orthodox church. A preacher must also remember that it is not his office to campaign against all imaginable false doctrines and heresies. He should consider, mention, and refute those that have already entered his congregation or are threatening to do so.

Third, with respect to rebuking and exhorting, a preacher should consider the special needs of his own congregation in applying God's Word. The main rule is that a preacher would rebuke all sins but especially those that are more prominent than others in his congregation. [Walther refers to Luther's preface to the Small Catechism.] A preacher must consider that, without considering the special needs of his congregation, little or nothing will be accomplished even by the most zealous and earnest rebuking. For example, if in a congregation in which there is little knowledge, he harshly rebukes the coarse sins and those which occur least in his congregation, he could easily produce more hypocrites than penitents. It shows up—and not seldom—that those for whom he cannot preach sharply enough are the worst Christians. They always want others rebuked, not themselves, and if they are once struck by it, they become hostile to the preacher. But if a congregation, according to the majority of its members, is still immature and ignorant, then it would be perverse, for example, to preach zealously against things which they, with their unsharpened consciences, do not yet recognize as sins, such as dancing and the like, as if these were the real, the worst and most horrible sins, without consideration for the status of the people's knowledge.

One should never rebuke in such a way as to give the appearance that he wants to lord it over the congregation and that he considers himself a great saint exalted over the sinners. He should never use common insults or ironic, sarcastic speech. He should never rebuke in such a way that he gives the appearance of misusing public preaching, when no one can talk back, to offend his opponents. He should never rebuke on Sunday things that have been reported to him the previous week.

As often as one must rebuke with any harshness, he would explain to the listeners the sad necessity for using harsh words. He should ask them not to become embittered but to remember that he must do it because of God's strict commandments (Ezek. 3:17ff.) and for their salvation. He should appeal to the testimony of their consciences as the judges. He should, for God's sake, not take sides. He should remember that rebuking usually accomplishes nothing if he gives even the appearance of living in the same sins he is rebuking (for example, greed, arrogance, irreconcilability, intemperance).

As for considering the special needs of the congregation in connection with applying God's Word for comfort, it is beyond doubt that, under all circumstances, the comfort-rich Gospel must predominate in the sermons of an evangelical preacher. But it is equally certain that in congregations in which there is still much carnal living or self-righteousness and false holiness, the sweet Gospel must be preceded by the sharpest, most serious preaching of the Law, clearly revealing human corruption and terrifying the conscience. As necessary as it is to lead a mostly frightened congregation to the green pastures of the Gospel, it would be just as perverse and dangerous to souls to try to bring people who do not yet know their deep corruption, to repentance by presenting their suffering Savior.

Here, too, Luther is a great example. The sweet doctrine of the justification of a poor sinner by grace alone through faith alone predominates in all his sermons, up to his death. But it cannot be denied that Luther's earlier sermons apply the Gospel even more abundantly than his later sermons. When Luther started, he found people who, though very ignorant, lived mostly in legalistic fear of God, death, eternity, judgment, and hell. Almost no Gospel but only

# The Requirements of Public Preaching

Law had been preached to them. The Gospel itself had been perverted into a Law; the Savior, into a terrifying Judge. In addition to the divine Law, an unbearable burden of human regulations had been laid on the people. So at that time Luther's preaching was primarily directed not to rebuke but to comfort, not to wound but to heal. But later, when the Gospel had released the people from the burden of the Pope, and many began to make evangelical freedom into a cloak for wickedness, we hear Luther rebuke and threaten in his sermons much more frequently than earlier. [Walther refers to Luther's Genesis Commentary on Genesis 21:15-16; Walch, I, 2143ff.]

## Comment 6.

The fifth requirement of preaching is that it be timely.

It hardly needs to be mentioned that that does not mean that the preacher should determine the content and form of his sermons according to the spirit and taste of the time. Then in a time when people did not want to permit the saving doctrines of God's Word, he would preach to people that for which their ears were itching and be silent about certain doctrines of God's Word which were considered antiquated or offensive. Or he would have to modify them so that God's Word would no longer be offensive to those proud of [human] virtue nor foolish to those proud of [human] reason. God forbid! Woe to the preacher who would adapt himself to the time in this way!

By timely preaching we mean the exact opposite. No time produces better people than another. In every time people lie in that inborn corruption from which they can be rescued only through the pure, complete Word of God. But in every time the general corruption expresses itself in a specific way. Every time has its own specific, fashionable prejudices, errors, sins, vices, and dangers. So every time has its special needs. God has not only given His written Word as the source and norm of all doctrine but has also instituted the personal preaching office to apply His Word, which contains the medicine for the spiritual ills of all ages, to the specific conditions and circumstances of people in each age.

The preaching office should be the light of the world, driving away all darkness. It should be the salt that prevents the spiritual foulness of the world. If should be the dam and wall which sets a border to the stream of corruption.

The timely preacher is not content that his sermons contain only the pure Word of God but continually considers the prejudices, errors, sins, vices, and dangers which prevail in his time, which he knows to be touching, endangering, and infecting his listeners. Anyone who wanted to deliver the same sermons which a distinguished servant of God of an earlier time had delivered with great blessing for his time, would not be doing what his office required of him in his time. The more timely the earlier preacher was, the less timely his sermons can be now. For although people today are still the same, lost damned sinners as centuries ago, our time still suffers from specific, characteristic, spiritual illnesses which need to be treated accordingly.

There was never a more timely preacher than our Luther. The constant treatment of the Pope, monasticism, self-chosen works, and the like in his sermons may now give the impression that he overdid it. But that is a testimony to Luther's serious concern not only to preach God's Word purely but also to work against the specific corruption of his time. A preacher of our time is following Luther only if he learns from him to consider the contemporary time as he did.

Reason has taken the place of the Pope. [Human] virtue with its secret societies [lodges] has taken the place of monasticism. Works of humanism and philanthropy, temperance and abstinence, have taken the place of the self-chosen works of fasting, penance, indulgences, pilgrimages, the mass, etc. Unbelief, the mocking of religion, rationalism, atheism, and materialism have taken the place of superstition. The swindle of liberation, self-deification, and the deification of the human mind have taken the place of human authority and the deification of the saints.

If we want to be Luther's faithful students, we must again and again consider contemporary dangers and the prevailing spirit of the time in our sermons, writings, and periodicals. We preachers are primarily responsible for the unopposed corruption of our time. Who should speak and work against it? If we do not do so, who can see through it by the light of God's Word and victoriously combat it with the powerful weapon of God's Word? In our time we should lift our voices like a trumpet against the errors and sins of our time. We should not be concerned that this testimony brings us nothing but scorn, ridicule, and persecution by the world, even if it seems that we are hindering the spread of the church and the salvation of souls by zealously opposing what all the world considers noble, progressive, and an achievement of civilization.

Woe to the preacher who does not touch the sore spots of his time! A double woe on the head of the preacher who otherwise knows God's Word well but has let himself be infected with the spirit and the ideas of progress, this dirt soup of all times; who prostitutes himself with the progressive people of our time instead of throwing himself against them with an iron breast [an image of knightly combat; "iron breast" recalls armor]! Woe to him who gushes and agitates with them for the beginning of the time of liberation from all "barbarism," of complete light, of complete freedom and equality!

It is true that we few, poor preachers will not hold back the flood of the end time. According to the prophecies of holy Scripture, it will finally cover and swallow everything until the Lord ends the misery by his appearing. But woe to us if we do not let God's voice of thunder resound into the raging storm "as testimony" against God's enemies and a call to salvation for all who will still be saved! For where the salt has lost its savor, how can it be seasoned [Matt. 5:13]?

## Comment 7.

The sixth and seventh requirements of preaching are that it be well organized and not too long.

a. It is true, as Spener writes somewhere, that those who are concerned only about the form of a sermon are like "those who only practice the stitching of shoes but do not care about leather and have to accept paper." It is also true that it is not the artistry, which is the preacher's contribution, but the Word of God contained in the sermon that has the power to edify Christians, to build them on the rock of salvation. But as all doctrine revealed in holy Scripture, and every part of doctrine, forms a wonderfully organized, cohesive whole, it is not the preacher's job to split it like dry wood but to present it in its wonderful order and living coherence, as much as he can by God's grace.

If he does not do that; if his sermon is nothing but an unorganized, incoherent collection of divine truths; the Holy Spirit may yet bring this or that truth into the heart of this or that listener and make it fruitful. But the preacher himself is hindering his listeners and keeping the sermon from reaching its blessed goal in them. A clear organization furthers the understanding of the divine truth, awakens attention, and helps the listeners remember what has been presented. Disorder in the sermon must cause confusion, inattention, and boredom, and keep people from remembering what they have heard.

A sermon should not be a collection of godly thoughts. As it is supposed to pursue a specific goal, it should also deal specifically with a main truth. Everything in the sermon should relate to it and serve to impress it on the people. That is not possible without a good, natural organization of all the subject matter. Experience shows that sermons which contain many different things in poor order, even if they contain much that is glorious, as a rule make less of an impression and have less of an effect than well organized sermons that form a strict unity, even if they are less full. God is a God of order, Who does everything Himself in wise order, and has formed the human spirit in such a way that it needs to be taught and learned in a definite order.

b. About the necessary brevity of a sermon, the following passage from Luther's Table Talk may find a place here: "Some plague the people with sermons that are too long, but listening is a tender matter and [the listener] soon becomes bored and tired of one thing. Doctor Pommer [Bugenhagen] always quotes this passage and makes it an excuse for his long sermons: 'He that is of God heareth God's words' (John 8:47), but moderation is good in all things.—The office and sign of a good speaker is that he stops when people most want to hear and think he is just getting started. But if people are bored and unwilling to listen and would like him to stop and come to the end and conclusion, that is a bad sign. So also with a preacher, if one says: I would liked to have listened to him yet a while longer, that is good; but if one says: he got started chattering and could never stop, that is a bad sign" (Erlangen, LIX, 222f. 242).

[Dr. Johannes Bugenhagen—called Pommer or Pomeranus because he was from Pomerania—was Luther's own pastor and confessor. Hearing that Bugenhagen had torn his robe on a nail getting out of the pulpit, Luther reportedly said something like: "I always thought he was nailed in."]

## Comment 8.

There is one more thing we must remember about preaching. There are many sermons about which one cannot say that they

## The Requirements of Public Preaching

contain false doctrine nor that they offend against any of the main requirements of preaching, but they still lack one of the most important characteristics of a good sermon. They do not reach the hearts and consciences of the listeners. Either their arrows go over the heads of the listeners, or if they do strike the listener, they do not hold him firmly but let him escape again as an open net lets the fish go. They terrify, or they awaken pleasure and pleasant feelings, or they produce a beneficial doubt, or they fill with wonder—but they do not bring the listener to a definite resolve. It takes heavenly wisdom for a sermon to reach its goal. That cannot come from any homiletic study but must be learned from one's own Christian experience and must be requested in prayer every time.

That is why Melanchthon said humbly: "Preaching is no art. Otherwise I could also do it." [Philip Melanchthon was a great scholar and lay theologian—but not a pastor. In view of all Walther says here based on God's Word, it should be clear that laymen should never preach, though one might read a sermon if necessary when a pastor cannot be present. A theological student preaching under a pastor's supervision is preparing for the pastoral office, not despising it.]

Anyone who is not a Christian; who has not learned and is not still learning the profound corruption of the human heart and the nature of the Holy Spirit's work in his own soul; anyone who does not pray when he approaches his text that, by comparing its contents with the conditions of his listeners, he may find the main topic; who does not pray when he approaches the details; who does not pray when he wants to memorize; who does not pray when he enters the pulpit—in short, who does not beg every sermon from God, cannot present any correct sermon as it should be.

It may be that after a born [proper] sermon no one calls out: That was a sermon! Those souls that are not hardened may only leave the church quietly and not say a word to anyone about it. They may feel compelled to speak about it that much more with God. Do not think that this effect if powerless. It is rather the best effect, which every sermon should have. The bestowing of great laurels [complimenting the preacher] is frequently a suspicious sign. Only too often it ends with—nothing.

# 12

## The Administration of Holy Baptism

The valid administration of Baptism includes that the one to be baptized be dipped into water, have it poured on him, or be continuously sprinkled with it in the name of the Father and of the Son and of the Holy Spirit.

**Comment 1.**

Baptism does not become invalid if the word "God" is added once or three times (when each Person is named). But either is unnecessary. It should preferably not be done. Baptism is not made invalid by the formula of the Greek church: "The servant of God, N. N., is baptized in the name of the Father, etc." But the formula customary in our church in the first person, "I baptize thee etc.," is certainly more fitting and completely conforms to Matt. 28:19; 3:11.

As for the Baptismal formulas "in the name of Christ," "in the name of the Lord," or "in the name of the Holy Trinity," a Baptism performed in that way is not to be considered absolutely no Baptism. But these formulas are to be avoided as highly questionable.

Luther writers: "I consider that, when he says, 'In the name,' he means thereby the Person of the Founder. It does not only mean to apply the name or to call upon the name in the work but to carry out the work as being done in the place of and in the name of another (Matt. 24:5; Rom. 1:5). I follow this meaning so gladly because it gives such abundant comfort and powerfully strengthens faith to know that one is not baptized by a human being but by the very Trinity, though a human being who carries it out in that name" ("On the Babylonian Captivity of the Church"; Walch, XIX, 72f.).

Brenz writes: For there are very important reasons, which it would be superfluous to enumerate, why the use of these words

## The Administration of Holy Baptism

should be carefully retained. And yet one must also understand this use correctly. For Christ has not based His Baptism on certain definite letters, syllables, words, or expressions. For He has not instituted a magic action which is bound to a definite form of words and gestures (*ritus*). Rather He has instituted heavenly Sacraments, which stand on His mind and will, which He designates for us through these or those words. For when Christ gave the command to baptize all the heathen, He was speaking Hebrew or Aramaic with His followers. So what? If Baptism were bound to specific letters and syllables, it would obviously be permitted to baptize only in the Hebrew or Aramaic language" (*Catechismus, pia et utili explicatione illustratus* (Frankfurt, 1551), pp. 55-57).

About the formula "in the name of Christ," the use of which, in the opinion of most Lutheran theologians, makes the Baptismal action invalid, the Leipzig theologian J. A. Scherzer writes: "We note that Baptism carried out in the name of Christ (Acts 2:38; 10:48; 19:5) does not exclude the most holy Trinity. But because Christ explicitly said that one should baptize in the name of the Father and of the Son and of the Holy Spirit (Matt. 28:19), no one has the right to disapprove of this formula, although we reject the opinion of those who maintain that one baptized in the name of Christ is to be baptized again conditionally" (*System. theol.*; 1689, p. 356; see pp. 358-359).

Deyling is certainly correct in taking the expression, "in the name of Christ" or "in the name of the Lord" in the Book of Acts, as indicating not the Baptismal formula but the authority by which Baptism was carried out. About Baptism with the words, "in the name of the holy Trinity," he writes the following: "We indeed admit that none of the power or substance of Baptism would be missing if someone baptized in the name of the Trinity, since the Father, the Son, and the Holy Spirit are the glorious and most holy Trinity. But Christ doubtless had important reasons for expressing the names of the individual Persons in this initiation formula and wanted Them to be explicitly named. So it is not permitted for a servant of the Word to depart from it according to his private judgement" (*op. cit.*, p. 366).

It does not need to be mentioned that we are not showing why certain differences in the form of Baptism do not make it absolutely invalid so that the preacher can act arbitrarily here but so that he may know whether or not to accept as baptized those who have allegedly been baptized by others.

Finally also grammatical errors do not deprive Baptism of its power and validity. Gerhard writes: "The question arises whether a Baptism is to be considered valid if one or the other letter or a syllable in the words is changed. I answer: If the meaning is not changed or falsified, and nothing was intentionally falsified, such a Baptism is to be considered valid, for Christ's institution is to be understood not as much of the sound as of the meaning of the words" (*Loc. de bapt.*, Sec. 93).

About the question of saying, "into the name" or "in the name," Gerhard answers: "Each of the two formulas is found in Scripture: the former (*eis to onoma*) in Matt. 28:19; 1 Cor. 1:13, the other (*en to onoma*) in Acts 2:38; 10:48. In our church the current custom is to say "in the name," which custom should not be needlessly changed so that others are not offended" (*op. cit.*).

## Comment 2.

Deyling writes about the material element of Baptism: "It does not matter whether the Baptismal water is drawn from a spring, a river, the sea, or a pond, whether it is rain water or dew water, whether is is cold or lukewarm, because there is no determination about it in holy Scripture. It is enough that one uses true, natural, pure water, which is suited to present the purifying power of Baptism.

"Those who want to replace it with another liquid and use, for example, artificial nutmeg water or rose water, upon which foolishness prominent and rich people sometimes come from arrogance, or to use wine, milk, or beer under the claim that it is an emergency, should be told that the Sacrament is falsified in this way because true water is necessary for the essence of Baptism since it is the washing of water by the Word (Eph. 5:26; John 3:5; Acts 8:36; 10:49). . . .

"The early church always denied that there could be a valid Baptism without water. Also our Evangelical [Lutheran] Church denies that Baptism can be administered without true water. . . . [Deyling is amazed that the Scholastics and the Reformed (for example, Beza) permitted Baptism with other liquids.] For it is not permitted to invent a Baptism without water any more than a Supper without bread and wine. For as soon as an essential part

## The Administration of Holy Baptism

is removed, the essence of the whole cannot remain intact. In general, if something of a foreign liquid, for example, oil or ointment, is accidentally mixed with the natural water, the Baptism still remains intact" (*op. cit.*, pp. 360ff.).

When it was suspected in 1542 that a midwife at Cahla and other places had allegedly baptized children "with God's Word alone, without water," Luther and Bugenhagen explained in a letter to the Elector [of Saxony] that such an undertaking "certainly came from a false doctrine." They advised a strict investigation, proved that the action was nothing but mocking God, and instructed that the children should be baptized (Walch, X, 2614-2617; Erlangen, LXIV, 316ff.).

Hollaz writes: "The expression 'pure water' excludes mixed, muddy, and dirty water such as an alkaline solution, also a broth mixed with bread and bits of meat, salty water, and the like. But it does not mean; total and complete purity, in which there is nothing of another element, but rather common and natural purity. So impurities should be removed from the Baptismal water with the same care with which people generally avoid muddy water if it is to be used for washing or drinking" (*Exam. theol.* P. III, s. 2, c. 4, q. 7. p. 1084).

For the sake of inexperienced preachers, it may be noted that, for reasons which are easy to guess, the water used should be neither too hot nor too cold.

## Comment 3.

The word *baptizein* used in the original text of the words of institution [of Baptism] means every type of washing (Mark 7:4). [Footnote: To maintain that *baptizein* can always mean only "to immerse" because of its root word would be just as perverse as to maintain that the word "to handle" [German: *handeln*] can, because of its root word, designate only an action in which the hand is used.]

Since the external form of Baptism is to indicate not only being buried (Rom. 6:3-4) but also the washing away of sin (Acts 22:16), the outpouring of the Holy Spirit (Titus 3:5-6), and being sprinkled with Christ's blood (Heb. 10:22; see Exodus 24:8; Heb. 9:19; 1 Cor. 10:2); since even in Baptism the washing of the body is not effective through the application of the water (1 Pet. 3:21) but is only supposed to indicate the washing of the soul by means of the Word; and since the power of Baptism does not lie hidden in the water, and so a lot of water has no more power than a little water; Baptism is valid when administered in each of the forms mentioned, *caeteris paribus* (if everything else is correct).

Immersion is not to be rejected even though it pictures being buried better than it pictures being washed or being sprinkled with Christ's blood. So pouring or continued sprinkling are not to be rejected although they less clearly represent being buried. But a minister of the orthodox church could conform to its custom all the more because still today the Anabaptists, contrary to Christ's Word and truth and especially contrary to Christian freedom, want to turn these adiaphora into essential parts of Baptism (Gal. 2:4-5).

It is intentionally not said that every form of sprinkling is a valid form of Baptism. Only continual sprinkling is a valid form. If the sprinkling is done in such a way that one hardly knows whether water has really been applied to the one to be baptized, such an alleged Baptism is not to be considered valid. In the Constitution of the Consistory at Wittenberg, which Luther composed with several other theologians, it says; "The abuse that some do not dip the children into the water nor pour it on them, but only wipe a little drop on the body or the forehead, should by no means be observed" (see Porta's *Pastorale Lutheri*, chapter on Baptism, sec. 1, Cramer's edition, p. 632f.). So the preacher should be concerned each time to fill his hollow hand appropriately with water and to pour it abundantly on the one to be baptized. See Deyling's *Institute. prud. past.*, P. III, c. 3, sec. 26, p. 372: "A more abundant pouring with water should properly be used so that it pictures and presents the washing away of the filth of sin (Acts 22:16)."

To the question whether the immersing or pouring is to be done once or three times, Gerhard answers: "We consider that an adiaphoron. In the early church a threefold immersion was customary. . . . In our churches the threefold pouring is also observed." (*Loc. de bapt.*, sec. 97).

To the question whether the immersing or pouring should be total, that is, whether the whole body should be washed, Gerhard answers: "That is also an adiaphoron since there is no prescription about it in the words of institution [of Baptism]; since in the sacramental action the giving and the manner of giving, the receiving and the manner of receiving, are to be distinguished; and finally since the purpose of Baptism is not the removal of the filth of the flesh so that the whole body would have to be washed and scrubbed, but rather regeneration and the spiritual cleansing from all impurity of sin [see 1 Pet. 3:21].

"But although that regeneration relates to the whole person, it is still not necessary for the whole body to be washed by the water of Baptism since the power of regeneration does not come from the water but from the Holy Spirit through the washing of one member of the body with the water of Baptism, as has been explained above with the example of circumcision. The people were sprinkled even though not the whole body was sprinkled (Ex. 24)" (*L. c.* sec. 98-99).

**Comment 4.**

About the movements in carrying out Baptism, Chr. Tim. Seidel writes: "The preacher grasps the child to be baptized on his left arm in such a way that the child's head rests on the left hand and his face is turned toward heaven. The child's body lies on the preacher's arm; but he will do well to enclose it as much as possible between the left side and the left arm so that he does not run the danger of dropping the child, which can very easily happen if he is not careful. At some places it is customary for the godmother to carry the child to the preacher and for him to carry out Baptism without touching the child. That does not remove anything essential from Baptism, but we consider it more fitting for the preacher to gather Christ's lambs in his arms" (*Pastoraltheologie*, ed. F.E. Rambach, pp. 119f.).

# 13

## The Persons to Be Baptized

The preacher is to baptize: 1. all unbaptized adults who desire it, if they have the knowledge necessary for salvation and confess the correct faith in word and deed (Act. 2:41; 8:27-39); 2. all unbaptized children who are brought to Baptism by those who have parental authority over them although, because of their age, they are not yet able to express their faith (Mark 10:13-16; Acts 2:39), as long as they do not belong to another parish (1 Pet. 4:15).

**Comment 1.**
Before carrying out a Baptism, the preacher should always ask whether the individual to be baptized has already been baptized. It has sometimes happened that alleged converts, for the sake of shameful profit, have had themselves baptized repeatedly. Parents sometimes conceal an emergency Baptism of their children, in part because in their ignorance they consider Baptism by a regular preacher more certain and more powerful, in part for other, less pure reasons.

**Comment 2.**
We must consider unbaptized, not only those who have allegedly been baptized but obviously not according to Christ's institution, but also all those: a. who have been baptized by heretics who, with their fellowship, openly deny what belongs to the essence of Baptism; and b. whose Baptism is uncertain.

a. Indeed, neither the faith nor the intention of the one baptizing or of the one being baptized belongs to the essence of Baptism (Rom. 3:3), but only water and the Word, according to the Augustinian principle: *Accedat verbum ad elementum et fit Sacramentum (Tract. 80 in Joh.* [Augustine's words mean: "The

## The Persons to Be Baptized

Word falls upon the element, and it becomes a Sacrament"; they are frequently quoted by Lutheran theologians and in the Lutheran confessions.]).

So it would seem that Baptism by any heretic would be real, valid, and powerful as long as he has applied water and used the formula: "I baptize thee in the name of the Father and of the Son and of the Holy Ghost." But God's Word is not the sound of the words contained in holy Scripture; rather [it is] the meaning expressed by them.

If it depended on the sound, only the words of the Hebrew and Greek original text would be God's Word. But the words of a Bible translation contain God's Word, as long as they represent the meaning of the original text. And one is not preaching God's Word if he uses the words, signs, and sounds that are in the Bible but explicitly uses them in a different sense than they are used in the Bible.

The spoken words do not have their meaning in themselves. Rather it depends not only on the nature of the language but also on the usage in a region and in a society of people. Not only do Latin words have a completely different meaning from German words that sound exactly the same, but many German words have different meanings in different regions, depending on regional usage and agreement. [Walther gives examples such as *laus*, which is spelled and pronounced exactly the same in Latin and in German; in Latin it means "praise"; in German, "louse."]

So if a heretical preacher baptized with the same sounds as orthodox preachers but teaches publicly, with his whole fellowship, that by the Father he means a god who does not exist in three Persons; by the Son he means a mere human being; and by the Holy Spirit he means the spirit of the times or of the Enlightenment or only some attribute or work of God; then even with sounds he is not baptizing in the name of the most holy Trinity. Such a heretical preacher is baptizing not only without faith but also without God's Word. He admittedly retains the sound but as the designation for a completely different meaning.

So the alleged Baptism of all preachers in Antitrinitarian fellowships is not to be recognized as a true Baptism. It is no better than a Baptism for joking or mocking. Those who have allegedly been baptized by them are to be [actually] baptized for the first time.

Friedrich Balduin (d. 1627) writes: "If they (the Arians) may even retain the words of institution [of Baptism], the sound of the words should still not be considered. For we do not attribute any magical power to them but consider the true meaning which Christ intended when He instituted Baptism. In the congregations of the Arians, who overthrow the article of the Trinity, there is therefore no true Baptism. So those who have received their baptism are to be considered unbaptized" (*Tractat. de cas. consc.,* p. 200 sq.).

Paul Tarnov (d. 1633) writes: "It is asked whether the heretics administer a true Baptism. I answer with a double distinction, first between heresies, second between people who adhere to them. For the one kind of heresy offends against the essential parts of Baptism, such as that of the Antitrinitarians, Arians, Photinians, Macedonians, Manicheans, Valentinians, and such, who deny and blaspheme the Trinity, in Whose name Baptism is to be administered. The other kind of heresy offends against the purpose and effect of Baptism, such as the Calvinists. [This category includes all the Reformed, all non-Lutheran Protestants]. The third kind of heresy, in addition to this error about the purpose and effect of Baptism, adds human traditions to its ceremonies, such as the Papists.

"Of these, the last two can baptize legitimately because they do not change the true Baptism for its essential parts. But the first [can baptize legitimately] only if the error and heresy is held only by the preacher or by a few people, privately and secretly (or is contradicted or at least not approved by the congregation). But if the error spreads freely and publicly and takes in the whole church, its minister can by no means administer true and legitimate Baptism.

"The ground of proof, on which this our judgment rests, is this: the nature of a church's Baptism is the same as the nature of its faith about the essential parts of this article, as is seen from the institution, Matt. 28:19. . . . For if the faith of those heretical churches...is not true in those essential parts, so also their baptism [is not true]. The same proof is valid in the other direction, with respect to an orthodox church and its heretical ministers. For Baptism is a possession of the church, not of the minister" (*Thesaur. consil.* by Dedekennus, Vol. II, P. 2, fol. 29).

Fecht says the same and shows that Athanasius, when he said that the Arians did not baptize in the name of the Father and the Son but in the name of the Creator and a creature, did not mean

## The Persons to Be Baptized

that they had so altered the Baptismal formula but they baptized in this altered meaning even though they retained the formula used by Christ (*Philocalia sacra. Thes. ex th. patrist.*, p. 219sq.).

Deyling writes: "He who is a Lutheran at least according to outward and public confession, and presents himself as a Lutheran preacher, administers not his own Baptism but the Baptism of God and the Church. And his Baptism is considered not a private action of the minister but a public action of the church. The matter stands differently with one who has been baptized in the fellowship of the Arians or Photinians or Sabellians and the like, who overthrow the mystery of the Trinity. For although they use the formula prescribed by the Savior and baptize the child with water in the name of the Father, the Son, and the Holy Spirit, they still falsify and destroy an essential part of the Sacrament with their opinion and in the name of their church by their public doctrinal confession.

"For an adherent of Arius recognizes three essentially different and unequal persons of the Trinity. The Sabellian understands by Father, Son, and Holy Spirit, not three Persons but only three designations for one person. So if a Socinian [Unitarian] comes to our church, he must receive the holy washing even if he has been baptized by his own people with the application of the customary formula. . . . Merely saying the words of institution is not enough, but it is required that it occur within a church that believes correctly (on this point), to which [church] Christ has bound His blessings (Matt. 16:18-19). But the sect of the Socinians is not a true (real) church" (*Inst. prud, past.*, ed. Kuestner, p. 347 sq.).

What is said here about being baptized by the Socinians naturally holds true also for being baptized by the Swedenborgians, Unitarians, Cambellites, the free thinking fellowships, and other sects that do not belong to Christianity.

If a person had baptized himself in an emergency, it should not be recognized as a legitimate Baptism. Just as no one can give birth to himself, no one can baptize himself, as most of our theologians correctly remark.

b. A preacher should indeed not immediately baptize those who are in doubt about their Baptism. But if absolutely no certainty can be attained, those who stand in doubt are to be baptized as unbaptized persons. They are not to be baptized as the Papists do, who say in such a case, "If thou, N. N., hast not been baptized,

I baptize thee in the name, etc." For that is not Baptism according to Christ's institution but with a condition.

Even if a person had already been baptized but did not know it, this second Baptism is not to be considered a re-baptism. Kromayer remarks: "It is better to repeat Baptism than to be in doubt about the one that had once been received" [no reference]. Luther writes: "Foundlings should be treated the same (that is, be baptized). Even though a note is included, reporting that the child has been baptized, such a Baptism, administered without witnesses of the church, is still not a public sign or Sacrament. Also, it cannot be believed with certainty because it cannot be proven" (1539 letter to J. Schreiner; Walch, XXI, 1289).

Luther says in the Table Talk: "Such a Baptism should not be considered a re-baptism, for the Anabaptists attack only the public Baptism of children.—But if the situation is such that a woman gives birth so quickly, and the child is so weak that it is a concern that he may depart before she could call anyone, in his case she may baptize the child alone. If he dies, he has died well and received the correct Baptism, which the mother should not doubt at all. But if the infant remains alive, the mother should not report to anyone about the Baptism she has performed. Rather she should keep quiet and bring the child again to public Baptism according to Christian order and custom. And this other Baptism should not and cannot be considered a re-baptism, as he has also been said above about foundlings. For it is done only because the mother, as an individual, cannot be believed [with absolute certainty] in such an important matter, on which the soul's salvation depends, and this, her Baptism has no witness. Therefore public Baptism is highly necessary" (Erlangen, LIX, 56f.). [Luther is applying the Biblical principle that at least two witnesses are required to certify a matter publicly.]

## Comment 3.

The mother also has the parental authority, on which children brought to Baptism are to be baptized, even if the father does not want to have the child baptized (1 Cor. 7:14). So do foster parents, step-parents, adoptive parents, guardians, and parents who are apostate or excommunicated or are members of an erring confession, provided that they do not state that they want to raise their children in error.

## The Persons to Be Baptized

Hartmann writes: "It is right to administer Baptism not only to the children of Christians but also to those of unbelievers if they come under the authority of Christians and there is hope that they may be raised in true faith and godliness. . . . But as long as the children of unbelievers remain with their parents, they may not be baptized contrary to their [the parents'] will, and Christian authorities must not dare to presume the authority to tear their children away from the Jews living here and there among the Christians and to baptize them.

"God certainly did not will that the faith should be spread and the Sacraments administered to anyone to the detriment of parental rights, for He saw that otherwise great confusion would follow and the heathen would be moved to hate the Gospel and the Sacraments. So the apostles never tore children away from their parents against their [the parents'] will. But if ever a child would be removed from the authority of his parents by accident, by shipwreck, or in another way, and the parents either knew nothing at all of him or had to give up all hope of recovering him, the child is certainly to be baptized.

"So Baptism is also to be administered if only one of the parents, even if it were only the mother, agrees, although the father is against it, for Paul assures in 1 Cor. 7:14 that children born of such parents, of whom only one is a believer, are 'holy.'

"Finally, if Baptism has already been administered to a child against the parents' will, then it is nevertheless valid and powerful if all essential elements of Baptism were present, for which the consent of the parents is not absolutely necessary. For here the rule of the lawyers has a place that many things would hinder a marriage that was about to be entered which would not dissolve a marriage that had been entered. So some things pertain to the administration of Baptism which would not render invalid a Baptism that had been administered.

"So a minister of the Word can baptize also the children of heretics, namely if they do not insist that they want to raise the children under their parental authority in that heresy and if they do not want any alteration in the Baptismal action. But heresies are to be distinguished, and it is to be considered whether they involve essential or non-essential elements of Baptism. Baptism is to be administered not to the children of the former but to the children of the latter because the children of those heretics who retain the essential elements of Baptism have been born in the church. For where there is a true [real] Baptism, there is a true [real] church, but every child born in the church is to be baptized.

"Therefore also the children of an apostate who still lives in the parish are to be baptized since the refusal of Baptism is not a legitimate means to bring a person back and convert him, and the son is not to bear the father's guilt (Ezek. 18:20). Indeed, even the children of excommunicated person are to be admitted to Baptism, no matter how much the especially stubborn among the Reformed may snarl against it" (*Pastoral ev.* pp. 639-641).

In 1623 the theological faculty at Wittenberg was asked for and gave its opinion on the question: "Should Jewish children of twelve to fourteen years of age be instructed and baptized at their request even against their parents' will?" [The answer it gave was that Jewish children were not to be taken away by force but that they should be instructed and baptized if they came voluntarily.] (*Consil. theol. Witeberg.* II., f. 115).

## Comment 4.

Also living miscarriages are to be baptized if they have a human head; Siamese twins [are to be baptized] doubled [that is, each one once]. Deyling remarks: "Premature children are also to be baptized if they have human form and are alive" (*Instit. prud. past.*, p. 356 sq.).

## Comment 5

Here in America, where so many reach a certain age without Baptism, it is especially important to ask up to what age children can be baptized without first being fully instructed as is required with adults. Here it is not possible to indicate the year [of age] for all cases. In general, it may be said that smaller children who can understand some but not all instruction in the chief parts [of Christian doctrine, the catechism] should be instructed about the meaning of Baptism to the extent that they can grasp it and should be baptized if they are not already openly malicious. In that case the questions are to be answered by the sponsors in place of the children.

## The Persons to Be Baptized

**Comment 6.**

As soon as he has been asked to perform a Baptism, the preacher should neatly enter the relevant data into the church book: day and time of birth; name or names of the child to be baptized; names, status, and current residence of father and mother; and the names of the sponsors. He should leave blank the time of the Baptism, which is to be added only after it has been performed. A preacher who is not careful in this matter is loading himself with a serious responsibility, for after some time the church book can be the only certain documentation that the child has really received Baptism.

# 14

## The Liturgical Customs of Baptism

Among the Baptismal customs observed in our church are: 1. a reminder of original sin; 2. the giving of the name; 3. the so-called minor exorcism; 4. the sign of the cross; 5. prayers and the pronouncement of a blessing; 6. the major exorcism; 7. the reading of Mark 10:13-16; 8. the laying on of hands; 9. the Our Father; 10. the renunciation [of the devil] together with the Apostles's Creed; 11. the employment of sponsors; 12. the benediction.

**Comment 1.**

Joh. Gerhard writes about Baptismal customs in general: "We divide the ceremonies and customs usual in the administration of Baptism into three classes: 1. some were commanded by God; 2. some were freely used by the apostles; 3. some were added by ecclesiastical persons. With respect to the specifics, the following rules are to be observed.

"1. The Baptismal customs instituted by God are to be carefully distinguished from those used by the apostles and from those added by ecclesiastical persons for the sake of decency, order, and godly remembrance. For the former are essential and necessary, but the latter [two categories] are non-essential and, in a certain sense, free. Christ has commanded that Baptism be in the name of the Father and of the Son and of the Holy Spirit (Matt. 28:19). So wherever water is applied according to Christ's command and the apostolic model, in the name of the Father and of the Son and of the Holy Spirit, there true and legitimate Baptism is administered even if outward ceremonies invented by people are not added. .

"2. The customs freely used by the apostles in administering Baptism, although they are not necessary to the same degree as the first category, instituted by God, are nevertheless to be distinguished from merely ecclesiastical customs, and are to be

## The Liturgical Customs of Baptism

carefully observed. From the Acts of the Apostles one concludes that, in the administration of Baptism, they used statements of the doctrine of the Sacraments, exhortations, prayers, giving of thanks, etc. (Acts 2:38ff.; 8:37ff.). We retain these customs also in our church because the Sacraments are not mere, empty spectacles but were instituted to state the promise [of the Gospel] more clearly and to strengthen faith. So the doctrine of their nature, use, and effect should be presented and explained from God's Word to those present in the language known to them so that they are made aware of the correct and beneficial reception of the Sacraments. But it is to be noted from where the explanations, exhortations, prayers, and giving of thanks are to be taken, namely from the institution and doctrine of Baptism as it is delivered in God's Word. But no definite verbal form is prescribed. Rather this is left free, as the circumstances may require for edification, as long as the basis is retained.

"3. The customs added by the ecclesiastical men are adiaphora. So they are not to be absolutely rejected, but they are also not necessary to the same degree as the usages commanded by God. In those customs which God neither commanded nor forbade (*in ritus adiaphoris*), the freedom which Christ dearly purchased and gave to His Church is to be firmly held. So they may be observed in freedom, without being considered necessary. But they may be removed and changed in an orderly way, with the agreement of the church, especially if they cease to be useful, do not attain their beneficial purpose, or degenerate into misuse and superstition. But in removing them, offense is to be avoided, and so changing these customs is not to be permitted to the frivolous arbitrariness of every private person, but it should be left up to the public opinion of the church" (*Loc. th. de bapt.* sec. 255, 256).

### Comment 2.

About giving the name, Deyling writes: "It is a very old custom, which is correctly retained still today, that children are given names at Baptism, which at one time was done in circumcision, so that they have in it remembrance of the Baptism they have received and so that the covenant thereby entered into with God, as well as the writing of their name into the Book of Life (Phil. 4:3), may continually be called to their minds. So the minister of the church should see that he does not omit the name of the child or give a masculine name to a girl or *vice versa*" (*Institut. prud. past.* p. III. c. 3. sec. 19. p. 359).

[Footnote: So that this does not happen, it is advisable to write the names of the child clearly on a slip of paper and to put it into the agenda so that one can easily read off the names. If one has to baptize several children at the same time, it should be arranged that the boys are baptized first, then the girls, and both [sets] in alphabetical order.]

Seidel makes the not superfluous comment: "The teacher himself should consider this: 1. that he speak to the parents and sponsors before anything else about giving the children Christian and reasonable names and names in which they will have a beneficial remembrance" (*Pastoraltheologie*, Th. 1, Cap. 6, sec. 8, p. 121).

## Comment 3.

About making the sign of the cross, Gerhard remarks: "The sign of the cross is made on the forehead and on the breast, which was already customary in Baptism at an earlier time, as Tertullian testifies in his book on the resurrection of the flesh. That is not done out of superstition, or because of some supernatural effect, but as a testimony that being received into grace and being regenerated to everlasting life is established for the baptized child only by virtue of the merit of Christ crucified. It is also a reminder that the child has been received into the number of those who believe in Christ crucified; that the old man in him is to be crucified in Baptism (Rom. 6:6); and also that he himself will be subject to the cross in this life" (*L. c.*, sec. 261).

## Comment 4.

About the benediction added to the prayers, Rudelbach remarks: "Before the one to be baptized came to the baptistry with the sponsors, yet on the threshold of the "house of blessing." as the ancients called the vestibule for that reason, he was accompanied according to ancient custom by the Davidic benediction from Ps. 121[:8]: 'The LORD shall preserve thy going out and thy coming in from this time forth, and even for evermore.' One must admit that it is the only suitable point at which this wish can be taken up; but it also stands right there at the correct place, where the church opens itself with the Baptismal covenant to the one to be

## The Liturgical Customs of Baptism

baptized. The delay of this passage, as in the new Saxon agenda, where this benediction appears at the conclusion of the Baptism, is not to be approved" (*op. cit.*, pp. 54f.).

**Comment 5.**
As far as the so-called exorcism is concerned, the minor one, which consists of the words: "Depart, thou impure spirit, and give place to the Holy Spirit"; is distinguished from the major one, with the words: "I adjure thee, thou impure spirit, in the name of the Father and of the Son and of the Holy Spirit, that thou depart and withdraw from this servant of Jesus Christ, N. N. Amen."

John Gerhard expresses his conviction with respect to the exorcism in the following words: "One should guard himself, 1. that this ceremony is not considered an essential and necessary part of Baptism; 2. that one does not thereby think of the child being bodily possessed, since it indicates only a spiritual captivity in the kingdom of Satan...; 3. that the use of the exorcism is considered significant but not effective as if the child were freed from the kingdom of Satan by the power of these words, for that is to be ascribed exclusively to the Sacrament of Baptism.... As concerns the actual matter represented by the exorcism, as well as the explanation of the words used in this ceremony (namely that it is a reminder and a testimony of the spiritual captivity of the child in the kingdom of Satan, of the misery into which we have been placed through the fall of the first parents, and of the saving effectiveness of Baptism, etc.), then it cannot simply be rejected since it is similar to faith. But since the words are somewhat harsh and without that explanation indicate that the child has been possessed in a certain sense, from which it is freed through that ceremony, therefore, as Dr. Chemnitz speaks in his *Locis*, 'The church has the freedom to present and explain that doctrine of original sin, of the power and kingdom of Satan, and of the effectiveness of Baptism with other words more in keeping with Scripture.'... But that the church may in fact employ, in the case of the exorcism, this freedom to remove an adiaphorous ceremony, may not be useless, for reasons that are not to be despised" (*Loc. de bapt.*, sec. 264-266).

[Walther notes that this ceremony had actually been dropped in most of German-speaking Lutheranism because of doctrinal indifference and Rationalism. Since it required an explanation, it was not to be reintroduced where it had fallen into disuse, but it

## Pastoral Theology

was not to be hastily done away with where it still existed.]

## Comment 6.

The use of godparents (*sponsores* or *fidejussores*; Greek: *anadochoi,* guarantors; *susceptores,* those who "lift" [the child] out of Baptism) is very ancient. Tertullian already took from it a reason to oppose infant Baptism (*De bapt.*, c. 18).

The following are not to be admitted to this office: those who have been excommunicated, blasphemers, enemies of the church, notorious unbelievers, and wicked persons, also children who are not communicants.

The pastor should indeed work for this purpose that only upright Lutherans are chosen and so should accustom his congregation to talk to him about the Baptism before the godparents are asked. But if well-intentioned heterodox persons have already been asked or come to the Baptismal font, the pastor should not turn them away, thereby shaming them publicly and awakening in them a lasting aversion to our church and its ministry. [Walther says that the heterodox may be witnesses that the Baptism performed is legitimate.]

How many sponsors are to be accepted? Gerhard answers: "At some places, one is asked; at others, three; at others, even more. But although nothing is added to or subtracted from the completeness and effectiveness of Baptism by the number of the sponsors, and it is therefore an indifferent matter whether one or several are asked, yet no offense is to be given, and the custom of each church should be respected.... Because the testimony should be certain and the child must be educated, namely, so that the child may be raised in a godly way if the parents die or one of the sponsors dies, it seems to be better to take three rather than one (Num. 35:30; Deut. 17:6; 19:5)" (*L. c.*). [Walther adds Matt. 18:16].

It is advisable to give the sponsors a sign when they are to answer. If they do not do it, one should remind them in a clear but friendly way what they are to do.

It is not to be rejected that the parents themselves take the place of sponsors at the Baptism of their children. But it is to be advised against as unsuitable and to be hindered as much as possible. For it is the sponsors' duty, if necessary, to take the place of the parents as *compatres* (co-parents).

There is no reason not to permit sponsors by proxy under certain circumstances. When Luther asked Prince Joachim von Anhalt to be a godfather in 1534, he himself suggested to him that a representative [proxy] be named (Walch, XXI, 377ff.).

**Comment 7.**
About the renunciation [of the devil] and [saying] the [Apostles'] Creed, Rudelbach writes: "How else would the Baptismal word receive its whole content if it did not refer to a confession of the Triune God in Whose name we are baptized? And how can we believe with the heart if we have not first rejected everything ungodly?" (*Die Sacrament-Worte*, pp. 25-32 [whole context; Walther quotes material before and after what is given here]. See Luther's Church Postille; Walch, XI, 834f.)

**Comment 8.**
The pastor should see to it that an emergency Baptism by a lay person does not become necessary through his own fault. So he should instruct his congregation to be prompt with Baptism, and if he is asked to perform it, he should accomplish it without grumbling, even at night. [Footnote: Luther writes: "One must, as much as possible, oppose delaying Baptism so that this custom of constantly holding back from Baptism does not become the rule" (XXI, 1339). This reminder is nowhere more necessary than right here where the corrupt sect of the Anabaptists [Baptists] has been so wide-spread and has had such a powerful influence. We have here made the firm ordinance that, except in a case of emergency, every congregation member has to have his new-born child baptized, at the latest, on the second Sunday after his birth.]

If an emergency Baptism has been administered, it should be formally confirmed (Walch, XXI, 1288f.). So that the congregation and especially the mid-wives should be instructed about correctly performing an emergency Baptism.

The congregation should be accustomed to bringing those to be baptized to the church where, if possible, a Baptismal hymn should be sung. The preacher should seriously work against having Baptisms at home, except in case of emergency, not only because of the Baptism itself but also because of the precious time of which the preacher would be robbed by having many Baptisms in the houses. [The time constraint to which Walther refers was obviously a matter of travel time when the pastor traveled on foot, on horseback, or in a horse-drawn carriage.]

**Comment 9.**
The more often a preacher has to administer Baptism, the greater is the danger that he will not carry out this most holy action with the proper devotion. So everyone should listen to what Luther says in the preface to his *Taufbeuchlein* ["Baptism Booklet"]: "But out of Christian faithfulness I ask all who administer Baptism, bring children [to it], and stand by [as sponsors] that they take to heart the excellent work and the great seriousness which is in it. ... I am concerned that it goes so ill with people after Baptism because one has dealt with them so coldly and negligently, and one has prayed for them in Baptism without any seriousness." Above all the preacher should not express the words that belong to the essence of Baptism in a lazy way but with a formally elevated voice.

**Comment 10.**
The members of the congregation should be accustomed to thanking God publicly for the healthy birth of a child within the congregation and for the healthy ending of the mother's confinement, if she belongs to the congregation, and to publicly interceding for them.

# 15

## The Communicants: Announcement

Since the preacher is not to be only a teacher but also a shepherd, bishop, and watchman (Eph. 4:11; 1 Tim. 3:1; Heb. 13:17; Ezek. 3:17-21); not only a distributor of the holy Sacraments but also a steward of them (1 Cor. 4:1); and has the earnest command not to give that which is holy to dogs and not to cast his pearls before swine (Matt. 7:6); he has the holy duty to hold those who want to receive the holy Supper to personal announcement in advance and to use it faithfully and wisely for an exploration. (See above, Chapter 6, Comment 7.)

**Comment 1.**
First, concerning the necessity of confessional announcements, there is an essay in *Der Lutheraner*, Vol. IV, No. 21. Its title is: "Something About the Custom, at the Celebration of the Holy Supper, of Inviting the Participation Even of Those Who Have Not Confessed." At the head of the article is Chrysostom's statement: "I myself would rather lose body and life than allow the body of the Lord to be given to someone unworthily; and I would rather have my blood shed than to permit His most holy blood to be given to an unworthy person" (*Hom.* 83 on Matt.). The essay follows [in abridged form].

Not a few preachers in this country have the custom, when they begin the celebration of the holy Supper, of turning to all those assembled and encouraging everyone to participate, even members of other confessions who are present. Especially the German Methodist preachers here use this means to gain access to the German Protestants who are scattered here. The latter have often had to do without public preaching and the reception of the Supper for years. Now if a Methodist preacher comes to them in their isolation and not only preaches but does not make the slightest difficulty about celebrating the Supper among them and admitting them to it without further ado, then he has usually already won the people for himself. He uses the holy Supper as bait, as a means of luring the people into the net of his fanaticism [*Schwaermerei*] and sectarianism.

But do not many so-called "Lutheran" preachers follow a similar practice! We have sadly experienced that not a few of the preachers who call themselves Lutherans, when they have prepared the holy table for the Sacrament, invite to this means of grace anyone who wants to come and admit them without any examination of their faith and life (in the opinion that this is truly evangelical). It is to be feared that many act this way for impure reasons, to be considered really "nice, broad-minded" men and to be praised. It is to be feared that many give the holy Sacrament to everyone, even to those who are manifestly godless, do not want to lose their pastoral position, which may bring them a good income.

There is hardly anything in all pastoral care [*Seelsorge*] that gives a faithful minister of the church more trouble than if he wants to act conscientiously in admitting people to the holy Supper. If an orthodox Lutheran preacher takes over a new congregation and wants to admit no member to the Lord's Table until he has spoken to each individual and has learned from his mouth that he knows what the holy Supper is; that he acknowledges that he is a miserable sinner; that he in his heart believes in God's Word; that he desires grace and the forgiveness of sins in Christ's Blood; also that he earnestly intends to follow Christ in a holy life, unspotted by the world, and the like; what harsh resistance he usually meets right away! How many enemies he usually makes right away! How seldom it proceeds without divisions arising! How often he sees himself required to travel on right away and to hear it said that he wanted to lord it over the congregation.

How is that? Is a preacher doing right if he would rather let all that happen to him, would rather give up his office, than admit anyone to the holy Supper without examination? Is the liberality of many preachers of this land in this respect really so blameworthy? We answer: Yes! To be able to judge correctly here, it is necessary to consider the real state of affairs with the holy Supper.

The situation is totally different from that of preaching God's Word. For the Word is presented not only to strengthen a believer

## The Communicants: Announcement

in the faith but also to awaken people first from the sleep to sin; to bring them to acknowledge their sins and to repent; to convert them to faith. Without the Word, that is all impossible. So no one can or should be turned away from [hearing] God's Word, for that would mean closing to him the only door to grace.

That is not the situation with the holy Supper. It is not the means first to bring a person to repentance and faith but [the means] to strengthen him in it. It is not the means for a person first to receive grace and become a Christian but [the means] to seal the grace he has received through the Word and to keep, preserve, and further him in Christianity. Through this food a person is not first awakened to faith but is nourished and refreshed when he is already spiritually alive.

Whoever wants to receive the holy Supper in a worthy way and for his salvation must already first have come to repentance and faith. He must already first have received grace and become a true Christian. He must already before have been awakened and reborn to life from God.

[Footnote: Luther writes in his Church Postille: "Christ also did it this way. He let the sermon go to the crowd, to everyone, as also the apostles [did] later, so that all heard, believers and unbelievers. Whoever grabbed it, grabbed it. We must also do it that way. But the Sacrament should not be cast in that way among the people in crowds, as the Pope did. If I preach the Gospel, I do not know whom it may strike; but here I should see to it first that it has struck the one who comes to the Sacrament. There I must not put it into doubt but be certain that the one to whom I give the Sacrament has grasped the Gospel and believes uprightly just as when I baptize someone, just as the one who receives it or is baptized should not doubt" (Easter Day, "On the Reception of the Holy Sacrament").]

Only he should receive the holy Supper who has already become a child of God through the washing of regeneration, holy Baptism, just as in the Old Testament only he could receive the Passover lamb who had already been received into the divine covenant of grace through the sacrament of circumcision.

Receiving the holy Supper is not something good in and of itself. It depends on how one receives it. It does not work *ex opere operato* ["by the work worked," the Romanist doctrine that the mere outward action bestows spiritual benefit]! It is not like a medicine that only needs to be taken so that it works. It is rather a treasure chest, the treasures of which can be taken only by the hand of faith. He who has no faith receives the real and whole Sacrament, not only bread and wine but really and truly, by mouth, in, with, and under these elements, the body and blood of Jesus Christ as a precious pledge of grace and forgiveness. But he leaves without the blessing that is there for the salvation of his soul. How can even such a precious and valuable pledge help a person, how can it serve for his assurance in a matter, if he does not believe that it is such a precious and valuable pledge?

Whoever receives the holy Supper without the correct faith, and so [receives it] in an unworthy manner, not only does not receive the grace that is in it, but finds in it instead of grace—anger; instead of life—death; instead of a blessing—a curse. He becomes, as St. Paul writes, "guilty of the body and blood of the Lord. . . . For he . . . eateth and drinketh damnation to himself, not discerning the Lord's body" [1 Cor. 11:27, 29]. So horrifying is the sin he commits, and so terrifying is the judgement he draws down on himself who receives the holy Supper unworthily. The people who say, "One should nevertheless be glad that the people still come to the holy Supper," thereby reveals the sad state of his knowledge of this holy Sacrament.

The holy Supper is one of the marks, one of the banners of the church, one of the seals of the doctrine and the faith (Rom. 4:11; see 1 Cor. 10:21; Ex. 12:48). In whichever church one receives the holy Supper, one is confessing that church and its doctrine. There cannot be a more inward, brotherly fellowship than that into which one enters with those in whose fellowship he receives the holy Supper. The apostle says, "For as often as ye eat this bread, and drink this cup, ye do shew the Lord's death till He come" (1 Cor. 11:26). And "For we being many, are one bread, and one body: for we are all partakers of that one bread" (1 Cor. 10:17).

There is a big difference between once hearing a sermon with them in a strange [foreign, *fremd*] church fellowship and participating there in the celebration of the holy Supper. One might sometimes hear the sermon there, perhaps to become familiar with their doctrine, without participating in the false-believing worship. But the holy Communion is an act of confession. If one communes in a strange church, one is actually joining it, presenting himself as a witness for its doctrine, and declaring its members to be his

## The Communicants: Announcement

brothers and sisters in the faith.

On the basis of that understanding, what is to be thought of inviting everyone present, without distinction, to receive the holy Supper, and admitting them without examination?—It is quite natural for that to be done by preachers who do not believe that the body and blood of God's Son is present in the holy Supper and is received by all communicants; preachers who consider the holy Supper a mere memorial meal, a mere ceremony, such as the Reformed, the Methodists, and most of the Union-Evangelicals. But it is inexcusable if those operate this way who want to be Lutheran preachers and are convinced of the truth of the Lutheran doctrine of the holy Supper.

Such preachers are acting against God's command not to "be partaker of other men's sins" (1 Tim. 5:22). Anyone who could prevent a sin and does not prevent it but furthers it, is making himself a participant in it. If those preachers could admittedly prevent the horrible sin of the unworthy reception of the holy Supper but do not do so, partly because they are afraid of people and partly because they want to please people, but further that sin by their frivolous invitations: oh, how horrifying their responsibility for it will one day be! How they will one day be terrified when God reckons as their own all the guilt against the body and blood of Christ which all those impenitent, unbelieving, and falsely believing people, whom they have admitted without examination, have loaded upon themselves! If unworthy communicants are one day damned, those who have lured them to it will have to suffer a ten-fold damnation.

In his instruction to the church visitors, Luther writes: "One should also not let anyone go to the holy Sacrament unless he has individually been examined by his pastor, whether he is prepared for the holy Sacrament. For St. Paul says in 1 Cor. 11:27, that those who receive it unworthily are guilty of the body and blood of Christ. Now the Sacrament is dishonored not only by those who receive it unworthily but also those who, through lack of diligence, give it to the unworthy" [no further reference].

Such a preacher would be sinning especially severely in that he is thereby making himself an unfaithful, careless, and unconscientious pastor [*Seelsorger*]. The Word of the Lord in the Prophet Ezekiel (3:17-18) holds true for every preacher: "Son of man, I have made thee a watchman unto the house of Israel:

therefore hear the Word at My mouth, and give them warning from Me. When I say to the wicked, Thou shalt surely die; and thou givest him not warning, nor speakest to warn the wicked from his wicked way, to save his life; the same wicked man shall die in his iniquity; but his blood will I require at thine hand."

True for every preacher is the Word of the Lord spoken to Peter in Matt. 16:19: "And I will give unto thee the keys of the kingdom of heaven: and whatsoever thou shalt bind on earth shall be bound in heaven: and whatsoever thou shalt loose on earth shall be loosed in heaven." True for every preacher is the apostolic Word: "Study to shew thyself approved unto God, a workman that needeth not to be ashamed, rightly dividing the Word of truth.... In meekness instructing those that oppose themselves; if God peradventure will give them repentance to the acknowledging of the truth; and that they may recover themselves out of the snare of the devil, who are taken captive by him at his will" (2 Tim. 2:15, 25-26). It is said of all upright preachers: "They watch for your souls, as they that must give account" (Heb. 13:17).

He is doing the opposite of all his obligations as a pastor [*Seelsorger*] if he admits anyone to the holy Supper without examination. He should proclaim to the godless, "Thou shalt surely die." But by admitting him to the table of grace, he is saying to him, "Thou shalt live." He should bind the impenitent, and he is loosing them. He should rebuke the opponents so that they may repent, and he is telling them that they are right so that they become that much more hardened. He should watch over souls, but he is showing himself, according to Is. 56:10, a voiceless dog that cannot bark but is lazy and wants to lie down to sleep. He should help souls out of sin and damnation, and he is strengthening them in their impenitence and shoving them deeper into sin, wrath, death, hell, and damnation, and he is strengthening them in their impenitence and shoving them deeper into sin, wrath, death, hell, and damnation. If a preacher is otherwise ever so zealous but does not do everything he can to prevent souls from receiving the most holy Sacrament unworthily, that one thing will already make him reprehensible and draw down upon him a heavy judgement as a hireling, as a faithless pastor [*Seelsorger*], as a soul-destroyer [*Seelenverderber*].

Luther writes in his incomparable 1540 "Admonition to the Pastors, to Preach Against Usury": "If such usurers want to get

## The Communicants: Announcement

mad because you do not absolve them, nor administer the Sacrament to them, no give them [Christian] burial, . . . then say: You are firstly forbidden by God to consider a usurer a Christian. . . . And how should I come to the point of laying my soul on the line for you and in your place and damn myself for your sin because you are such a miser?. . . . So it would not help you at all and would damn me if I would just absolve you. For God and the Emperor do not accept it in their law. So repent and do right. Otherwise you can simply go the devil doubly without my absolution. No, fellow, it is this way: you go, and I will stay here. I am not a pastor in order to go to the devil with everyone but to bring everyone to God with me" [no further reference].

A preacher has to consider that he has been appointed by God to be a "steward of the mysteries of God" (1 Cor. 4:1). A steward cannot, without severe responsibility, do whatever he wants with that which has been entrusted to him. He has to act according to the instructions he has received for the administration of his office. But in holy Scripture we preachers have the most precious instructions for the correct administration of the holy Sacraments. It is prescribed for us there with clear words who can be admitted to it and who cannot. Among other things, Christ says: "Give not that which is holy unto the dogs; neither cast ye your pearls before swine, lest they trample them under their feet, and turn and rend you" (Matt. 7:6). Christ also says: "But if he neglect to hear the church, let him be unto thee as an heathen man and a publican" (Matt. 18:17).

St. Paul writes: "But now I have written unto you not to keep company, if any man that is called a brother be a fornicator, or covetous, or an idolater, or a railer, or a drunkard, or an extortioner; with such an one do not eat. . . . Therefore put away from among yourselves that wicked person" (1 Cor. 5:11, 13 [v. 13 refers to Deut. 17:7 and related passages]).

The same apostle writes: "And if any man obey not our word by this epistle, note that man, and have no company with him, that he may be ashamed" (2 Thess. 3:14).

Finally John writes: "If there come any unto you, and bring not this doctrine, receive him not into your house, neither bid him God speed: for he that biddeth him God speed is partaker of his evil deeds" (2 John 10-11; see 2 Thess. 3:6; Rom. 16:17; 1 Tim. 6:3-5; 2 Tim. 3:1-5; Titus 3:10-11; 2 Cor. 6:14-18).

Accordingly Christians should not deal with any manifest sinner, with any despiser of the Christian congregation, with anyone who would not submit to discipline, or with any unbeliever or false believer as if they stood in brotherly faith fellowship with him. Here every preacher has the precise instructions that God's Word gives him about the administration of the Sacrament. It is obvious that all those with whom Christians cannot maintain any brotherly faith fellowship, should also, according to God's Word, not be admitted to the reception of the Sacrament, by which the most inward brotherly faith fellowship is established and expressed.

What are those preachers doing who admit anyone without distinction? They are proving that they are unfaithful, frivolous stewards over God's mysteries. They are interfering with God the Lord in His office and setting themselves up as lords over His holy Sacrament, when they should only be its ministers. If they do not come to their senses in time, woe to them forever and eternally! There will come a day when they will have to suffer horrible for robbing the Lord of His goods and misusing them for impure purposes. The Lord will summon them before Him and call out to them: "How is it that I hear this of thee? give an account of thy stewardship; for thou mayest be no longer steward" (Luke 16:1-2).

Will some now say: What should a preacher do to rescue his conscience? I want to let Luther speak about that. He writes this way in his 1523 writing, "A Christian Way to Go to God's Table": "Here one should have the same manner or ordinance that one keeps with Baptism, namely, that first the bishop or pastor is shown who they are who want to receive the Sacrament, and they themselves should ask him to administer the Sacrament to them, so that he learns their names and may know what kind of life they lead. Then, even if they ask for it, he should not admit them before they have given an account of their faith and especially have answered the question: whether they understand what the Sacrament is, what it benefits and gives, and what they want to use it for, that is, whether they can say the words of the Sacrament and their explanation by heart; and they indicate that they are going to the Lord's Table because they are plagued, on account of sins, with a burdened conscience or the fear of death or with any other assault of the flesh, the world, or the devil; that they hunger and thirst to receive the word of grace and salvation from the Lord Himself through the office of the minister so that they may be comforted and strengthened, as Christ has given and instituted it out of inexpressible love in this Supper, with these words: 'Take, eat, etc.'

"But I consider it enough that one who desires the Sacrament be asked and questioned in this way once a year. Indeed, he may be so sensible that he might be asked only once in his life or not at all. For by this ordinance we want to prevent it that worthy and unworthy run to the Lord's Table at the same time as we saw before under the Papacy where nothing else was desired but just to receive the Sacrament. But there was neither talk nor thought of faith, comfort, and the correct use and application of the Sacrament. Indeed, they were even very diligent in hiding the Words of the Sacrament, that is, the bread of life. Indeed, they dealt with it with great nonsense as if those who receive the Sacrament were doing a work that was good because of their own worthiness, not that they received faith and were strengthened by Christ's goodness. But we certainly want to separate and exclude from the fellowship of this Sacrament those who do not know how to answer about the above-mentioned parts as those who lack the wedding garment [see Matt. 22:11-14].

Accordingly, if the pastor or bishop sees that they understand all this, he should also consider whether they prove their faith and understanding with their life and morals—for even Satan understands all that and can even speak about it—that is, if he sees a fornicator, drunkard, gambler, usurer, slanderer, or someone else suspected of public vice, he should certainly exclude him from the Supper unless he proves by publicly giving notice that he has changed and amended his life. But the others who sometimes fall and return and are sorry that they fell, should not only not be denied the Sacrament but should know that it was instituted primarily for this purpose that they may be refreshed and strengthened. For we all fail in many ways (James 3:2), and it is proper for one to bear another's burden because we can be burdensome to each other (Gal. 6:2). For I am speaking here of those who despise, of those who sin without shame or fear, and yet boast great things about the Gospel. [Luther is distinguishing between open and manifest sinners, who sin out of malice and should come under church discipline, and upright Christians, who sin out of weakness and should be absolved and communed.]

"I believe now as I have taught before about private confession, namely that it is neither necessary nor required, but that it is beneficial and should by not means be despised" (Halle, X, 2764-2767).

What Luther says here privately [in a book that is only his own] we find also in our public confessional writings. Article XXV of the Augsburg Confession says: "We retain the custom of not administering the Sacrament to those who have not first been examined and absolved." Article XV of the Apology says: "Among us the Sacrament is received willingly without coercion, every Sunday, by the people who have first been examined, whether they have been instructed in Christian doctrine and know and understand something of the Our Father, the Creed, the Ten Commandments."

So far the essay.

Confessional announcement is especially necessary where private confession is not practiced, which, among other things, was retained in our church for the same purpose which confessional announcements are to achieve. [The theological faculty of Wittenberg wrote in 1619 that private confession had been retained in order to give the pastor the opportunity to speak individually with people; to give people the opportunity to speak to the pastor about specific concerns or problems; and to apply God's grace and the forgiveness of sins for Jesus' sake individually to penitent sinners (*Consil. Witebergens.* II, 139).]

## Comment 2.

A faithful and wise use of confessional announcement consists in this that the preacher consider only the salvation of those who want to commune and primarily explore:

1. whether the person considers God's Word to be God's Word;
2. whether he knows what is necessary for salvation;
3. whether he recognizes himself to be a miserable sinner, finds comfort only in Christ's merit, and has no wicked intentions (Ps. 66:18);
4. Whether he believes in the mystery of the holy Supper and seeks in it forgiveness as well as strengthening in faith and godliness;
5. whether he confesses the Lutheran faith, as it is laid down in Luther's Small Catechism, as the correct Christian doctrine.

With all diligence the preacher should guard against deterring

## The Communicants: Announcement

people with a formal attitude and against turning a friendly discussion into a rigorous examination and torture session. If possible, the preacher should find out what he needs to know without giving the person the impression that he is being examined.

The greater the prejudices that are present in a new congregation against the institution of confessional announcement, which has become strange [foreign, *fremd*] to them, the more the preacher must avoid everything that could make this institution suspicious and repugnant to the members. In order to win over those who oppose it out of misunderstanding, the preacher must not shrink from visiting those who refuse to come to him and starting the necessary exploration in the most careful way.

Luther writes to Pastor Balth. Thuringen in Coburg: "I have written to the pastor that he should not torture the ignorant by long examinations when they want to go to the holy Supper and yet [he should] not admit them entirely unexamined and unquestioned. For it is no use [*nichts nuetze*] to admit them unexamined. We accuse the opponents of serving the belly [Rom. 16:18]. But our people are harsh and incur wrath. So I ask you, for God's sake, to give our greatest efforts so that the Gospel may be preached properly" (Walch, XXI, 1348).

It is an atrocity if a preacher uses confessional announcements to find out secret sins or family matter.

## Comment 3.

It is not only not necessary to examine each person before each Communion (it is enough to do it from time to time, perhaps once a year), since the examination is not based on a law but on the needs of souls; in the cases of those who are known to be knowledgeable, upright, and proven Christians, the examination can be omitted entirely.

Luther writes: "Along with this freedom, we retain this manner that a parishioner [*Beichtkind*, one coming to his *Beichtvater* for confession] may tell some sins which oppress him the most. And we do not do that for the sake of those who understand well; for our pastor, chaplain, and Master Philip [Melanchthon] know well what sin is. From them we do not require any [confession]. But because the dear youth grow daily so and the common man understands little, for their sake we retain this custom so that Christian discipline and understanding may be increased. [Luther himself regularly went to his pastor, Johannes Bugenhagen, for private confession and Absolution.]

"For such (private) confession is not done only so that sins may be told but rather so that they may be examined whether they know the Our Father, the Creed, the Ten Commandments, and the rest of the Catechism. For we have certainly experienced how the people and the youth learn little from the sermon if they are not individually questioned and examined. But when can that be better done, and when is it more necessary, then when they want to go to the Sacrament?

"Indeed, it is true that if the preachers administer only bread and wine for the Sacrament, it does not matter much to whom they administer it or what the recipients know and believe.... But because we intend to educate Christians as our posterity and to administer Christ's body and blood in the Sacrament, we do not want to and should not give this Sacrament to anyone unless he is first examined as to what he has learned from the Catechism and whether he wants to abandon sins he has done against it [against the Ten Commandments contained in the Catechism]...

"For because a pastor should be a faithful minister of Christ, he must, as much as is possible for him, not cast the Sacrament before sows and hounds, but hear who the people are. Then if they deceive him and do not tell him rightly, then he is excused and they have deceived themselves" ("Admonition to Those at Frankfurt," 1533, XVII, 2499ff.).

**Comment 4.**

If an evil rumor is going around about those who announce, or if they are accused of a sin, it should be presented to them. But if they deny the charges, and their guilt is not otherwise proven, perhaps by several witnesses, they are not to be suspended from the Supper but to be treated as innocent, according to the principle: *De occultis non judicat ecclesia* ["The church does not judge about hidden matters"]. Even those who are conducting a presumably legitimate lawsuit, namely against non-brothers [Walther assumes that Christians will not sue each other (1 Cor. 6:1-8)], are not to be turned away from the holy Supper for that reason, though they are to be warned earnestly against all vengefulness and irreconcilability.

[Walther presents a case with which the Wittenberg theological

## The Communicants: Announcement

faculty dealt in 1624. A woman confessed to committing fornication with a man who denied it. She seemed to be sincerely penitent. He denied that it had happened at all. The faculty said that neither could be denied Absolution and Communion but that both should be strictly warned. The faculty said: "The ministry cannot judge hidden sins; mere suspicion can also deprive no one of the Sacrament" (*Consil.* II, 125).]

J.L. Hartmann writes: "We say that no suspicion is sufficient to turn a person totally away from the holy Supper. But we are speaking of a suspicious person who has been diligently examined but insistently denies the deed. For a person is not always guilty of a crime of which he is accused by a rumor.... So Luther's opinion is valid here: If someone comes to confession and is suspected of a crime, then I must (if I am acting as father confessor [*Beichtvater*]) inquire accordingly about the circumstances. But if he denies it, I should think more highly of his denial [literally: "his No"] than of my suspicion. And if he insists on being admitted to the holy Supper, I am obligated to administer it to him" (*Pastorale evangelicum*, p. 791).

[Footnote: Confession before people is necessary only when not confessing would harm the neighbor, as when an innocent person would have to suffer because the guilty did not confess. Except in that case, the preacher should never himself ask a suspected person whether he has committed a sin. For he would be forcing the guilty person either to lie or to reveal a sin that is still hidden.]

# 16

## The Communicants: Private Absolution

The Augsburg Confession explicitly testifies: "confession is not commanded by Scripture but rather was instituted by the church" (Article XXV); but it also confesses: "On confession it is so taught that *privata Absolutio* [private Absolution] should be retained in the churches and not be allowed to fall into disuse" (Article XI). The Apology says: "We also retain confession for the sake of the Absolution, which is God's Word, through which the authority of the keys absolves us of sins; therefore it would be contrary to God (*impium esse*=it would be godless), to remove Absolution from the church, etc. Those who despise Absolution do not know what the forgiveness of sins is nor what the authority of the keys is" (Article on Confession and Satisfaction). A preacher cannot demand the introduction of private confession as a *sine qua non* of the Lutheran congregation or let it be robbed of the pure preaching of the Gospel and perish rather than not have private confession introduced. He must rather guard against introducing it in a disorderly way where it has already fallen into disuse or insisting on its exclusive existence at any cost where the abolition of its exclusive use is requested. But in an evangelical way, through instruction and exhortation, and through praising it, [he should] work toward the goal that it be diligently used in addition to general confession and that, where it is possible and advisable, it be finally reintroduced as the exclusive custom and that it be properly preserved where it exist. But by all means he may under no circumstances yield to a congregation which does not want to permit the use of private confession and Absolution even on the part of the individual members, for "to remove Absolution from the church" would certainly be "contrary to God."

## The Communicants: Private Absolution

**Comment 1.**

We see how highly Luther regarded private confession [and Absolution, *Beichte*] from his 1523 writing, "Admonition to Those At Frankfurt to Guard Against Zwinglian Doctrine": "If thousands and thousands of worlds were mine, I would rather lose everything than to let the least little part of this confession [and Absolution, *Beichte*] leave the church.... For it is the Christians' first, most necessary, and most useful school in which they learn to understand and practice God's Word and their faith, which they do not do so powerfully in public readings and sermons" (*Luther's Volksbibliothek*, IV, 61; see 54-66).

In 1522, while Luther was kept hidden at the Wartburg, Carlstadt began his iconoclastic reforming at Wittenberg and, among other things, did away with private confession. Luther hurried from his refuge, although the Elector had forbidden it, so that as a faithful shepherd he could resist the wolf that had broken into his fold. Arriving in Wittenberg on March 6, he delivered a sermon every day from *Invocavit* to *Reminiscere* [the first and second Sundays in Lent] and with God's help quickly restored order in everything which Carlstadt's wild fanatical spirit [*Schwarmgeist*] had thrown into confusion. In the last of his eight sermons Luther comes to speak of private confession [and Absolution]:

"Third, there is a confession [*Beichte*] where one confesses to another and takes him to a place alone and tells him what his trouble and concern is so that he may hear a word of comfort from him to still his conscience. The Pope strictly commanded it and made it a requirement so that one should take pity [on the people]. I have rejected and harshly attacked this requiring and coercing when I have preached and written about confession. And just for that reason I do not want to go to confession because the Pope has commanded it and wants to have it. For confession should be left free to me and not be made into a coercion and command, which he has no power or authority to do.

"But nevertheless I do not want to let anyone take private confession away from me and would not exchange it for the treasures of the whole world, for I know what strength and comfort it has given me. No one knows what private confession can do except one who must often fight and battle with the devil. I would long ago have been conquered and killed by the devil if this confession [and Absolution, *Beichte*] had not sustained me. For

## Pastoral Theology

there are many doubtful and erring matters with which a person cannot well deal nor understand alone. When he now stands in such doubt and does not know how to get out, he takes a brother to a place and presents to him the trouble that lies upon him, complains of his weakness, his unbelief, and his sin; and asks him for comfort and advice. For what does it hurt him if he is humbled and shamed a little before his neighbor? If you there receive comfort from your brother, accept it and believe it as if God Himself had said it to you. . . .

"But whoever has a firm, strong faith in God and is certain that his sins have been forgiven him, he may well omit this confession and confess to God alone. But how many are there who have such firm, strong faith and confidence in God? Let everyone look to himself that he does not mislead himself" (Erlangen, XXVIII, 249f.).

On Luther's advice, in almost all of the church orders of the sixteenth century churches in fellowship with the Wittenberg church, the exclusive use of private confession and Absolution was established, and general confession was not permitted. In the 1542 church order, signed by Luther, it says: "If any preacher should assemble those who want to commune in the morning and speak a general Absolution to them: that should by no means be done."

If anyone does not believe that Christ has already completely redeemed the whole world, and that the glad message of the Gospel is nothing other than an Absolution, which is based on that accomplished redemption, which is to be brought to the whole world, and which calls for nothing other than faith; or if anyone has never experienced the distress of sin; he cannot be convinced of the value of private confession and Absolution. If, as sadly! often happens, the preacher himself does not make use of this glorious means of comfort and so cannot speak from experience about its glory, it is not amazing if his teaching about this institution remains without results in his congregation.

We refer to an article in *Der Lutheraner* (Vol. VI, No. 15) with the title: "How Great and Harmful Is the Error of Those Who Deny to Preachers of the Gospel the Authority to Forgive Sins on Earth."

## Comment 2.

As high as private confession and Absolution has always been held in our Lutheran church, it has not always been practice in all Lutheran churches, not have our orthodox fathers denied that

## The Communicants: Private Absolution

a church was Lutheran if it did not introduce this institution. [Walther cites sources. Balthasar Meisner says that general Absolution is still true and effective but that private Absolution is more fitting (*Colleg. adiaphorist. disput.* 7. 1616. E. 2. b.).]

Luther writes (with Melanchthon and [Justus] Jonas) in giving advice for the discussion at Smalcald: "Although we do not want to force and push anyone to (private) confession by [making its omission] a mortal sin, also not to obligate them to tell every sin, torturing consciences as happened under the Pope; nevertheless it is just as little to be tolerated that anyone would want to forbid confession and so remove Absolution from the church. . . . What is Absolution other than the Gospel spoken to an individual person who thereby receives comfort about the sin he has confessed?" (Walch, XVI, 2177f.).

**Comment 3.**

Private confession should be held in an open and accessible place, where the one hearing the confession and the one making it can be seen, but at such a distance from others present that they cannot hear what is said.

**Comment 4.**

The preacher indeed has the duty of asking one who comes to him for confession about an evil rumor he has heard. But he should not deny him the Absolution if he maintains that the rumor is groundless and it cannot be proven. It is contrary to his office to seek out secret sins.

In the Saxon General Articles it says therefore: "The servants of the church should not ask of their parishioners [*Beichtkinder*] that which is not confessed to them, for this confession was not instituted to be an inquisition into secret and hidden sins, but rather primarily and alone for the teaching of the simple and the comfort of the troubled and assaulted conscience" (*op. cit.,* fol. 297).

To the question: "Whether a pastor in the confessional may also present something to a person on the basis of the common cry?" the following answer is found in Dedekennus: "Yes, certainly, for it stands in Luke 16[:1] that the unjust steward had been accused to his lord that he had wasted some of his goods. From that the lord took occasion to speak with him and says [v. :2] 'How is it that I hear this of thee?' He does not say: 'I find it to be the case that you are not being a proper steward for me.' So it would certainly not be fitting for a pastor, because he is the people's watchman and will one day have to give account to them, to be quiet if he hears something evil, that one of his parishoners is not being a proper steward.

"In 1 Cor. 1[:11] we read: 'For it hath been declared unto me of you, my brethren by them which are of the house of Chloe.' In 1 Cor. 11[:18]: 'I hear that there be divisions among you.' In 1 Cor. 5[:1]: 'It is reported commonly that there is fornication among you.' Here Paul takes occasion from the common cry to write to the Corinthians.

"Luther writes: 'If someone comes to confession, and I have suspicion and distrust, then I should diligently ask about all circumstances. If he totally denies it, I should respect his denial [literally: 'his No"] more than my suspicion, and if he continues and requests the Sacrament, I should administer it to him' [no further reference].

"Chemnitz in *The Examination of the Council of Trent*, p. 365, where he deals with the benefit and correct use of private confession, sets down these words: 'One asks them also if one believes that they are stuck in certain sins.'

"What if a pastor would also have causes that would drive him that he would have to present the evil cry to his parishoner? For Paul says that one should not lay hands suddenly to anyone in 1 Tim. 5[:22]. Again Dr. Luther: 'The Sacrament is dishonored not only by those who take it unworthily but also by those who administer it unworthily. But if I should learn whether someone is worthy, then I must ask him about what I hear of him, and then hear from his answer whether he is worthy, whether he is sorry for his sin and wants to amend his life. For if he still wants to defend the sin and is in general an impenitent sinner, then the pastor cannot absolve him' [no further reference].

"What if now in the confession the blessed little hour may come when God wanted to work the knowledge of sin? For people cannot recognize their sins on their own even if they know that they have done them and know that they have thereby done wrong, even that it is known to man: yet they do not consider it and go to the Sacrament anyway. Indeed, as Dr. Luther has written, many cover their sins, shames, and vices by receiving the Sacrament. For while the people themselves do not recognize their sins nor sorrow over them, God must instead work repentance and sorrow. But He does not work repentance and sorrow without but rather through means. Therefore it is necessary that a pastor speak with his parishoner about the evil reports that have gone forth about him, so that God may give repentance through his office [the ministry of the Word], that the parishoner may begin to look within himself and may gain repentance and sorrow for his previously committed sins" (see *Thesaurus Consilior.* by Dedekennus II., fol. 752).

Already Augustine writes: "We can turn no one away from Communion unless he confessed voluntarily or has been accused and convicted in a secular or ecclesiastical court. For who may presume to be both someone's accuser and his judge?" (*Serm.* 351, sec. 10.).

**Comment 5.**

No preacher has the authority absolutely to exclude a member of his congregation from the holy Supper on the basis of his own knowledge. But cases can occur in which a preacher would sin severely, profane the holy Supper, participate in the sin of unworthy reception of the holy Sacrament by the communicant, and cause great offense if he would without further ado admit to Communion someone who announced for the Supper. That would be the case under the following conditions: if the one announcing had fallen into or lived in manifest mortal sin and showed himself impenitent; if he had committed theft and did not want to restore what had been stolen; if he had offended someone or been offended by someone and did not want to be reconciled (Matt. 5:23-25; 18:28ff.; Luke 17:3), etc. Then the preacher is in a situation in which he cannot administer the holy Supper to a person, although he does not have the authority to excommunicate a member of the congregation. Under such conditions there occurs the necessity of the suspension from the holy Supper, by virtue of which a member of the congregation is denied the holy Supper, not absolutely as if he had already been excommunicated, but only for a certain time until the matter has been settled, that is, until he shows penitence or is reconciled with his neighbor or whatever.

As certainly as a preacher must not participate in another person's sins (1 Tim. 5:22), so certainly must he have the right to suspend a person from the holy Supper in those cases in which, by admitting someone to the Lord's Table, he would knowingly assist in the commission of a grievous sin. So as definitely as our old orthodox theologians deny to preachers the right to excommunicate without [the participation of] the congregation, so definitely do they also ascribe to them the right to suspend people from the holy Supper. [Walther quotes several Lutheran theologians to this effect. Suspension may be the first stage in church discipline according to Matt. 18:15-20].

**Comment 6.**

If the preacher has strong doubts whether the one confessing is penitent and upright, without being able to convict and reject him, the preacher may not try to help his conscience by adding any kind of conditions, or even warning or threats, to the formula of Absolution. Deyling writes: "It is the almost universal opinion of our theologians that the formula of Absolution should as a matter of order be phrased categorically and should be without any added condition. For everyone making confession is presumed to be a penitent and a believer if the opposite cannot be known to us most certainly and without any doubt (which can very seldom be the case). For one who was previously the worst rascal can now have come penitently to true repentance and have a different attitude" (*Institut. prud. pastor.* P. III, c. 4, sec. 38, p. 447).

Nevertheless that is not intended to deny that every Absolution, even the absolute one, is fundamentally conditional in a certain sense. Luther writes in his 1539 letter to the Council of Nuremberg: "That also the intended Absolution is *conditionalis* [conditional], is the same as for the public preaching and every Absolution; both, public and private, have the condition of faith; for without faith it is no release, and therefore it is not an erring key. For faith is not based on our worthiness but is only as much as to receive and affirm the Absolution" (Walch, XXI, 424f.).

**Comment 7.**

The preachers must not reveal what has been confessed to him. In Luther's's Table Talk it says: "Someone asked Dr. M. Luther and said: If a pastor and father confessor had absolved a woman who had killed her child, and it was later revealed and made known by other people, would the preacher also have to testify to the judge if he were asked about it? Then he [Luther] answered: Absolutely not! For one must distinguish between churchly and worldly

## The Communicants: Private Absolution

government since she has confessed it not to me but to the Lord Christ, and if Christ keeps it secret, I should also keep it secret and say nothing more than: I have heard nothing; if Christ has heard something, let Him tell it" (XXII, 879).

When Luther was told that the [city] council of Venice had sentenced to be burned a monk who had absolved someone for a murder he had confessed to him and had then let himself be moved by bribery to reveal it, Luther stated: "This is a correct, good, reasonable sentence and wise decision of the council, and the monk is properly burned as a betrayer" (*op. cit.,* 880).

A preacher who gossips about what has been confessed to him has forfeited his office and deserved to be deposed. Fecht writes: "That obligation (not to break the seal of confession) is based on a tacit contract between the one hearing and the one making the confession. For if a minister of the church were not obligated to the strictest silence, the listener would be acting very foolishly if he confessed anything to him that could be damaging, . . . . Also in this action the minister of the church is not considered to be an accuser, an investigator, or a judge. Finally not only the Roman church but also our whole Lutheran church commands that this silence be considered holy. With reference to the seal of confession, however, it should also be noted that it extends not only to what occurs in the confessional chair itself between the one hearing and the one making the confession, but also to all other private actions which the father confessor undertakes pastorally [*seelsorgerisch*] with the one making the confession unless he had explicitly recognized what he was speaking to him in a different relationship [in other words, the whole pastoral relationship is confidential]. (*Instruct. pastoral.,* Cap. XIII, sec. 33, p. 151).

The preacher should guard his tongue with all seriousness. Even if he presents a case without names for instruction, he should see to it that he does not do it in such a way that others can guess about whom he is speaking. He should destroy letters that contain confessions as soon as their purpose has been fulfilled.

The doctrine of the *sigillum confessionis* [the seal of confession] has been exaggerated by some. Cardinal Petronius approved the horrible statement of a French Jesuit: "If the Lord Jesus were still walking around on the earth, and someone confessed to him in confession that he wanted to kill Him, he would rather let the Lord Jesus be killed than to reveal what had been confided in him" (see

*Der gewissenhafte Beichtvater* (Leipzig, 1692), p. 49).

It should be noted first that if a person confesses a sin that is yet to be committed, that does not at all belong in the category of confession. Even such admissions should not be revealed without the most urgent necessity. But if that which has been revealed relates to a sin that would harm another person or perhaps the whole community, an intended murder, perhaps regicide, poisoning a well, starting a fire, treason, and the like, there must indeed first be every kind of appeal to the conscience of this blinded person so that he will desist from his intention. But if that does no good, the matter should be told at the proper place [to the proper people]— without the name if the danger can be avoided in that way, but also by name if that is not the case.

Fecht explains: "Those sins which, if they are not talked about, result in the destruction either of a whole community or of several persons, are not to be kept secret, because there is to be more consideration for a whole community than for an individual person. All theologians are unanimous here. But in such revelation, one should proceed as considerately as possible, as the holiness of the confessional seal requires. One must spare the persons as long as and as far as can be done" (*op. cit.*, p. 152).

Deyling writes: "We distinguish between sins that have occurred and those that are yet to be committed. The former are correctly kept secret and covered with complete silence if the general well-being and the command of the highest authority does not require something else, ... There are fewer reservations about future sins that are yet to be committed. For if a [future] crime revealed under the seal of confession and the concealing of the same would work for the harm of the highest authority or the state or the neighbor, for example, if conspiracy, treason, poisoning a well, or starting a conflagration were confessed, and if the one confessing persisted in his evil intention in spite of the admonition of the preacher; in this case he cannot be absolved because he is impenitent, nor can his horrible crime be kept silent if the one hearing the confession did not want to act contrary to the law of nature, which command that we prevent any harm to the neighbor, and if he did not want to participate in the same sin and make himself guilty of shedding innocent blood. . . ." (*op. cit.*, sec. 43, p. 456 sq.).

Dannhauer writes: "Indeed, what has been intimated in the

## The Communicants: Private Absolution

confession is to be kept quiet according to natural obligation (Prov. 11:13), according to the ancient practice of the church, and because the preacher stands in Christ's stead and so, since the Latter covers the sins of the penitent, the absolver may not reveal the same, especially those that are secret and are not vicious [would not harm others by being kept secret]. But if silence would harm the state or be against love for the neighbor (for example, if conspiracy, treason, poisoning a fountain, or danger of a conflagration were confessed), then the one who has confessed is to be urged either to reveal the same himself or explicitly to permit that it be revealed. Otherwise he is not to receive the benefit of the loosing key. If he does not want to do that, one is to bear more concern for the society than for an individual person, and there is no seal in the divine Law which could be imposed upon the mouth in this case" (*Hodomor. Spirit. Papaei*, p. 1456).

### Comment 8.

The preacher himself can, if necessary, go to the holy Supper without confession, but he should not let that happen except in a case of necessity. Every preacher should rather choose his own father confessor, confess to him regularly, and receive absolution from him. The preacher also needs this important means. How can he expect his listeners to respect the holy preaching office if he himself gives the appearance of despising it [by not having a pastor of his own]?

[Footnote: Luther writes in his 1538 "Instruction to the Visitors": "And I, Dr. Martin, sometimes go to it [Communion] without having confessed so that I do not make it a custom necessary to my conscience. But again I use confession and do not want to do without it, most especially for the sake of the Absolution (which is God's Word)" (X, 937ff.).].

# 17

## The Administration of Holy Communion

The valid administration of the holy Supper includes that bread and wine be blessed (consecrated), distributed, and received.

**Comment 1.**

It is an adiaphoron whether the bread is leavened or unleavened; whether it is rye, wheat, barley, or oat bread, whether it has this or that form; as long as it is baked from water and the flour of some grain. It is also an adiaphoron whether the wine is red or white; whether it is totally pure or is mixed with water (such as the Lord probably used according to the custom in that country); as long as it is from the fruit of the vine according to Matt. 26:29.

It is an error when the Greek and Roman churches want the holy Supper celebrated only with wine mixed with water; or when the Reformed Beza, following Calvin, wanted to permit the holy Supper to be celebrated with any substituted elements similar to the bread and wine; or when the Gnostic Enkratites from the second to the fourth centuries forbad wine and used only water it its place, even in the holy Supper, in which they have recently been followed in America by certain temperance fanatics [*Schwaermer*].

It is proper for us Lutherans to stay with the hosts or consecrated wafers, which were customary already in the fourth century as mentioned by Epiphanius, because they are very convenient, and because the Reformed, who do not recognize Christian freedom, want to make it a sin on our part (Gal. 2:3-5). The holy Supper is not a ceremony by which the Lord's suffering and dying are only symbolically represented, not a mere memorial meal, but rather a holy Sacrament in which, under the bread and wine, Christ's body and blood are to be given and received as a pledge of the forgiveness promised by the clear divine words. Christ broke the bread only in order to distribute it. So breaking the bread

## The Administration of Holy Communion

is not an essential part of this action any more than the plastered room in which the Lord first held this holy meal (Luke 22:12 [Luther's translation calls it a "plastered" room]). So we Lutherans properly omit the breaking of the bread, all the more so because the Reformed insist on it as something essential and necessary and make it a sin to omit it.

**Comment 2.**

About the consecration, Gerhard writes: "Since at the institution of the holy Supper, Christ explicitly commands that we do what He did when we administer it, it follows that the ministers of the church, when they want to celebrate the holy Supper, must repeat the Words of Institution, consecrate the bread and wine in this way, and distribute them to the communicants. So when the minister repeats the Lord's Words of Institution, consecrates the bread and wine with them, and distributes them to the communicants, that is not merely a historic repetition of what Christ did, as when those words are customarily repeated to the people in sermons to be presented to them.

"Instead: 1. through this formal repetition of the institution, the minister of the church publicly confesses that he wants to celebrate the most holy testament of Christ according to His institution, ordinance, and command, and so does not want to act according to his private opinion but as a steward of God's mysteries.

"2. Precisely through this action he is separating the outward symbols of the bread and wine from common and vulgar use, so that they were no longer mere bread and wine but instruments, carriers, and means through which the flesh and blood of Christ are to be distributed.

"3. He is earnestly praying that Christ be present in his sacramental action according to His promise and distribute His body and His blood to the communicants by means of these outward symbols.

"4. He testifies that, by virtue of the ordinance and institution of the truthful and almighty Christ, the consecrated bread is the Communion of His body and the consecreated wine if the Communion of His blood.

"5. He is therefore exhorting all who approach the Sacrament of the Eucharist [*Danksagung*] to believe the Words of Christ against every contradiction of opposing reason, and to approach in true repentance, upright fear of God, proper respect, and the serious intention to amend their lives.

"With special emphasis, the holy apostle in 1 Cor. 10:16 calls the cup of the Supper 'the cup of blessing which we bless,' in which, by repeating it twice, he includes both Christ's blessing and ours. . . .

"This consecration of the Eucharist is 1. not a magic spell which, by the power of certain words, essentially changes the bread into the body and the wine into the blood of Christ; as the Papist priests pretend that for the sake of their being shorn and anointed, by virtue of the cannon law and the intention [to act] according to the faith of the church, they bring the Sacrament about *ex opere operato* ["by the work worked," merely by the outward action] and change the outward symbols essentially into the body and blood of Christ.

"2. It is also not only a historic repetition of the institution; as the Reformed consider the recitation of the Words of Institution unimportant (see Bucer on Matt. 26) and insist that it is directed only to the people and by no means has the purpose of consecrating the elements (Calvin's *Instit.* IV, 17, 39).

"Rather, 3. it is an effective consecration by which, according to the command, ordinance, and institution of Christ from the first Supper, the consecration is applied (*derivatur*) also to our Supper and the elements are specified for this holy use so that Christ's body and blood are distributed with them.

"Indeed, we do not ascribe to the Words of Institution this power to make the body and blood of Christ present by a hidden power adhering to the words (as the magicians recite their poems . . . with specific words), much less that they essentially change the outward elements. Rather we believe and confess uprightly that the presence of the body and blood of Christ depends exclusively on the will and promise of Christ and on the constantly continuing effectiveness of the first institution.

"Meanwhile we add yet that the repetition of the original institution, which is done by the minister of the church at the celebration of the holy Supper, is not merely historical and does not consist merely in teaching, but is rather consecrating; and that through it, according to the ordinance of Christ, the outward symbols are truly and effectively specified for the holy use so that in the distribution they themselves are the Communion of the body and blood of Christ, as the apostle explicitly says in 1 Cor. 10:16.

## The Administration of Holy Communion

The Son of God Himself is repeating the once spoken Words of Institution through the mouth of the minister and thereby hallows, consecrates, and blesses the bread and wine so that they are the means of the distribution of His body and blood" (*Loc. th. de Sacra Coena*, sec. 149-151).

The words of Chrysostom, quoted in the Formula of Concord, serve to clarify the relationship: "As this saying, 'be fruitful and multiply, and replenish the earth' [Gen. 1:28], was said only once but is always powerful in nature, that it grows and multiplies; so also this saying ('This is My body,' etc.) was spoken once but is powerful to this day and into the future and has the effect that His true body and blood are present in the Supper of the church" (Epitome, Article VII).

Christ's body and blood are not conjured into the outward elements by virtue of the speaking of these words because some mysterious power resides in these words. For in that case the body of Christ would be present wherever those words were spoken over bread, even in a blasphemous joke.

If the Words of Institution are not at all spoken over the elements, so that the elements are not blessed or consecrated, one is not doing what Christ commanded. So He does not fulfill there what He promised; one is not celebrating the meal instituted by Christ; Christ's body and blood are not present; and nothing is distributed and received except bread and wine.

[Walther presents the case of a deacon who said that there was no difference between consecrated and unconsecrated bread. Luther said: "Let him go to his Zwinglians" ([Walch] XXII, 908; [Erlangen] XXI, 1561). If there is a shortage of bread or wine and more must be brought, it should also be consecrated. There should be more bread and wine in the church than is thought to be needed. If a preacher forgets or omits a word or two from the Words of Institution, that does not render the Sacrament invalid.].

## Comment 3.

From the fact that the recitation of the Words of Institution does not work magically but is necessary only to obey the command of Christ, "This do," and to complete the action in which the Lord has promised the presence of His body and blood, it follows that the mere recitation of the Words of Institution does not make the Sacrament real if the consecrated elements are not also administered to communicants and received by them. For the necessity of the former, the axiom holds true: *Accedat Verbum ad elementum et fit Sacramentum* [Augustine: "The Word falls upon the element and it becomes a Sacrament"]. For the necessity of the latter, the axiom holds true: *Nihil habet rationem Sacramenti extra usum divinitus institutum*, that is, nothing has the nature of a Sacrament outside of the divinely instituted use (see the Formula of Concord, Epitome, Article VII).

Luther writes: "Just as Baptism is nothing other than mere water if there is no child there to be baptized, so we also maintain quite certainly that nothing other than bread and wine is present if there are not people eating and drinking according to Christ's institution, even if one would recite the words a thousand times" (XXI, 1589).

Quenstedt writes: "The sacramental union does not happen except in the distribution. For the elements, bread and wine, do not sooner become the means of receiving the body and blood of Christ until through the addition of the distribution they are eaten and drunk.... Christ also does not say absolutely of the consecrated bread but rather of the bread broken and given to be eaten that it is Christ's body. For He said first, 'Take and eat,' then He said, 'This is My body'" (*Theol. did.-pol.*, Cap. de Coena S. 1187, 1268).

**Comment 4.**

The great majority of our theologians, Luther in the forefront, believe that the holy Supper should never be administered privately by one who is not in the public preaching office, by a layman. That is partly because no such necessity can occur with the holy Supper, as with Baptism and Absolution, that would justify a departure from God's ordinance (1 Cor. 4:1; Rom. 10:15; Heb. 5:4); partly because the holy Supper "is a public confession and so should have a public minister"; partly because schisms can easily be brought about by such private Communion (see Luther's 1536 letter to Wolfgang Brauer, pastor at Jessen; Walch, X, 2735ff.; see XX, 2191; Gerhard, *loc. de sacra coena,* sec. 17. and *loc. de sacram.*, sec. 29.).

It is a different question whether it pertains to the reality and validity of the holy Supper that the administrant be legitimately called and ordained to the public preaching office; whether the "office" or the authorization to administer the public office makes the Words of Institution powerful so that the essence of the

## The Administration of Holy Communion

Sacrament includes not only the Word and the elements along with the use but also a quality of the administrant. That is the doctrine of the Roman church, which is rejected and opposed by all theologians generally recognized in our church as orthodox.

Most of the same [orthodox Lutheran theologians] state that the administration of the holy Supper by a layman is never *recta* and *legitima* [correct and legitimate]. But none denies that it can be done *rata* and *de facto* [with validity and in fact]. When Luther enumerates the offices of the spiritual priesthood in his letter to the Bohemians, he writes: "The third office is to bless or administer the holy bread and wine. Here those who hear the tonsure boast a special triumph; here they are gloriously defiant and say: no one else has this power, neither the angels nor the Virgin, the Mother of God. But let us dismiss their nonsense and say that this office is also common to all Christians as the priesthood" (X, 1841ff.). Luther did not teach this only in earlier times, as some want to maintain, but rather until his death. For example, in 1533, he writes in his writing, "Of Private Masses and the Consecration of Clerics": "Our faith and Sacrament must not be based on the person, whether he is pious or wicked, consecrated or unconsecrated, called or having snuck in, the devil or his mother" (XIX, 1551).

Here Luther did not want to state that a layman would be doing right if he would arrogate to himself the administration of the holy Supper. As has already been mentioned above, Luther much rather declared himself to be against that with all earnestness. With that doctrine he only wanted to oppose the error that the preachers of the New Testament constituted a special, holier estate of priests, who alone could make real the means of grace of the New Testament by the power of their consecration.

Gerhard writes: "Bellarmine scourges Luther for having taught that every baptized person has the power and the right to administer the Sacraments. But Bellarmine knows that we by no means approve of disorder in the church and ascribe to no one the power to administer the holy Supper except to him who has been legitimately called, not even in an emergency, since Baptism and the holy Supper are in a different relationship. As far as Luther is concerned, he does not ascribe to all baptized persons unconditionally and absolutely the power to administer the holy Supper; rather he speaks of a certain general capacity which the

Christians, as distinct from the unbelievers, have with respect to the Sacraments, because they have been received into God's covenant through Baptism and are fit and capable for this office if they have been called to it. Luther sets this capacity over against the priestly character about which the Scholastics and Papists argue that through the sacrament of ordination a certain spiritual power has been worked and caused in the soul of the recipient, through which the priest becomes capable of making the Sacrament of the Altar so that it can by no means be made without it, and because they say that a character has been impressed on the soul as a sign of this power" (*Loc. de sacram.*, sec. 29).

How far the teachers of our church are removed from the horrible doctrine that only a legitimately called and ordained preacher is capable of effecting the presence of Christ in the holy Supper, which would destroy all certainty of the holy Supper, is shown by the fact that a whole series of our unquestionable, strictly orthodox Lutheran theologians have taught that, in an (assumed) case of necessity, the holy Supper could be validly administered by a layman not only *de facto* but also *de jure* [not only actually but also rightfully].

About the words of the Council of Trent: "If anyone would say that all Christians have the authority of administration in the Word and all Sacraments, let him be accursed," M. Chemnitz writes: "Concerning the meaning of this canon, as the words are put down, I answer definitely and clearly that if some believe that every Christian, without distinction, without a special and legitimate call, is given the power to use and exercise the office of the Word and the Sacraments in the church, they are correctly condemned. For they are contesting against that divine rule: 'How shall they preach except they be sent' [Rom. 10:15]. Further: 'I have not sent these prophets, yet they ran' [Jer. 23:21]. Further against St. Paul's rule that everything be done decently and in order in the church [1 Cor. 14:40]. Nevertheless the church has always excepted the case of necessity as Jerome testifies against the Luciferians and Augustine testifies to Fortunatus" (*Exam. Concilii Tridentini* II, cap. de ministris sacram. f. 223).

Johannes Corvinus, professor at Erfurt, as quoted by Gerhard in his *Methodus* of the doctrine of the holy Supper (1579 [*sic*]), affirms that a layman is permitted to administer the Lord's Supper in a case of necessity: 1. since Christ gave the authority to forgive

## The Administration of Holy Communion

and retain sins, not to the disciples alone, but to all the pious, and because the command is a general one, to the brethren, who ask that the Gospel be preached; 2. because laypersons are permitted to baptize in a case of necessity (*Loc. de s. coena.*, sec. 17).

Joh. Gallus, professor of the Augsburg Confession at Erfurt (d. 1588), on the question: "Whether it is permitted also for a layman, in a case of necessity, to administer the holy Supper, and where such administration is valid?" writes with almost the same words: "Since Christ gave the authority to remit and retain sins not to the apostles alone but rather commanded all the pious and godly in general to proclaim the Gospel to their penitent brothers; therefore it is permitted not for the servants of the church alone but also for laypersons, in the greatest and most extreme case of necessity (that is, at a time when no servant of the church can be had and one [a layperson] is sought and requested by other fellow Christians), to administer the holy Supper, as well as to baptize and to speak the Absolution. If the Baptism and Absolution of a layman are valid in the most extreme case of necessity, why should not in the same way also the administration of the most worthy Supper be valid when it is done by a layman in a case of necessity? For there is no difference between these things, baptizing, absolving, and administering the Supper" (*Bidembachii consil. Decad.* 3. p. 148 sq.).

Further Tilemann Heshusius (d. 1588) writes: "In a case of necessity, since one cannot have regularly called servants of the church, there is no doubt that every Christian has the authority from God's Word and is authorized according to Christian love to carry out the service of the church with the proclamation of God's Word and the administration of the Sacraments. . . . But here we are speaking of that case of necessity when one cannot have true Christian and upright servants of the church and what is then up to a Christian. As if some Christians are at a place where there are no called pastors [*Seelsorger*]; if some Christians were in prison for the sake of the truth or were in danger on the sea; or if some Christians were under the Turks or the Papacy where there were no correct pastors; if some Christians were under the Calvinists or Schwenkfeldians or Adiaphorists or Majorists, from whom, as from false teachers, they must separate according to God's command; or if some Christians were under such pastors or such church servants who practiced public tyranny and horribly persecuted the correct confessors of the truth so that they [the former] would then also sufficiently reveal that they were not members of the true church, and that godly Christians were then obligated to withdraw from their fellowship in order not to strengthen their tyranny and help condemn the innocent Christians: in such and similar cases of necessity, which happen quite often, that one cannot have true servants of the church, whose doctrine and confession is upright and agrees with God's Word, it is permitted also for an individual private person and believing Christian to absolve the penitent sinner of sins, to comfort the weak with God's Word, to baptize babies, and to administer Christ's Supper...." (*Ibid.*, pp. 135-140).

The strict champion of Lutheran orthodoxy, Johannes Fecht, writes: "If it happened that, in a case when a pastor could absolutely not be had, someone in the greatest danger of death, with the good intention of strengthening his faith, appealing to the fact that the Sacrament was instituted to be added to the Word for confirmation in a case of weakness, would constantly ask for it from someone who was familiar with the administration of the Sacrament, and [the one in danger of death] would not be calmed by his exhortation, then I would not accuse such of disturbing good order. Since the Sacraments are fundamentally given to the church; and it is agreed that it [the church] in a case of necessity baptizes, teaches, and absolves through a layman; and although very rarely—more often with respect to other actions—a case of necessity arises; then I confess that I cannot judge otherwise than that it should be done, if the case is as just described" (*Instruct. pastoral.* e. 14., sec. 3, p. 157 sq.).

Zach. Grapius, professor of theology at Rostock (d. 1713), writes: "The laymen are priests but are suited for all official churchly actions only through an inward capacity and so also for the administration of the holy Supper; so that we do not think that it would be a less true Sacrament which a laymen may have given, perhaps through necessity or in error" (*System. noviss. controvers.* IV, p. 89).

No one doubts that the administration of the holy Supper by a layman who had been temporarily called by a whole congregation in an emergency, although not ordained, would be valid and legitimate. Grapius writes: "The theologians do not doubt that in a time of pestilence, when all regular ministers have been taken away by death, also in times of public disorder when the order of

## The Administration of Holy Communion

the church is dissolved, or in foreign places where one lives among unbelievers and errorists, one person can be called provisionally with the agreement of the Christians present, that he may teach the Word only through reading aloud, as well as give the holy Supper to those who desire it, until they are again provided with a regular minister. But in this way the layman is administering it not as a layman but as a minister who has been truly called for a time" (*L. c.,* p. 86).

**Comment 5.**

The administration of the holy Supper is not made invalid and powerless by the unworthiness, unbelief, or false intention of the administrant (see the Augsburg Confession, Article VIII). But those false teachers who, with the agreement of their congregation, publicly pervert the Words of Institution and give them a meaning according to which the body and blood of Christ are not really present in the holy Supper and are not distributed nor received—those who therefore retain the sound of the words but take away what makes them God's Word, namely the divine meaning, and so deny and suspend the essence of the holy Supper, such as the Zwinglians and Calvinists—they do not celebrate the Lord's Supper, even if they ostensibly retain the consecration. They distribute only bread and wine.

Luther writes in his general confession, with which he closes his 1528 "Large Confession on the Supper": "I speak the same way and also confess the Sacrament of the Altar, that there the body and blood of Christ in the bread and wine truly are eaten and drunk by mouth, even if the priests who administered it or those who received it did not believe or otherwise misused it. For it does not rest on human faith or unbelief but rather on God's Word and ordinance. But it would be different if they first changed God's Word and ordinance and interpreted it differently, as do the current enemies of the Sacrament. They admittedly have only bread and wine, for they also do not have the words and the instituted ordinance of God but have rather perverted and changed them according to their own opinion" (XX, 1381 [in footnote, Walther notes that this comment by Luther has confessional validity for Lutherans because it is incorporated into Article VII of the Epitome of the Formula of Concord]).

Luther says in his "Admonition to Those at Frankfurt am Main, to Guard Themselves Against Zwinglian Teaching and Teachers": "Whoever knows of his pastor [*Seelsorger*] that he teaches in a Zwinglian way, he should avoid him and rather do without the Sacrament his whole life long than to receive it from him, indeed, [he should] rather also die and suffer everything for this point" (XVII, 2440).

Compare Luther's Table Talk, Chapter 19, No. 26 (XXII, 906. f.), where Luther says: "If the Words of Institution of the Supper are publicly heard by the church, then the danger lies on the neck of the godless preacher, not on the church, which believes the words and receives what they say, and faith holds it to be that and believes it. But one should pay attention that he does not publicly preach and teach against the Supper. . . .

"So where the public confession of the Word is, no matter that the rascal may be as he wants, then nothing is taken away from the Sacrament. And this is the reason: if a rogue also swears by the name of the Lord, it is still the true name of the Lord; he would not be sinning if it were not the true name of God by which he was swearing. . . . But the Sacramentarians take the substance totally away; therefore they also have nothing in the Supper except bread and wine."

[In a footnote, Walther notes that most Lutheran theologians deny that Calvinists administer the body and blood of Christ but that a few Lutheran theologians disagree.]

## Comment 6.

[Luther said that one may consecrate both elements and then distribute both—or consecrate and distribute the bread, then consecrate and distribute the wine (X, 2761). But Deyling notes that it is more practical to consecrate both, then distribute both, especially if there are many communicants, in order to be sure that no one receives only one element (*Institut. prud. past.* III, 5, 32, pp. 504f.).]

## Comment 7.

As the words of consecration are God's Words, which constitute the Sacrament, the words of distribution should contain the confession of the church. There is indeed no single distribution formula which alone is justified. But any one [formula] is to be rejected which does not contain a confession that Christ's body and blood are here present and are distributed and received; or which purposely tries to circumvent any such confession, such as the distribution formula of the [Prussian] Union Church: "Take and eat; Christ says, 'This is My body, 'etc.,'" which leaves it up to everyone to believe what he wants and so makes doubt the confession at the Lord's Table, where His death is to be proclaimed.

With this distribution formula the Unionists make themselves like the Jews who did not want to tolerate the inscription on the cross, "This is the King of the Jews," because they did not believe it, and wanted instead, "He said, 'I am the King of the Jews'" (Luke 23:38; John 19:19-22).

But if the Unionists and pseudo-Lutherans raise the objection that it is an addition to God's Word when we Lutherans say, "This is the true body," etc., that [objection] is based on a confusion of the Word of God that constitutes the Supper and the confession of the church in the celebration.

It is proper for the preacher to follow the distribution formula that is predominant in the ecclesiastical fellowship to which he belongs. The formula: "Take and eat; that is the true body of your Lord and Savior Jesus Christ, given into death for your sins; may it strengthen and preserve you in the true faith until eternal life. Take and drink, that is the true blood of your Lord and Savior Jesus Christ, shed for the forgiveness of your sins; may it strengthen, etc." has been accepted in several Lutheran church orders since the end of the sixteenth century (see *Sacramentworte* by Rudelbach (Leipzig: Tauchnitz, 1837), p.78).

**Comment 8.**

With respect to the outward peripheral actions at the consecration, Chr. Tim. Seidel writes: "When the words are spoken, 'He took the bread,' the preacher lays his hand on the plate of wafers and lets it rest there until the words come, 'This is My body,' when he makes the sign of the cross over bread. When later the words are spoken, 'He took the cup,' he touches the cup with his hand and lets his hand rest there until the words come, 'This is My blood,' when the sign of the cross is made again over the cup" (*Pastoralth.* I, 8, 8.).

If there are so many communicants that not all the necessary wafers can be laid on the paten, and not all the wine can be poured into the cup, the rest should be put into a wafer box and a wine flask, suitable for churchly use, made of metal if possible, both of which are to be opened before the consecration, which are to be placed right there, and over which the sign of the cross is to be made at the appropriate time, to indicate that also this part of the elements belongs to what is being set aside [for sacramental use].

**Comment 9.**

[With quotations, Walther recommends great care with the elements—not to drop a wafer but still to use one that has been dropped; if a fly or spider falls into the consecrated wine, it should be fished out with a knife or, better, a spoon with holes in it; if a person dies with the wafer on his tongue, the wafer should be burned; the preacher should turn the cup as he moves from one person to the next at distribution; someone with an infectious sore on the lip should commune privately.]

**Comment 10.**

As baseless as it is when the Reformed do not want to let the mere reception with the mouth be considered a true reception (see John 19:30), and so as little as a Lutheran preacher may let himself be moved unnecessarily to depart from this form of reception which has become customary in our church for good reasons, yet what Seidel writes is quite correct: "Nothing is taken away from the essence of the Sacrament if the communicants take the bread and the cup from the hand of the preacher (into their hands) and eat and drink in this way. In the case of elderly preachers who may happen to have trembling hands, it is rather to be advised that such be done than that one must be in constant fear, especially that the wine may be spilled" (*op. cit.*, Th. I, C. 8. sec. 9). The same holds true then, for example, if sick communicants can assume only such a bodily position that one cannot himself bring the cup to the mouth without spilling some. See Luther's letter about this matter to Duke Johann Friedrich of Saxony, when Carlstadt offended the weak in Wittenberg by introducing the practice that one take the consecrated elements with his hands (X, 2740f.).

In any case, since some communicants take an awkward position, especially when receiving the cup, the preacher should be very careful that each of them really receives some wine.

## The Administration of Holy Communion

**Comment 11.**
As to the sequence of the communicants and the order of the distribution, Deyling writes: "In the distribution of this Sacrament, a servant of the church should proceed most carefully with respect to order, that he not only distribute first to the men, then to the women, but also that he first administer the consecrated bread and then the wine. The eighth of the general orders prescribes 'that first the men and bachelors, and then the spinsters, but after them the wives, should present themselves in an orderly way for Communion' if it is not already otherwise customary" (*L. c.*, sec. 32). Therefore it is not completely indifferent, not only because everything should be done in good order in the church, but also so that all opportunity for a controversy about rank may be avoided, which is nowhere more vexatious than at the Lord's Table.

Seidel remarks: "It is not an indifferent matter if someone wanted to administer first the cup and then the wine or may have done that by mistake. Such a reception of the Supper would have to be declared invalid because the words of the Founder have the force of a testament, which has been sealed by His death" (*op. cit.*, I, 8, 9.). Dedekennus communicates an opinion of the Marburg theologian Hyperius, according to which a preacher who had absent-mindedly made himself guilty of this reversal of order in the administration of the Supper would have to repent publicly before the church and so remove the offense which has been given (*Thesaur.*, Vol. I, P. 2. f. 257.sqq.).

Luther considers it proper for the communicants to stand at a separate place. He writes: "If Communion is administered, it would be fine for those who want to go to the very worthy Sacrament to stay together and to stand apart at a separate place; for the two, the altar and the chancel, have also been built for that. Not that it matters to God whether one stands here or there, nor that it adds something to faith, but it is necessary for this reason that the persons may be seen and recognized by those who receive the Sacrament as well as by those who do not go, so that afterwards their lives may be that much more seen, proved, and revealed. For the reception of this Sacrament in the congregation is a part of the Christian confession so that those who go to it confess before God, angels, and people that they are Christians. For that reason it is to be diligently observed that none sneak secretly to the Sacrament and afterwards, mixed among other Christians, cannot be seen whether they live well or wickedly. But also here I do not want to make a law but only to indicate that Christians, who are certainly free, should freely and without coercion do and observe everything which is honorable and orderly (1 Cor. 14:40)" ("How to Hold a Christian Mass," 1523, X, 2766.f.).

**Comment 12.**

Deyling remarks: "The elements consecrated by the pastor can neither be preserved nor sent to those who are absent, which was an evil custom of some in the ancient church. For the sacramental action, which consists of consecration, distribution, and reception, must be completely uninterrupted" (*Instit. prud. past.* III, 5, 13.). Pruckner raises the question: "What should a minister of the church do if the consecrated bread would be distributed but not the consecrated wine, for example in case of fire or enemy attack?" He answers: "Those elements are to be consecrated anew and distributed to the communicants with the bread in the consecration and would become conscious again only after several hours, he should anew be given the consecrated bread and wine" (*Manuale mille qq. Cent.* IV, q. 19. p. 274).

**Comment 13.**

[With quotations, Walther notes that Communion should be received in church, in the public assembly, with the exception of those who cannot be present: someone who is ill, someone in prison, a woman waiting to deliver a child, a person undertaking a dangerous journey before the next public celebration.]

Those who do not commune and yet are present in the divine service are in general to be admonished not to depart during the celebration of the Supper. Deyling writes: "In many churches the great misuse has become prominent that almost only the communicants are present during the celebration and distribution, and the others go out right after the sermon has been concluded just as if the sacramental action did not concern them. So the people are to be instructed about the importance of the matter which is being handled here and to be reminded that the celebration of the holy Eucharist is a major part of the divine service and is devoted to the remembrance of the passion [of Christ]. Those who do not themselves receive the Sacrament by mouth should yet receive it by faith, spiritually receive the body and blood of Christ, praise God

# The Administration of Holy Communion

with hymns, and not leave the church before the divine service and the thanksgiving have been concluded, as happens with the blessing of the people" (*op. cit.*, sec. 36).

**Comment 14.**

If something remains of the consecrated elements, the wine should be drunk by the communicants, the elders, etc., perhaps in the sacristy. By no means is it to be mixed again with unconsecrated wine or used to commune the sick, but without being mixed with unconsecrated wine. It is to be consecrated again. Consecrated hosts may be saved for the next celebration of the Supper since they do not become mixed like the wine. But it is self-understood that they must be consecrated again.

When in 1543, Simon Wolferinus, pastor in Eisleben, mixed the remainder of what was consecrated with what had not been consecrated, Luther wrote him two very serious rebuking letters. Therein he even remarked: "Maybe you want people to consider you a Zwinglian." So it also seems that Luther believed that the consecrated elements were still the body and blood of Christ outside of the instituted use (XX, 2008-2015). But is seen from Luther's opinion in another case that this is only the appearance, that Luther rather rebuked that procedure so seriously because it looked bad and could give offense. For when, the next year, wafers were burned because a preacher had put consecrated and unconsecrated ones together and had used them, Luther wrote to Amsdorf: "It would not really have been necessary to burn them since nothing is a Sacrament outside of the actual use; just as the Baptismal water is not Baptism outside of the use" (XXI. 1561).

Seidel makes the remark, which may not be superfluous: "We consider it dubious for the preacher to drink the remaining wine because he could thereby put himself under suspicion, as if he wanted to be served a drink and had intentionally taken more wine than was necessary for the communicants" (*op. cit.*, sec. 10).

**Comment 15.**

[Someone prevented by illness from receiving the holy Supper after confession and Absolution could be given the Sacrament the following Sunday without confessing again.]

# 18

## The Persons to Be Communed

As far as the communicants are concerned, only those are to be admitted to the holy Supper: 1. who have already been baptized; 2. who are able to examine themselves; 3. about whom it cannot be proven that they are non-Christians or erring believers and who would therefore receive the Sacrament unworthily; and finally, 4. in whom no reason is found that they first need to be reconciled or to make restitution.

**Comment 1.**

Since holy Baptism is the Sacrament of regeneration to the kingdom of God and of initiation, and the holy Supper is the Sacrament of strengthening, only those who have been baptized are to be admitted to the latter, according to the analogy of the Passover meal, to which, according to Ex. 12:48, only those were to be admitted who had been received into the covenant of grace through circumcision.

**Comment 2**

Since according to God's Word everyone who wants to go to the Lord's Table should first examine himself and discern the Lord's body (1 Cor. 11:28-29), the holy Supper is not to be administered to children who are still incapable of doing so. It was an obvious misuse when it [communing children] was rather generally done, from the third to the fifth centuries, out of a misunderstanding of John 6:53, which was [incorrectly] understood as referring to receiving the Sacrament. This misuse was also practiced by the Bohemian Hussites and is the rule still today in the Greek church.

Luther writes: "I cannot consider it right that the Bohemians give the same (the holy Supper) to the children, even though I do

## The Persons to Be Communed

not call them heretics because of it" (1523 letter to Hausmann; XXI, 841).

The category of those who cannot be admitted to the holy Supper because they cannot examine themselves includes also the sleeping, the unconscious, those who cannot deliberate because they are in the last movements [the last gasps before death], the insane, and the like.

[Walther quotes John Gerhard (*Loc. th. de s. coena.*, sec. 225) to the effect that insane and even possessed people may be communed if they have lucid intervals during which they are able to examine themselves.]

Even deaf-mutes, if they have signs of faith and of understanding the holy action, are not to be turned away from the Lord's Table. Luther writes: "Some have asked whether the Sacraments should be administered also to the [deaf-]mute. Some intend to deceive them amicably and think that they should be given unconsecrated hosts. This insult is not good and will also not please God, Who has made them Christians as well as us, and the same is fitting for them as for us. So if they are rational and one can perceive from definite signs that they desire it from the correct Christian devotion, as I have often seen, one should leave the Holy Spirit's work to Him and not deny Him what He requires. It may be that they internally have greater understanding and faith than we, which no one should maliciously resist" ("Sermon on the New Testament"; XIX, 1302f.; see Deyling's *Instit. prud. past.* III, 4, sec. 45). [In Luther's day and Walther's day, the deaf could not be educated as well as they can be today.]

In a case in which one who desired the holy Supper had become so weak in understanding and memory that he could undertake the self-examination only with the preacher's help and could only repeat what was said to him, but had shown himself to be an upright Christian when he had greater mental powers, the theological faculty at Jena advised that he be admitted [to the holy Supper] (see Dedekennus, *Thesaur. consil.*, Vol. I, Th. 2, f. 357).

**Comment 3.**

It is good to note that a preacher does not have to be certain that those whom he wants to admit to the holy Supper are Christians standing in living faith. For who could do that? Rather [he must be certain] only that it is not provable or obvious that they are non-Christians. To act according to his moral conviction in admitting people or turning them away is an inexcusable lordship over the conscience. Even the Lord, Who according to His omniscience knew that Judas was receiving the holy Supper to his judgment, nevertheless admitted him because he was not yet manifest to people [as a non-Christian].

Gerhard writes: "Christ certainly admitted Judas at the same time as the others to the use of the holy Supper, as is concluded from Luke 22:20-23. For although Judas already then intended in his heart to betray Christ, indeed, had already then been paid for unrighteousness, yet this very serious sin was known to Christ alone but was by no means known to one of the apostles at this time, for they asked one another 'which of them it was that should do this thing' (Luke 22:23). So after a foregoing serious warning to desist from that sin, Christ admitted Judas to the holy Supper at the same time as the others. So according to Christ's example, a minister of the church should not exclude from the holy Supper those whose sins are still hidden but should seriously warn the unworthy before the harmful reception and admonish them to true repentance" (*Loc. th. de s. coena.*, sec. 223; see sec. 235 about Judas' reception of the holy Supper).

## Comment 4.

Anyone who does not confess the faith that the true body of Jesus Christ is truly and really present in the holy Supper and so is received by all communicants, worthy and unworthy, cannot discern the body of the Lord (1 Cor. 11:29) and so is not to be admitted to the holy Supper under any circumstances (see Gerhard, *op. cit.*, sec. 222). But even one who confesses that cannot ordinarily be admitted if he is and wants to remain, not a member of our orthodox church, but rather a Separatist, Romanist, Reformed, so-called Evangelical or Unionist, Methodist, Baptist, in short, a member of an erring fellowship. For the Sacrament, as it is a seal of faith, is also the banner of the fellowship in which it is administered. [Footnote to "ordinarily" [*ordentlicher Weise*]: Namely, except for the case of the fatal emergency, with which we will deal later.]

Mich. Mueling writes: "The holy Sacraments are symbols, watchwords, ensigns of the Christian confession of the heavenly truth, of the living faith, and of the true fellowship of the Church of Christ. So those who assent to false, erring doctrine cannot use the holy Sacraments without an evil conscience and name, indeed, without giving offense to those weak in the faith" (Dedekennus' *Thesaur.* Vol. I, P. 2. f. 364). [Footnote: See "Thesen ueber Abendmahlsgemeinschaft mit Andersglaeubigen," in the Proceedings of the 1870 convention of the Western District of the Missouri Synod.]

**Comment 5.**

Those who have angered or offended others (whether an individual person or a whole congregation) and have not yet been reconciled to them or who have been angered or offended and have not yet sought reconciliation, are to be suspended from the holy Supper, on the basis of Matt. 5:23-25, until they have fulfilled their duty and done what depended on them to bring about reconciliation.

If reconciliation in person is not possible, it can also be done in writing or through other persons. If even this is not possible, it is enough that one indicates an honest desire for it since God alone knows the hearts. Balduin writes: "If the offended one is

**Fig. 6: Walther's Study**
Courtesy of Concordia Historical Society

present, the offender is obligated to go to him and ask for forgiveness, according to Christ's words in Matt. 5, and no one is absolved if he has not made amends to the other person whom he has offended. But if he is absent and no discussion with him can be undertaken, the inward reconciliation of the heart or the testimony before others that he is ready to ask for forgiveness is enough" (*Tractat. de cas. consc.* IV, 17, 5, p. 1256).

Those who are living in an ungodly status are to be suspended from the holy Supper until they abandon this status and devote themselves to a God-pleasing profession. But a status is not to be considered ungodly only because what it produces is mostly misused. [Walther presents quotations in which the professions considered ungodly include: actors, jugglers, sorcerers, occultists, whoremongers, boxers, and tight-rope walkers.]

The category of those who are to be turned away from the Supper includes all who have been excommunicated, until they reconcile themselves to the church, unless they suddenly come into a fatal emergency. The Lower Saxon Church Order says of this case: "If it happens that the excommunicated person, before he lets an improvement be sensed in him, is overcome with harsh, severe, fatal illness, that person's friends as well as the pastor should with all possible diligence use admonition and the remembrance and indication of divine wrath on such a sin, so that he will consider and confess his sin and desire forgiveness of his sins by God through Christ, in addition to reconciliation with the church he has offended. If that is the case and occasion, the pastor should absolve him in the presence of witnesses and administer the holy Supper, with the understanding that if the Lord raises him up again from his bed [grants him recovery], he does not want to omit public repentance and absolution in the presence of God's congregation" (Dedekennus' *Thesaur.* Vol. I, Part. 2, fol. 687).

## Comment 6.

The well-known proverb: *Non remittitur peccatum, nisi restituitur ablatum* (The sin is not forgiven unless what had been stolen is restored) is certainly correct. A person is a thief as long as he illegally retains another person's possession. So long as he does, he cannot worthily receive the holy Supper. Dannhauer writes: "One must restore the whole; one must restore either the thing itself or something of equal value, corresponding to the extent of the damage that was done (such a case would be a retraction if one had to restore someone's good name). One must, if he can, make restitution to the one from whom the thing had been stolen; if he cannot, then to his heirs; if even this is not possible, then to the poor (naturally secretly). If the one who is obligated to make restitution cannot do so, he must make restitution in the sense of the wish and the promise to do so if he gets into better circumstances, the restitution can also be done through other people without the one from whom it has been stolen learning who is restoring to him had been stolen.

**Comment 7.**

If two preachers are distributing the holy Supper at the same time, and the first has already given a communicant the consecrated bread, the latter should not deny the communicant the consecrated cup, so that he does not mutilate the Sacrament, even if he otherwise has a well-founded reservation about doing so. (See G. Koenig, *Casus catech.* P. I, c. 6, cas. 5. pp. 467-476; and Hanneken, *Opus novum,* fol. 578).

**Comment 8.**

[Walther considers the question of whether the preacher may commune himself. The consensus of Lutheran theologians is that he may not do so privately, apart from the congregation, which is the meaning of the Smalcald Articles II, 2. But he may commune himself in the public service, which was especially necessary in nineteenth century America where many preachers were quite isolated and so would otherwise have to go without the Sacrament for a long time.]

# 19

## The Wedding and Marriage

When those who are entrusted to a preacher's spiritual care intend to marry, he has a threefold duty: 1. to consecrate the marriage only of those whose marriage is contrary neither to a human (that is, civil) nor a divine law; 2. to carry out the consecration in a correct way; 3. to guard against the marital bond being dissolved contrary to God's will.

**Comment 1.**

In the preface to his *Traubuechlein* [Wedding Booklet], Luther does indeed write that weddings and marriages are worldly [civil] matters, which it is not up to ministers of the church to regulate (X, 854). In his 1530 "Writing on Marital Matters," he writes: "I am horrified by the examples of the Pope, who was the first to mix himself into this game and grabbed such worldly matters to himself to such an extent that he became nothing but a worldly ruler over emperors and kings. So I am concerned here, too, that the dog may learn from the scraps to devour leather and may be misled with good intentions until we finally also fall out of the Gospel into mere worldly doings. For if we begin to become judges in marital matters, then the farm machine has grabbed us by the sleeve and will tear us away so that we have to pass verdicts. If we are to pass verdicts, then we must judge about life and possessions. Then we will be down under the wheel and will drown in the water of worldly business" (X, 893f.).

But these and similar statements are directed only against Papocaesarism, by virtue of which the Papistic priesthood declared civil marriage mediated by a priest to be real marriage, and that to be a sacrament. It also wanted to decide what concerned the state's marriage laws and what could or could not be allowed or permitted by it (see Matt. 19:8).

## The Wedding and Marriage

But since in marital matters the conscience is to be advised according to God's Word, no servant of God's Word can completely avoid them. Everything that is to be decided according to God's Word belongs within the duties and the authorities of the [pastoral] office. Luther not only delivered many wonderful sermons about marriage but also wrote and issued whole books about it.

Joh. Gerhard expresses himself very thoroughly about this matter: "Necessity itself requires it that, along with other articles of the Christian faith, also the doctrine of marriage be treated and clarified in the church, including showing the true and firm reasons for orthodox judgment and refuting the dreams of the opposed opinions and errors. But in particular it pertains not only to jurists and politicians but also to theologians and ministers of the church to make that doctrine known with a diligent spirit that shies away from no effort, so that when they are called upon to render judgments in marital matters, in controverted and doubtful cases, they can show the true foundation from God's Word and correctly

**Fig. 7: Mr. and Mrs. C.F.W. Walther. Mrs. Walther was born Emilie Buenger.**
Courtesy of Concordia Historical Institute.

advise consciences. . . .

"For that ministers of the church are also to be called to render judgments in marital matters we prove:

"1. From the nature of marriage. Although marriage is not really a so-called sacrament, it is still an estate regulated by God and so a matter of conscience, which depends on the divine institution and on the revealed divine laws. So the ministers of the church, as those to whom the care for souls and consciences is committed, cannot be absolutely excluded from rendering judgment in marital matters.

"2. From the Scriptural norm of this doctrine. Everything that is taught and presented in holy Scripture is to be expounded primarily by the theologians and the ministers of the church. But the doctrine of the institution and the laws of marriage, of the forbidden degrees, of divorces, of polygamy, etc., is presented in holy Scripture. So it is primarily to be expounded, and judgements based on it are to be rendered, by the theologians and ministers of the church.

"3. From the Christian and apostolic practice. Christ expounded the doctrine of the cause of divorce (Matt. 5:31-32), and when the Pharisees brought Him a question about marriage (Matt, 19:3), He did not direct it away from Himself and to the government as He did when he was asked for advice about dividing an inheritance and answered: 'Man, who made Me a jude or a divider over you?' (Luke 12:14). Rather He presented a thorough explanation of it from the words of the divine institution. In 1 Cor. 7:10ff. Paul dealt with the question of marriage between a believer and an unbeliever. In the ancient church, when the pious bishops were asked for advice in marital matters, they presented their judgment from God's Word, etc." ( *Loc. de conjugio*, sec. 7).

# 20

## The Persons to Be Married: Civil Laws

Before the preacher officially consecrates a marriage, he should not only be sure that he is authorized for that function according to the laws of the state but should also familiarize himself with the laws of the state in which he is. Observing them is required for a valid and legitimate marriage, and he should proceed according

Fig. 8: Courtesy of Concordia Historical Institute.

to them insofar as they are not contrary to God's Word.

**Comment**

In some states, only preachers who have been ordained or belong to a synod [church body] may perform weddings. In some even these may do it only if the engaged couple has gotten a government marriage license. In some, as in Missouri, that is currently not necessary, but they must, under threat of punishment, register the marriage that has taken place within ninety days on a specific form with the Court of Common Pleas.

In some states the preacher can or should have the engaged couple swear that they are aware of no legal impediment to their marriage. Responsible witnesses are always required. In some states, parental permission is always necessary, even after they [the engaged persons] have attained their majority [have come of age]. In most states there is a severe penalty for performing a wedding involving a minor without permission from parents or guardians.

Laws vary even about the degrees of relationship that prevent a marriage and about the age required for marriage. In some states it is still forbidden at this time [in Walther's day] to unite [in marriage] a white and a person of color. In some states a repeated proclamation of the banns is necessary for a legitimate marriage. Also the reasons for divorce are not the same in all states, etc.

[Some of these laws may be only of historical interest today, but the relevant advice is that a pastor must know the laws of the state, must register with state or county authorities to perform weddings, must know how soon before the wedding the license must be procured, etc.]

# 21

## The Persons to Be Married: Forbidden Degrees

If persons ask the preacher to consecrate their marriage, he should certainly investigate whether they are related to one another in a degree which, according to God's Word (Lev. 18:1-30; 20:10-23; Deut. 27:20-23; see Matt. 14:3-4; 1 Cor. 5:1), prevents marriage between them. That includes not only the persons explicitly named but also all persons of the same degree of relationship as is required by the general rule that precedes all the prohibitions: "None of you shall approach to any that is near of kin to him" (Lev. 18:6; according to the Hebrew, "flesh of his flesh," *sheer besaro*), in which category are understood, in addition to siblings and everyone in direct line of ancestry or descent *in infinitum*, also all who are one flesh with those who are already one flesh with the person to be married; to which are added, according to Lev. 18:14; 20:20, the spouses of deceased siblings of parents, because of the *respectus parentelae* (because the relationship to these persons calls for respect).

**Comment 1.**
[Walther notes that it is important to distinguish between moral law and civil law in this matter. He presents a lengthy extract from Dr. Christian August Crusius, *Kurzer Begriff der Moraltheologie* (Leipzig, 1773), pp. 1612-1643 showing that incestuous relationships (parent and child, any ancestor and any descendant) can never be true and real marriages according to both Scripture and natural law. They would be contrary to human nature as created by God; the child would not be leaving father and mother to become one flesh with someone else (Gen. 2:24). That natural law forbids such relationships is shown by the fact that all civilized peoples know it (1 Cor. 5:1). Crusius shows that there are important reasons in moral purity, the love of the neighbor, and the well-being

of the human race for the Scriptural prohibitions of marriage between siblings or other close relatives. These prohibitions are moral law, not only Old Testament ceremonial law, for God punished the Canaanites for breaking them (Lev. 18:20-23).]

**Comment 2.**

[Walther quotes John Gerhard (*Loc. th. de conjugio*, sec. 281-282) to the effect that all prohibitions apply equally to both sexes and that they apply also to illegitimate relationships (for example, a man may not marry his half-sister, born as the result of an extra-marital affair on the part of his father, Lev. 18:9).]

**Comment 3.**

The relationship which arises as the result of a legitimate betrothal does not produce, according to God's Law, any prohibition of marriage, as one sees from the reasons which are always given for the prohibition in Lev. 18. So, for example, it is not contrary to God's Law for a man to marry his deceased brother's fiancee.

**Comment 4.**

It is very important for a preacher to instruct his congregation thoroughly in advance about the degrees of relationship that prohibit marriage, especially that the general rule of Lev. 18:6 forbids marriage with the deceased wife's sister, which sadly! often happens in our day. [That was an issue in small, isolated communities before professional day-care. If a woman with several children died, her sister/their aunt might be the only woman willing to care for the children. That put pressure on the widower to marry his sister-in-law.]

Gerhard writes: "That marriage with the deceased wife's sister is forbidden by God's Law we prove with the following reasons:

"1. From the explicit prohibition in Lev. 18:18; . . .;

"2. From the principle that in Leviticus not only [marriages with] the explicitly named persons but also [with] those who stand in the same degree of relationship are forbidden . . . ;

"3. From the rule set up and proven above that, as a relationship by blood, so also a relationship by marriage continues to exist and is not removed by the death of the one through whom it arose . . . ;

"4. From the general rule in Lev. 18:6: 'None of you shall

## The Persons to Be Married: Forbidden Degrees

approach to any that is near of kin to him.' But now man and woman become one flesh through marriage (Gen. 2:24; Matt. 19:5).

"5. So the wife's sister becomes near of kin, and consequently one must not enter a marriage with her. Brother and sister and so also two sisters are one flesh (Gen. 37:27). So the man who has become one flesh with one sister through the marriage relationship, cannot marry the other sister, who was one flesh with the first one through the closet blood relationship" (*Loc. de conjug.*, see sec. 347; sec. 347-350).

# 22

# The Persons to be Married: Previous Marriages

The preacher has to investigate whether those who are asking him to marry them are not already validly and legitimately betrothed to someone else or are already in another marriage that is still valid.

**Comment 1.**
A valid and legitimate betrothal has occurred when two persons capable of marrying have voluntarily and unconditionally promised to marry each other before witnesses or, if the parents are still alive, with their explicit permission; or, if the promise to marry was conditional, when the condition has been fulfilled. There is no validity to secret betrothals, that is, those done behind the back or without the approval of the parents, no matter how public they may otherwise be, even if they have been confirmed by oath.

**Comment 2.**
Secret betrothals have no validity because, according to God's Word, children are not their own masters (not *sui generis* [legally independent]). So not children but rather their parents give them in marriage (1 Cor. 7:36-38; see Deut. 7:3; Gen. 29:21; Ex. 22:17). For according to God's explicit ordinance, parents can break an oath made [by children] without or contrary to their will (Num. 30:4-6).

**Comment 3.**
[Quoting Gerhard and others, Walther discusses conditional betrothals. It would be wrong to make harmful conditions such as agreeing to prevent conception or to participate in crime. It would be acceptable to make honest and realistic conditions such as parental approval or financial ability. Sexual unfaithfulness would

break an engagement as it would a marriage, and faithfulness is therefore always a tacit condition of the betrothal.]

**Comment 4.**
[With various sources, Walther discusses aspects of parental consent. It would not be required if the parents' whereabouts were unknown or if the parents were not mentally competent to grant or refuse consent. There should be some recourse (in German "state church" conditions, it was to the consistory) if parents stubbornly refused to consent for no good reasons, for example, if a widowed father wanted to keep a single daughter home as a housekeeper. If father and mother disagreed, the father's decision would take precedence.]

**Comment 5.**
[Since betrothal must be voluntary, it is not valid if one party has been subjected to duress or deceit. One cannot become betrothed while drunk. Insanity, leprosy, epilepsy, or other infectious and incurable diseases, and criminality would invalidate a betrothal if the other party did not know about it in advance. Inability to consummate the marriage would invalidate both marriage and betrothal.]

**Comment 6.**
That a legitimate betrothal is to be considered as binding as a completed marriage is taught in God's Word when a fiancee is called the wife of her fiance (Gen. 29:21; Matt. 1:18-20), and when sexual immorality with an engaged woman is punished the same as adultery committed with the neighbor's wife (Deut. 22:23-24; see v. 22 and 28:29; Hos. 4:13).

It is a wicked error that the *vinculum coniugale* [marriage bond] arises only through the church wedding or even only through physical intercourse. The former only confirms the marriage, and the latter would be immoral if the marriage had not already been entered into. Rather the effective cause of marriage is a mutual consent. The marriage bond has been made as soon as that has occurred [in the public betrothal].

Gerhard writes: "The pastoral blessing of newly married people is not required for the essence of the matter, namely of the marriage, but for the public witnessing of the same, so that it may be known to everyone that the marriage has been entered in a legitimate and honorable way. Before the court of the conscience and before God, that marriage is true and valid which has been entered into with mutual, legitimate, and honest consent, even if the pastoral blessing is not added" (*L. c.*, sec. 412).

The theological faculty of Rostock writes in 1622: "So also the *benedictio sacerdotalis* [blessing by a pastor] is only an outward adiaphoron, ordained by the church, which does not belong to the substance and essence of marriage but is rather properly . . . kept so that everyone . . . may know that the two married persons are correct spouses who have entered the state of holy marriage according to God's will and ordinance; and then also so that the estate of the two young married people may be diligently commended to God in prayer and that they may be reminded of their office [duties]. If a marriage may not be correct or complete in itself, the *copula sacerdotalis* [wedding by a pastor] cannot improve it or make it a marriage" (see Dedekennus, *Thesaur.* Append. ad Vol. III, fol. 35 sq.).

From that it follows first that a legitimately betrothed person may separate [*scheiden*, the same verb used for "to divorce"] from the other party only if the same ground exist for which a marriage could legitimately be dissolved. Other contracts are suspended if both parties are willing to give up their rights under them. Not so the unconditional betrothal. Through it a bond arises on both sides before God since marriage is a divine estate, a divine institution.

[Walther notes that Gerhard is a bit more lenient about breaking a betrothal than about dissolving a consummated marriage. He gives the following reasons for breaking a betrothal: sexual immorality; an action that would result in sterility; malicious desertion; incestuous intercourse with a relative of the other party, in which case the betrothal must be broken; crime; impotence resulting from an injury or illness; insanity; incurable, infectious disease, also epilepsy or total paralysis; deformity; notoriety; a long absence for no good reason and contrary to the will of the other party (*op. cit.*, sec. 166-169). It should be noted that epilepsy could not be managed medically in Gerhard's day or Walther's day as well as it can in ours—but that, according to these principles, AIDS or HIV infection should be added to the list of diseases that would be valid reasons to break a betrothal, for the uninfected party would be risking his or her life in the marriage.]

It certainly follows from the concept of legitimate betrothal that legitimately betrothed persons who live together as man and wife before the wedding are not committing the sin of fornication. But they are nevertheless committing a great sin. For if they want to be wedded [to go through the wedding ceremony] as if they were [only] betrothed, they are deceiving the church, acting contrary to all Christian and civil honor, and causing a severe public offense, especially if the matter becomes known and the bride become a mother before the [proper] time. So they become subject to church discipline.

Menzer writes: "Although the sin which such a fiance commits cannot be called fornication or adultery, it is still at odds with the chastity which God requires in the Law and runs counter to many commandments of the divine Law. For such a fiance is transgressing the betrothal in which he has made a holy promise that he will honorably lead his bride to the church for the wedding. He offends against obedience to the churchly office, to the government, and to the parents. And while he should guard his fiancee, he takes away her virginal honor and robs her of what should be more precious to an honorable virgin than life itself. He is pretending that he is a chaste youth and is violating his fiancee as a chaste virgin. So this sin is not to be dismissed and excused" (*Opus novum*, f. 573).

Gerhard writes: "It is one thing to enter a betrothal, and a different thing to complete a marriage. For the betrothal is only a promise of marriage. So the fiance should not consider the fiancee as a wife who has already been given to him but as a spouse who has been promised to him.... Otherwise they would be letting their marriage, which they had already previously begun, be announced to the church as a future one. They would be asking that they be joined together and their marriage blessed by the hand and mouth of the minister of the church, as by God Himself, when they had already long completed it...." (*op. cit.,* sec. 475f.). Gerhard then warns the ministers of the church against presuming evil and proceeding rigorously in cases of early birth or late birth (with respect to widows) [a bride might give birth prematurely, or a widow might give birth belatedly, without a sin having been committed, and they should be given the benefit of the doubt.]

## Comment 7.

A preacher should, with all earnestness, advise against marriage between orthodox persons and errorists. [In a footnote, Walther notes the importance of this advice in America in his day when an erring or unbelieving husband often moved his wife to a place where there were either no churches or only sectarian churches.] But if the decision had been made, he should no longer try to prevent it.

Gerhard writes: "Although we consider it most certain, best, and most advisable for those persons to marry who agree in the true knowledge and confession of the true religion, so that they can serve the true God and call upon Him with one mouth and one heart, according to the prescriptions of the divine Word; nevertheless when unbelievers or errorists are not also blasphemous and stiff-necked, but there is almost certain hope that they will be converted; then if the other party, who is Christian and orthodox, has a good understanding of the Christian religion, and so there is no danger of being misled and persuaded; marriage may be permitted, namely if the man is Christian and orthodox, who through marriage attains dominion over the unbelieving or erring wife.

"Here it can be applied to some extent that God, in Deut. 21:11, allowed the Israelites to marry women captured in war from other nations because it was improbable that a prisoner-of-war would bring her master to renounce his paternal religion. Further there are the examples of Judah and Joseph (Gen. 38:1; 41, 45).

"But if it is a question of such an unbelieving and heretical person who combines blasphemies with his unbelief or his heresy that overthrows the basis of the [true] religion, and who explicitly confesses that he wants to remain in his heresy, then we say that every believing and orthodox person should hold back from marrying that other person. And we can hardly be brought to accept it that marriages between persons of different religions are to be permitted" (*Loc. de conjug.*, sec. 387-388).

In the following context, Gerhard gives several reasons why that is not to be permitted:

1. The explicit divine prohibition (Ex. 34:16; Deut. 7:3-4; Joshua 23:12; 1 Cor. 7:39);

2. The reasons given for the prohibition, which show that it is moral and not Levitical in nature (Neh. 13:23ff.; 1 Kings 11:2-4);

The Persons to be Married: Previous Marriages

3. The experience that the usual result is falling away (Gen. 6:2; 26:34f.; Judges 3:5-7; 1 Kings 16:31);

4. The disadvantages which arise from it, namely with respect to worship at home, the raising of children, etc.;

5. The nature of marital fellowship;

6. The evil appearance which is thereby given, that one despises the correct faith.

The Leipzig theological faculty gave the following advice in 1620: "To the question whether a Lutheran may marry a stiff-necked Calvinist who refuses to be corrected, . . . we believe that it is to be answered that it is by no means to be advised. . . since *matrimonia* [marriages] with persons who are devoted to false doctrine and religion never turn out well as a rule but bring with them a great deal of trouble, as in the examples in God's Word, especially in the alliance of the house of Jehoshaphat with the house of Ahab (2 Chron. 18-22) and in daily experience before our eyes. But if such a marriage has been entered between a Lutheran and a stiff-necked Calvinist, a preacher would not be able to deny them the wedding and the blessing (because it [the marriage] has nothing to do with religion itself, and the errorist may perhaps in time be won (1 Cor. 7:16)" (*Thesaur. consil.* by Dedekennus, III, 242).

Balduin writes: "Jews should absolutely not be allowed to marry Christian children because of the danger of misleading [the Christians]. Therefore in the *jus civile* [civil law— probably referring to the Code of Justinian] marriage between Jews and Christians is forbidden with capital punishment. But here it should be noted that this law speaks of a marriage which one intends to enter. But of a marriage which already exists, Paul speaks in 1 Cor. 7:13-14: 'And the woman which hath an husband that believeth not, and if he be pleased to dwell with her, let her not leave him. For the unbelieving husband is sanctified by the wife,' etc." (*Tractat. de cas. consc.*, p. 193). So no upright servant of Christ will agree to consecrate such a marriage. [This point is not about Jews as an ethnic group; it is only about adherents of the religion known as Judaism.]

## Comment 8.

If Muslims or heathens (Mormons) are converted, and have previously lived in polygamy, only the first wife is to be recognized as a wife, and it is to be urged that they dismiss the other alleged wives. Gerhard writes: "Bellarmine says: if the unbeliever who lives in polygamy comes to Baptism, he is to be required to dismiss all wives but the first because only the marriage with the first one is a true [real] marriage. This insistence is based on the foundation that polygamy is contrary to God's Law and natural law. But whatever is contrary to natural law is forbidden also to the heathen who are outside of the church. And there is no place for any dispensation since the lower cannot suspend the law of the higher. And we agree with this opinion as the one that is more certain for consciences" (*L. c.*, sec. 226).

**Comment 9.**
[With various quotations, Walther deals with the question of how soon a person who has been widowed may remarry. A year of morning was customary and had sometimes been required in Europe. A widower should wait in order not to give the appearance that he had not loved his deceases wife and had already sought another wife while the first one was alive. A widow should wait for the same reason with respect to her deceased husband and also to avoid confusion about whose child she might be carrying. This advice is valid today, but it was more important when, before modern medical and emergency services, it was more common for a person to be widowed while quite young. There was considerable pressure to remarry, for a woman was economically more dependent on a husband, and a man was domestically more dependent on a wife to care for his motherless children, than is the case today.]

**Comment 10.**
A preacher should not marry a widowed adulterer to the person with whom he had fallen [into sin] during the lifetime of the spouse. In any case, such person should move to places where their fall is unknown. [In "The Babylonian Captivity of the Church," Luther permitted such marriages (XIX, 123f.). Other Lutheran theologians and some civil laws opposed such marriages for the sake of decency and in order to avoid the temptation to murder the first spouse.]

**Comment 11.**
To the question whether the guilty party in a divorce may be allowed to remarry, Gerhard answers: "Some absolutely deny this. . . . Others decree the opposite. . . . We hold with those who go

## The Persons to be Married: Previous Marriages

a middle way in that they decree that the guilty party should not be granted the authority to contract a new marriage immediately or without further ado but also that it should not be absolutely denied.

"1. We say that the government should be earnestly admonished to establish the death penalty for adultery. Then this question ceases [is settled].

"2. The guilty party should also be earnestly admonished that his very severe crime is worthy not only of eternal death but also of temporal death; that he should live in true terror of conscience, in crucifixion [mortification] of the flesh, and in work and fasting; and that he should consider himself unworthy to be given the authority for a new marriage.

"3. As long as the innocent party is still living outside of marriage, and so there is hope for reconciliation, the guilty party may absolutely not be allowed to hurry to a new marriage.

"4. If it is a fact that his conscience is suffering necessity and he is obviously threatened with corruption if he is not advised [if sexual temptation is too severe], then he can be permitted to marry again, but under the following conditions: a. that the guilty person does not enter a new marriage on his own authority but first asks the approval of the government and the churchly ministry; b. that he is not permitted to contract a marriage with the person with whom he had committed adultery; c. that first the earnest repentance of the guilty person is examined for a specific time; d. that he be required to change his place of residence and to go where his shame is not known" (*L. c.*, sec. 622).

Wigand writes in his book on marriage: "If the guilty person would be allowed to remarry according to his preference at the same time, that would open the door and the window for all wickedness, and evil would gain a desired reward. So it is necessary for the sake of honor and peace that guilty persons either remain without marriage or be forced to move" (*op. cit.*).

Luther gives the same judgement: "Where the government is negligent and careless and does not execute (the adulterers), the adulterer may move to another, distant place and marry there if he cannot contain himself. But it would be better: dead, dead with him! in order to avoid the evil example" (see X, 723ff.).

## Comment 12.
[If parents stubbornly refuse to allow children to marry but have no good reason, permission may be asked from the government. A child should not be allowed "easily" to refuse a marriage urged by the parents.]

## Comment 13.
If a person has been publicly betrothed to two different persons, it is self-understood that the second betrothal must yield to the first one (see Luther, X, 922). [Luther says that it should be considered adultery to marry the second fiancee instead of the first (*op. cit.*, p. 932).]

## Comment 14.
[If a man has sexual intercourse with a virgin or a widow without any promise of marriage, he should either marry her or accept the burden of her financial support.]

## Comment 15.
[Investigation was required if a person claimed that he had only been joking when he consented to a betrothal.]

# 23

# The Public Announcement of a Wedding

Although public church announcement before the wedding is not of divine right, it is a praiseworthy custom with the purposes: 1. that the intended marriage may be publicly known in advance, and those who know of a hindrance to the marriage have the opportunity to report it in time; 2. that the Christian congregation intercede in fellowship for the betrothed persons. It is most fitting that the banns be published on three successive Sundays, indicating the names and residences of the engaged persons and their parents, or the name of the deceased former spouse, in order to prevent confusion. The proclamation concludes with an intercession. After an objection has been made, the publication of the banns proceeds only as an *actus notificationis* [act of notification, without intercession], but the wedding takes place only after the objection has been settled.

**Comment 1.**
Dannhauer is correct in criticizing the Roman Church for permitting the publication [of the banns] to be omitted in the *Tridentinum,* sess. 24. c. 1. He writes: "The omission can lead to offense and dishonoring holy marriage. Then the church cannot excuse itself by [claiming] ignorance. For it is obligated to be morally wise with all possible caution" (*Lib. conscient. apert.* I, 817).

**Comment 2.**
[Publishing the banns could also be done on the Second Christmas Day, Second Easter Day, Second Pentecost Day, when there were worship services, but by custom it was not done on the first day of such a festival.]
In some states, the publication [of the banns] is required by civil law for a legitimate marriage, recognized by the state. In that case,

the preacher has no authority to omit it. Otherwise in a congregation in which there are many weddings, for example in a big city, it is not to be expected that the banns will be published for all non-members who are married by the pastor.

**Comment 3.**
[When the banns are published for a marriage involving a non-Lutheran, the preacher should warn against such marriages. The Lutheran party should be admonished to have the other party promise that he will not try to turn the Lutheran away from Lutheranism and that the children will be raised Lutheran.]

**Comment 4.**
Here in America, where people often change professions and the previous life of new individual members is unknown to the church, it may not be advisable, when the banns are published, to add the character and the full titles of the persons, also not the so-called chastity predicates ("a spinster," "a bachelor"). Here the preacher should be guided by the desire and custom of the congregation.

# 24

## The Wedding Ceremony

The public church wedding or marriage ceremony is performed according to the orthodox agenda which has been introduced [in the congregation], with a consideration for the customs of the congregation in which it is taking place.

**Comment 1.**
To the question: "Is the churchly blessing of the marriage a matter of necessity?" Conrad Dannhauer answers: "It is not absolutely a matter of necessity, for marriage can be valid among the heathen without it, as a civil action. In his writing about marital matters, Luther writes: 'Indeed, no one can deny that marriage is an external, worldly matter, like clothes and shoes, house and land, subject to worldly government, as is proven by the imperial laws set up for it.' . . . But it is nevertheless a matter of necessity for a Christian, holy, blessed generally recognized marriage; as the petition for daily bread is not absolutely necessary but is necessary for it to be a bread received with thanksgiving, as the Catechism's explanation of the fourth petition says. [Dannhauer refers to Mal. 2:14; Heb. 13:4; 1 Tim. 4:4; Col. 3:17; even the heathen have religious observances at weddings.]

"Dr. Menzer writes: 'A Christian bridegroom must believe that in Adam's marriage a rule is prescribed for him, which he should follow. For as he received his Eve from the hand of God Himself (Gen. 2:22), he must certainly think that in the church God Himself, through His servant, is giving him the bride, uniting her with him, and blessing this, his marriage. He must consider it shameful to enter without the knowledge of the church a marriage from which future members of the church should be born.'" (*Lib. conscient.* I, 818ff.).

But as decidedly as all our orthodox theologians testify that no upright Christian can despise the churchly blessing of his marriage if he can have it and seek [only] a civil wedding ceremony; they still make an exception for a case of necessity. The Wittenberg theological faculty writes in 1612: "So this is our opinion that the legitimate consent of the persons contracting [the marriage] is absolutely necessary for a legitimate marriage. So if someone lives at such a place where he cannot have the pastoral blessing nor can get it in neighboring churches, that lack should not lead him to err in his conscience" [that is, he can in good conscience have a civil wedding] (*Consil. Witeb.* IV, 23).

[It is logically consistent that Lutherans do not have converts

**Fig. 9: Walther wanted to be a musician first. He had a standing invitation to play the organ on any Sunday when he was not preaching. His skill at the organ was such that he improvised preludes and postludes.**
Courtesy of Concordia Historical Institute.

## The Wedding Ceremony

who are already married go through another wedding ceremony. A civil wedding would be preferable to a wedding performed by a heterodox pastor.]

### Comment 2.
As a rule, the preacher who performs the wedding is the one whose parish the bride belongs. [The reason given is that the bride's pastor is usually the one within whose geographic parish the wedding takes place.]

### Comment 3.
Deyling writes about the place of the wedding: 'As a rule the blessing and wedding takes place in a public church assembly, in the presence of the parents of the groom and the bride, with guardians, relative, and other friends. An exception would be an emergency or when a speechless person is to be married" (*op. cit.*, sec. 20).

### Comment 4.
Whether the so-called closed times (*tempora clausa*), in which weddings are not to take place, namely Advent and Lent, are to be observed should be left up to the congregation since these are indeed in keeping with God's Word (1 Cor. 7:5; Joel 2:16) but are not *juris divini* [by divine law]. [The Bible passages cited are relevant as examples, for Advent and Lent are traditionally penitential seasons, which do not fit well with wedding festivities, but the closed times are not divinely commanded.]

### Comment 5.
[With a quotation from Dannhauer (*Lib. conscient.* I, 1048), Walther recommends a middle road between being too formal and being too informal in weddings as in all church matters. In the German culture of his day, with the tendency to heap up titles and to avoid the second-person singular form of address, the third person form would be used in a wedding.]

### Comment 6
[Walther notes that various Lutheran writers approve of the practice of a new wedding celebration for the fiftieth anniversary, the "golden wedding."]

# 25

## The Case of Adultery and Divorce

If one of the spouses breaks the marriage bond through sexual immorality, and if the guilty party shows true repentance, it is the preacher's duty to advise the innocent party to forgive the other for the sin and to remain in the marriage. But he has to place that decision within the goodwill of the innocent party, and he may not deny this person, after a certain amount of time, the consecration of another marriage, if this person has sought a legal divorce and can prove that it has been received. [Footnote: The preacher's authority to marry by no means includes the authority to grant a divorce.]

**Comment 1.**
Chr. Tim. Seidel writes: "The preacher is obligated to bring those who live in an unhappy marriage to the right way and to guard against any divorce as much as he can. Here he should carefully guard against setting himself up as a judge for every case. For as soon as he agrees with one party, he has most often made himself incapable of accomplishing anything. So he must bend every effort so that both parties trust him. It is very good to visit such persons often and unexpectedly, especially if one hears that discord has arisen. Experience teaches that it often has a beneficial effect if he kneels down with those who are at odds with each other and, together with them, presents the matter of God. The innocent party especially is to be exhorted to be patient and reconcilable" (*Pastoraltheologie*, pp. 193ff.).

**Comment 2.**
The Papists indeed insist that even adultery [*Ehebruch*, breech of marriage] through sexual immorality does not dissolve the *vinculum matrimonii* [marital bond] so that even the innocent party

## The Case of Adultery and Divorce

may not enter another marriage before the death of the guilty party (see *Concil. Trid.* sess. 24, can. 7). But that is part of [their] Anti-Christian sin-inventing, contrary to the clear letters of the divine Word, because of which, among other things, the Pope is called the "man of sin" (2 Thess. 2:3).

**Comment 3.**

It would be an error to interpret the Lord's Word in Matt. 19:9 as if He were commanding divorce in the case named there. Rather divorce if only thereby declared to be permitted under such circumstances. Dannhauer writes; "Although the case of adultery is a just cause of divorce, it is still not a necessary and binding one. Why should the offended party not be able to be reconciled with the offender, following God's example, and the latter be able to be received in favor again?" (*Lib. conscient.* I, 808).

Luther writes: "Accordingly I cannot and do not want to resist that, where one spouse commits adultery, the other party may be free, may get a divorce, and may marry someone else. But it is much better, where it can be done, that they be reconciled and remain with each other. But if the innocent party wants to, he may use his right in the name of God. And above all things, such a divorce should not happen in one's own power but should be spoken through the advice and judgement of the pastor or the government. An exception would be if he wanted to do it privately and leave the area like Joseph [Matt. 1:19]. Otherwise, if he wants to stay [in the area], there should be a public decree (*op. cit.*, pp. 949 f.). It is self-understood that that advice can be followed only if the innocent party does not want to marry again and, by moving away, does not run the danger of being treated as a *desertor* [malicious deserter].

In the following context, Luther earnestly urges the preacher to "use Scripture confidently" to encourage the innocent party to forgive the one who has fallen but is penitent and to accept the person again. [In a footnote, Walther quotes Gerhard to the effect that the guilty party should be accepted again especially if there is good hope that that person will be faithful in the future and if the adultery has not become public knowledge (*Loc. de conjug.*, sec. 613).]

If the innocent party has, in fact, forgiven the guilty party by continuing to live together in marriage after the fall [into sin] has become known, that person cannot later move for divorce *ex post facto* (see Gerhard, *Loc. de conjug.*, sec. 621). [If sexual relations are resumed, the innocent party has forfeited the right to a divorce based on the past adultery.]

**Comment 4.**

About the time that should pass before the innocent party may enter another marriage, Luther writes: "So that such divorces may be minimized as much as possible, the one [innocent] party should not be permitted to marry immediately but [should be required] to wait at least a year or half [a year]. Otherwise it has an evil appearance as if he wanted it, was pleased that the spouse committed adultery, and so happily grasps this opportunity to be free of the one, wants to take another right away, and so is exercising malice under the cover of right. For such villainy indicates that he has so willingly left the adulteress and so eagerly sought another not because of disgust with adultery but because of a grudge and hatred toward the spouse and out of desire for and interest in another" (*op. cit.*).

# 26

## The Case of Desertion and Divorce

According to God's Word, there is only one legitimate reason for a divorce, namely sexual immorality (Matt. 19:9). But according to a clear apostolic statement (1 Cor. 7:15: "But if the unbelieving depart, let him depart. A brother or sister is not under bondage in such cases.") there is another case in which the innocent party suffers a divorce: if a non-Christian spouse maliciously deserts (*malitiosa desertio*), that is, leaves with the proven intention not to return to the abandoned spouse and cannot be moved to return by any means. In that case the innocent party (naturally only after a legal divorce has been procured) cannot be denied another marriage, after a proper time, according to the statement of the holy Apostle, as one who is no longer "under bondage," that is, is no longer bound to the previous spouse (1 Cor. 7:15, *ou dedoulotai*, see Rom. 7:1-3).

**Comment 1.**

There have been theologians who thought that they could prove from 1 Cor. 7:15 that there were two reasons for divorce. But that is an error. According to Christ's explicit statement, there is only one reason for divorce, and the apostle by no means contradicts that. Gerhard writes with total correctness: "Christ's exclusive statement, which specifies adultery as the only reason for divorce, does not lose anything through the apostolic statement because the former is not dealing with one and the same question, nor with one and the same case, as the apostle. Christ indicates the case of procuring a divorce; the apostle indicates the case of suffering a divorce and becoming free again through unjust desertion. Christ speaks of one who procures a divorce; the apostle speaks of one who suffers a divorce. Christ speaks of one who leaves his spouse; Paul speaks of one who is left by his spouse. Christ speaks of voluntary divorce; Paul speaks of involuntary divorce" (*Loc. de conjug.*, sec. 607).

Luther explains 1 Cor. 7:15 in this way: "Here the apostle says that the Christian spouse is free and single where the non-Christian spouse separates form him [*scheidet von*, the same term used for divorce] or will not allow him to live in a Christian way, and gives him the right and power to marry another spouse. But what St. Paul says here of a pagan spouse is also to be understood of a false Christian so that, if he wants to hold his spouse to an un-Christian life and not let the person live in a Christian way, or separates from the spouse, the spouse is single and free to marry another" (1523 exposition of 1 Corinthians; VIII, 1114f.).

[Walther continues the Luther quotation to the effect that the abandoned spouse cannot be expected to wait to the point of endangering his soul through temptation. The concern is that the divorced spouse will face severe sexual temptation. Not being "bound" means being free to marry another. In a footnote Walther says: "For whether one spouse maliciously leaves the other or uses tyranny of conscience to force the other to leave is completely the same." See Comment 5. below.]

## Comment 2.

Malicious desertion does not occur if the one leaving is absent because of his profession or with the consent of the other. Gerhard writes: "One must distinguish between an absence that is necessary or approved or incidental and an absence that is malicious, voluntary, wicked, etc. For only he is to be considered a deserter who gets up and leaves with a wicked intention, not for any just and honorable reason, but either out of hatred of religion or thoughtlessness or for some other unnecessary reason; and will not let himself be moved to return, neither by private admonition nor by public citation; but wanders around here and there and goes to other regions and distant places so that there remains no hope for his return or for reconciliation with him. . . . As in other actions, so also in separation and absence, the intention is primarily to be considered. So one who is absent because of his profession and intends to return cannot be considered a malicious deserter unless he changed his attitude toward his spouse and broke the promise he had made [to return]. The will distinguishes between actions, and the causes change the nature of the matter" (*L. c.*, sec. 626).

## The Case of Desertion and Divorce

On the question when a person who has been maliciously deserted can remarry, Deyling writes: "Although malicious desertion dissolves the marital bond just as adultery does, it is not to be recognized as a true desertion resulting in the dissolution of the marital bond if the divorce has not been carried out and declared after a foregoing, public, legal summons and a legitimate court procedure.

"The judge himself should first institute a careful investigation of all circumstances before he permits or institutes a trial for desertion. Otherwise injustice could easily be done to a spouse who was absent for legitimate reasons, and he could be declared to be a deserter when he was not one. So it must carefully be investigated whether the case is one of malicious desertion or deceit by agreement, whether the cause of the absence is just, and whether the other spouse may have agreed to it. For in this case no trial for desertion may be permitted. . . .

"Finally a sufficient amount of time must have passed since the desertion itself. That certainly cannot be determined by legislation but depends on the opinion of the judge. A time period of seven, four, or two years is not absolutely required; but it is believed that under certain circumstances even one year, indeed, even half a year, can be enough. If the absent spouse or betrothed person is to be summoned before the court for such a trial concerning marriage, that is usually done by a citation that is repeated three times. . . ." (*Instutut. prud. past.* III, 7, sec. 32-34; pp. 621 sqq.).

What has been said here relates partly to civil laws about marriage. But a pastor can see from it in which case he should consider an individual to be a malicious deserter, after he has been declared such by the worldly government and the judicial divorce has then taken place. [Today's legal situation is different, but we see here how seriously these matters should be treated in church discipline.]

[Walther gives a long quotation to the same effect from Luther's 1530 "Writing on Marital Matters" (X, 951ff.). Merchants or military personnel are examples of men who might be justifiably absent from their families for considerable time. Luther says of a man who would abandon wife and child: "There is no rascal that I would rather have hanged or beheaded than such rascals."]

## Comment 3.

[With quotations from Luther and others, Walther shows that refusing sexual intercourse is a type of malicious desertion according to 1 Cor. 7:4-5. But it would have to involve the same kind of stubbornness that would have to be proven in other cases of malicious desertion, with the intention never again to consent to sexual intercourse, and it would have to be clear that no persuasion would make a difference.]

## Comment 4.

About cases in which it is uncertain whether the one who has left is a *malitiosus desertor* [malicious deserter], Gerhard writes: "It is asked how much time is required for it be concluded of a person that he is a deserter. We say with Chytraeus in his commentary on Deuteronomy: 'The imperial laws determine certain times and a certain number of years before a deserted person can be permitted to marry. Although that has been done with the best intention, the diversity of the cases and circumstances of abandoned men and women is nevertheless so great that it is difficult and dangerous to prescribe a specific time in law. It is much rather totally right to leave it up to the opinion of a wise pious judge to determine, according to circumstances, a longer or a shorter time for remarrying and, as much as it can be done without danger to the conscience, to encourage the abandoned person to wait until the death or repentance of the deserter can be proven.'" (*L. c.*, sec. 632). [The danger to the conscience is the danger of sexual temptation since one of the purposes of marriage is to avoid sexual immorality. (1 Cor. 7:2)]

## Comment 5.

A spouse may not seek a divorce because the other one has temporarily left out of anger, or because the other spouse has been angry and raging, even in a life-threatening way. Rather there may be a temporary separation, without remarriage, always being ready for reconciliation. The apostle speaks of these and other cases in 1 Cor. 7:10-11.

Luther writes: "But if one once leaves the other out of anger or impatience, that is a much different matter. That is also not a secret, treacherous abandonment. There one learns from St. Paul, 1 Cor. 7, what one should do, namely let oneself be reconciled again, or, if reconciliation will not succeed, remain without marriage. For such a case can well occur that they are better apart from each other than with each other. Otherwise St. Paul would not have admitted that they may remain without marriage if they will not be reconciled. And who can list all such cases or put them into a law? Reasonable people must judge here" (X, 953f.).

About the case of constant discord, Luther remarks in his 1522 "Sermon on Married Life": "If one here had Christian strength and bore the other's wickedness or evil, that would indeed be a fine, blessed cross and a correct way to heaven. For such a spouse well fills the office of a devil and purifies the person who can recognize and bear it. But if he cannot bear it, rather than doing something worse, let him separate and remain without marriage all his life. But if he wanted to say that it was not his fault but the other's, and wanted to marry another spouse, that is not valid. For he is obligated to suffer evil or to let God alone remove the cross from him because marital duty must not be renounced. Here the saying applies: Whoever wants the fire, must put up with the smoke, too" (Erlangen, XX, 73f.).

**Comment 6.**

Exile, imprisonment, and flight after committing a crime are not types of malicious desertion. So according to God's Word they are not grounds for divorce for the innocent party. Gerhard writes about such cases: "Since there are only two causes of divorce, adultery and malicious desertion, we say that therefore a woman cannot marry another man because the husband has fled or been deported as the result of a crime unless it has become known that the man who has fled has become involved with other loves (*alienos amores sectari*) or has completely given up the attitude of being married. For no human authority is permitted to add other reasons to those which are explicitly named by Christ and St. Paul because the way the Savior speaks is so emphatically exclusive" (*L. c.,* sec. 691).

**Comment 7.**

A divorce because of alleged adultery can be procured only if it is clearly proven. Aegidius Hunnius writes: "*Suspicio adulterii* (suspicion of adultery) is also not sufficient cause for *divortio* (divorce) because in important marital matters it cannot go as far as divorce on the basis of mere mistrust or suspicion but [only] on the basis of sun-clear arguments and proven testimonies. Otherwise everyone who wanted to be rid of his spouse could present such suspicion. That would lead to internal ruin of the married estate" (Dedekennus, *Thesaurus*. III, 514).

**Comment 8.**

If a married woman has been subjected to force, that does not dissolve the marriage. Gerhard writes: "For actions are to be judged according to the attitude, not according to the outward deed" (*Loc. de conjug.*, sec. 612). [In this context, "force," *Gewalt*, means rape. Rape is not adultery on the victim's part.] According to Gerhard, the case of those who are only betrothed is different (see sec. 112).

**Comment 9.**

If a spouse knows that the other party has committed adultery and nevertheless continues to live for a time with the fallen person as man and wife, the marriage has thereby been re-established, and the right to a divorce has been forfeited. See Dedekennus, *op. cit.*, fol. 519.

**Comment 10.**

[If both spouses commit adultery, neither may divorce the other according to a seventeenth century statement by the Wittenberg theological faculty (see Misler's *Opus novum*, fol. 603.]

**Comment 11.**

Disease, no matter how offensive, infectious, or chronic, even if it makes the person unsuitable for marriage [makes sexual intercourse impossible], and insanity do not dissolve the marriage. Luther answers the question whether one may procure a divorce in such cases: "Absolutely not! Rather serve God in the sick person and take care of him; consider that in him God has given you something sacred in your house so that you should attain heaven. Blessed are you and blessed again if you recognize this gift and grace and therefore serve your spouse for God's sake. But if you say: Indeed, I cannot contain myself; there you are lying. If you will serve your sick spouse with the earnestness, and recognize that God has sent it [the situation] to you, and thank Him, then let Him be concerned about it. He will certainly give you grace that you may not [have to] bear more than you are able. He is much too faithful to let you be robbed of your spouse by sickness without also taking away the wantonness of the flesh if you otherwise faithfully serve the sick person" (1522, "Sermon on Married Life"; X, 726f.).

**Comment 12.**
To the question: "Is the abandoned person to be absolutely denied the right to marry someone else if it is revealed that he himself gave some occasion [cause] for the desertion?" Gerhard answers: "Even if the deserted person may have given some kind of occasion for the desertion, he should still not be considered the effective and unavoidable cause of it" (*L. c.,* sec. 633).

**Comment 13.**
If one spouse has entered a second marriage in the mistaken notion that the first spouse was dead or had deserted, and if the one who had been believed dead or had mistakenly been considered to have deserted returns, the alleged marriage entered into the meantime is to be considered and declared null and void; and the first marriage is to be recognized as continuing.

**Comment 14.**
Alleged marriages that are incestuous must be dissolved. Baier writes: "If illegitimately united persons, for example those who are related by blood in degrees that are forbidden by natural law [to marry], are parted, that is not a divorce but rather a declaration that no marital bond was present in that union because the one person was not able to contract a valid marriage with the other person, being a near blood relative" (*Compend. th. posit.* III, c. 16., sec. 34).

[Walther presents several quotations showing that there is some disagreement among orthodox Lutheran theologians about situations in which a marriage has already been entered.]

It hardly needs to be mentioned that we have communicated the foregoing not to prove that a preacher himself is able to bless marriages that transgress the divine commands about the forbidden degrees of relationship. It is rather a matter of how a preacher is to conduct himself if people want to join his congregation and are already living in a marriage forbidden by God's Word, for example, with the brother's widow or the [deceased] wife's sister. Should the preacher make the dissolution a condition of reception [as communicant members] or Absolution? It is our opinion that the cases just named do involve marriages that have been entered against God's command but are not incestuous unions. They are real marriages and need not be dissolved. What convinces us of that is primarily levirate marriage with the wife of a brother who had died childless, which was instituted by divine dispensation. That dispensation would not be conceivable if this union were an incestuous non-marriage (Deut. 25:5; see Lev. 18:16; 20:21).

**Comment 15.**
[Walther notes that poverty does not dissolve a marriage. If necessary, parents might support their married children financially without separating the couple.]

**Comment 16.**
[A quotation from Luther's 1530 "Writing on Martial Matters" shows that not everything can be legislated in writing. One should get advice and do the best that can be figured out (Walch, X, 920-922; 958-960; Erlangen, XXIII, 117-119, 151-153). Walther recommends reading further in this writing by Luther, which he has often quoted in this whole section.]

# 27

## The Institution of Confirmation

Confirmation is an adiaphoron, not a divine institution, much less a Sacrament; but it is a churchly institution which, if correctly used, can be accompanied by great blessing. The preacher should be concerned to reintroduce it where it has fallen into disuse and to preserve it where it exists.

**Comment**
Deyling writes: "Confirmation is a very ancient custom. It was originally given to children as well as adults right after Baptism if a bishop was present, who pronounced formal prayers and the outpouring of the Holy Spirit on the one who had just been baptized and added to it the anointing with the laying on of hands and the sign of the cross. So the whole action was sometimes called chrisma (anointing), sometimes cheirothesia (laying on the hands) and sphragis (seal), which designations were much more well known than the name of confirmation itself. So Tertullian writes: 'Having come out of Baptism, we receive the holy anointing.' And: 'Then the hand is laid on and, with a benediction, the Holy Spirit is called on and implored [to come] down' (*De bapt.* c. 7.8.). So in the most ancient time, confirmation was by no means a separate sacrament but nothing other than a ceremony added to Baptism.

"In the course of time that ceremony began to be separated from Baptism and to be carried out apart from it. It consisted mainly in examining the adults, repeating the Baptismal convenant, and obligating the baptized person anew to persist steadfastly in the true faith. Later the Papists made a sacrament out of the ceremony, which was to be received by all who had passed the seventh year and which, as they say, had the effect of bestowing grace greater than Baptismal grace, strengthening the soul against the assaults of the devil, and conferring an indelible character through which

Pastoral Theology

the person was joined to Christ's army. But these are all pure inventions as M. Chemnitz clearly proved in his *Examination of the Council of Trent.*

"When the Evangelicals [Lutherans] rejected the Papistic sacrament of confirmation as a superstitious ritual, a certain type of formal confirmation was retained at various places. That is very commendable since it has been purified of all superstition. Reintroduced from the ancient church, it customarily precedes the first reception of the holy Supper and has no small benefit. For the children, if they have matured to some extent and have been sufficiently instructed in Christian doctrine, before they are admitted to the holy Supper for the first time, demonstrate their progress in the Christian religion in front of a public church assembly and renew their confession of faith. Then public prayer is made for them, and they are dismissed in peace as those who

**Fig. 10: Walther loved children.**
Courtesy of Concordia Historical Institute

have the nearest expectancy of [receiving] the holy Supper. One may consult the Mansfeld Agenda, Cap. 17, under the title: 'Of the Confirmation of Children Who Recite the Catechism and Should Now Be Admitted to the Most Worthy Sacrament'" (*Instit. prud. pastoral.* III, 3, 40, pp. 390-393).

Since our church rejected not confirmation itself but only the Papistic superstition connected with it (see the Apology, Article XIII), it happened that Bugenhagen, with Luther's approval, introduced a purely evangelical confirmation in Pomerania, which example was soon followed in the church of Electoral Brandenburg, Strassburg, and Hesse. It is said in the Protestants' answer to the document of the Regensburg Colloquy in 1541: "There is neither divine command nor promise for confirmation and anointing. And the opponents know that these customs are only leftover indications of the ancient gifts of the Holy Spirit. For in the beginning of the churches the manifest gifts of the Holy Spirit were given to the people when the apostles laid hands on them. So also the prophets and apostles healed various illnesses and diseases with prayer and anointing and other things that were available as medicine. The customs are still left over from the beginning. . . . But we wanted to exercise the catechism faithfully in the churches and to pray for the children after they had been questioned, had confessed their faith, and had promised obedience to the church. And we believe that this prayer would not be in vain, and we are not displeased that the laying on of hands is used for it as it is also kept in some churches among us" (Luther's Words, XVII, 879).

But confirmation was not a universal institution in our church in the sixteenth century. Even though M. Chemnitz recommended it urgently in his *Examen* [*Examination of the Council of Trent*], it declined through the confusion of the Thirty Year's War [1618-1648, a war involving various European nations but fought mostly on German soil causing great devastation] even where it had been introduced. One of the first who called attention to this institution and its blessing again was Dr. J. Quistorp, professor of theology at St. James Church in Rostock. For a more general introduction of the confirmation ceremony after 1666, Spener is known to have been active more than others. Loescher also calls it "a very praiseworthy and edifying ceremony," but adds, "which, however, cannot be introduced everywhere and is also not absolutely necessary" (*Unschuldige Nachrichten,* 1713 volume, pp. 694ff.).

# 28

## The Confirmation Instruction

It is the preacher's duty to prepare those who want to be confirmed by thorough instruction in the Small Catechism and to carry out the ceremony according to the guidance of an orthodox agenda.

### Comment 1

The constitution of the Missouri Synod says: "The district synod is to exercise supervision so that its pastors confirm catechumens only when they can at least recite the text of the Catechism verbatim, without the exposition, and their understanding of it has been brought to the point that they are capable of examining themselves according to 1 Cor. 11:28. The synod requires that more capable catechumens, where possible, be brought to the point of being able to prove the doctrines of the Christian faith from the clearest proof passages of Scripture and to refute the erring doctrines of the sects from them. Where possible, a hundred hours should be used to instruct confirmands. The preacher should also see to it that his confirmands have memorized a good number of those good, churchly, basic hymns that may serve to accompany them for their whole life."

### Comment 2.

About the age necessary for receiving confirmation, the end of the twelfth year would be the earliest for most [children] (Luke 2:41-42). For unconfirmed adults, especially those who are already married, it should be made optional [*frei*, free] whether they want to be confirmed publicly. But they should all first receive confirmation instruction before they are admitted to holy Communion.

## The Confirmation Instruction

**Comment 3.**

According to ancient custom, the day of confirmation is either Palm Sunday or Quasimodogeniti [the first Sunday after Easter]. The former is suitable because preparation for the first reception of the holy Supper belongs to the nature of Evangelical [Lutheran] confirmation. [The confirmands would then commune first on Maundy Thursday.] But Quasimodogeniti [is suitable] because on that day, according to very ancient custom, the newly baptized "were formally received into the church by a formal presentation, at which time they now first laid aside their white Baptismal gowns. Therefore this Sunday of the Easter octave itself was called *dominica in albis, kyriake en leukois* (the Lord's Day in white

**Fig. 11 Courtesy of Concordia Historical Institute**

gowns), *dies novorum* [the day of the newborn], *octava infantium* [the week of the infants], *dies neophytorum* [the day of the neophytes]; later—with different meaning—in the west, Quasimodogeniti ('as newborn babes,' 1 Pet. 2:2) according to the introit used in worship" (Guericke, *Archaeologie*, p. 175).

To choose a high festival day for it, for example, the Second Day of Pentecost, as some do, seems unsuitable since that would necessarily infringe on the festival celebration of the great works of God.

**Comment 4.**

The preacher should certainly guard against presenting confirmation as an action which completes and perfects a Baptism received when the child was unaware, as if the child first now has to make his own the confession and vow spoken by the godparents. Rather the action of confirmation should serve mainly to bring the glory of Baptism received already in childhood to the living memory of the confirmand and of the whole congregation.

**Comment 5.**

The certainty that the catechumen bears a true life of faith in his heart cannot be made a condition of confirmation. Only notoriously wicked children, if all faithful use of God's Word bears no fruit, should not be confirmed. They would consciously be taking God's name in vain. Just as little should those be admitted to confirmation and the Lord's Table who are still so ignorant that they cannot examine themselves according to 1 Cor. 11:28.

**Comment 6.**

On the Sunday before confirmation the confirmands should be urgently commended to the intercession of all Christians, especially their parents, godparents, and relatives.

**Comment 7.**

About the whole celebration of confirmation, see the rite in the agenda of the Missouri Synod.

# 29

## The Pastoral Care of the Youth

The preacher should care in a heartfelt way for the confirmed youth in his congregation; be serious about this group of Christ's sheep, who stand in special danger; and keep a watchful eye on them. He should institute regular church examination, do everything he can so that the youth willingly attend it, and see that they regularly attend worship; that they diligently use confession and the holy Supper and regularly announce for it in person; that they do not attend the worship services of false believers; that they avoid seductive society and dangerous get-togethers, in public (in bars and such) or in private (in this case, both sexes), also dishonorable or even indecent games (Prov. 7:13), and [that they avoid] attending the theater, public dances, circuses, and such; that they do not join godless clubs or those that would be dangerous because of their inexperience and immaturity (gymnastic or musical clubs and the like); that they do not fall upon soul-poisoning reading (godless newspapers, obscene or even overly intense novels and stories, or dramatic works of that nature, doctrinally erring or naturalistic writings, and the like), etc.

**Comment 1.**
The constitution of the Missouri Synod says; "The district synod is to make it a conscientious duty of its preachers not to lose sight of the catechumens after their confirmation but to be concerned about them in an especially paternal way and so, among other things, where possible, to institute public examinations about the Catechism every Sunday." ["Church examination" is an old Lutheran custom in which the confirmed, unmarried youth sat together at the front of the church and answered questions about the Catechism after the worship service but still in the presence of the congregation.]

## Comment 2.

The more inclined the youth are to withdraw from the supervision of their pastor [*Seelsorger*] after confirmation, and the easier it is to do so here [in America], the more necessary it is for the pastor to seek to learn how those he has confirmed are doing and to follow up with them. The pastor should see to it that he does not intervene only after the young person has already fled from church and fallen prey to the world. The preacher should observe with special diligence whether the confirmed regularly attend the worship services and the church examination and diligently come to [private] confession and the holy Supper. He should faithfully use the [Communion] announcement to learn how it is going inwardly and outwardly for those whom he has confirmed and to approach their heart and conscience.

It is always necessary for the preacher to guard against being morose in a legalistic way but to practice pastoral care [*Seelsorge*] with a truly evangelical attitude. That is especially necessary in dealing with youth (Col. 3:21; 1 Cor. 4:15; 1 Thess. 2:7). Luther comments on Eccl. 12:1: "Solomon is a very royal schoolmaster. He does not forbid the youth to be with people or to be happy as the monks did for their pupils. . . . But it is dangerous for young people to be alone in that way, to be separated so from people. Therefore one should let young people hear and see and learn all kinds of things, but they should be preserved in discipline and honor. . . . It is good for a young person to spend a lot of time with people but to be honorably raised in honesty and virtue and kept from all vices" (V, 2348f.).

If young people with a Christian attitude form organizations in the congregation, the preacher should gain access to their meetings and seek to make them not only harmless but also useful and at the same time interesting, entertaining, and pleasant. The preacher should watch that the organization not become the center of the craze for amusement, but he should not expect young people to be as serious as adults, nor should he deprive the organization of free self-government.

It is an important part of the preacher's concern for the youth to see that get-togethers of both sexes never take place without the supervision of parents with a Christian attitude or of [other] married persons who take Christianity seriously.

## The Pastoral Care of the Youth

**Comment 3.**

[With quotations, Walther recommends that the church examination be lively, practical, attention-getting; popular but not vulgar; both thorough and simple. The questions should be so phrased that they can be answered briefly, even with yes or no. The preacher should be friendly and encouraging, not intimidating. He should always be very well prepared for each session of catechizing. What is said here and below may apply equally well to confirmation instruction.]

Christoph Timotheus Seidel writes: "Whoever wants to have peace of conscience in this matter will consider the following:

"1) Has he prepared enough for each catechization and grasped the truths about which he wants to ask with his own understanding, with proper clarity, thoroughness, and order?

"2) Is he approaching the catechization with an attitude of true love for the souls entrusted to him, and does he therefore take a joy and pleasure in the work; or is it something forced, which he makes a burden to himself and carries it out unwillingly and with displeasure?

"3) Is he aware of anything in language and manner of speech which will be offensive to the catechumens?

"4) Has he adapted a physical posture and gestures which will cause people with a less mature mental attitude to show him the respect due him, which would otherwise be denied?

"5) Is he aware of anything unusual or unkempt about his clothing which would cause laughter and therefore offense?

"And out of these considerations we will deduce the following duties of a catechist toward himself.

"The first duty of a catechist toward himself is that a conscientious catechist must always prepare in his understanding a clear idea of the truths about which he wants to ask. He must impress upon himself the order in which he wants to ask questions so that he can accordingly hold his thoughts together as an orderly guideline and not make digressions from one topic to another, which will confuse the catechumens and finally also himself and will make him conclude and break off early in dismay, wishing to get away from such boring work. We consider it one of the duties of a teacher that he must prepare himself for every catechization with all forethought. . . .

"Each catechization must relate to the previous one. One must well consider what was lacking in the first one and how to make up for it in the following one. One must know how to imagine in a very lively way the condition of his catechumens and prepare in advance for each of them that which can promote what is truly best for him. One must use strong proofs in the later one [the next lesson] since in the first one he only prepared the understanding [of the students] for more important things by using a few images. And so no more testimony is needed that the catechist is obligated to prepare himself in advance for every catechization. . . .

"The second duty of the catechist toward himself is that he must encourage himself in every way possible to carry out this work with joy and pleasure. For if he undertakes it unwillingly and with boredom, he will lack the cheerfulness which is unavoidably necessary for this task, and no more dismal work than this one will be found. . . Therefore the teacher must encourage himself. Here he will be able to make use of our advice, which consists in the following:

"1) Above all, one must call upon God both for His help and for the joy for a work which seems so despicable to the world and to flesh and blood and for which true self-denial is required.

"2) One must place before himself the command of Christ, our Chief Shepherd [1 Pet. 5:4], Who has explicitly commanded that His lambs be fed [John 21:15]. He who knows in his spirit what an evangelical teacher is will never appear bored.

"3) One must know how, through a rational method of catechizing, to set in motion the love and interest of his catechumens. A loving relationship with them produces an uncommon joy in the work" (*In der Erfahrung gegruendete Anweisung, welches die Methode zu catechisiren sei* (second edition, Helmstaedt, 1748), pp. 124ff.).

# 30

## The Private Pastoral Care of Souls

A pastor must not think that he is carrying out his office satisfactorily through public preaching alone. He must not withdraw from the duty of private pastoral care [*Seelsorge*] and the necessary home visits if he wants to be found to be a faithful steward.

**Comment 1.**
Dr. Johannes Fecht writes about the necessity of private pastoral care [*Privatseelsorge*]: "For although the preaching of the divine Word and the administration of the Sacraments are correctly considered the most primary office of the preacher because of the divine character [*Goettlichkeit*] of the Word which is presented and because of the divinely mandated practice of public worship, yet it is not to be doubted that it is an extremely dangerous error that that includes the whole office of a pastor [*Pastor*] and watchman of the church. In the meantime it speaks for itself that private teaching and exhortation belong no less to the presentation of the divine Word and often promise just as much fruit because they reach the hearers more deeply by their more confidential manner and personal application, and the form of discussion awakens attentiveness, which is sometimes lacking precisely in the sermon" (*Dissertatio de domestica auditorum visitatione etc.* (1708), quoted by J. Glob. Pfeiffer in his *Miscellanea th.* (Leipzig, 1736), pp. 725ff.).

Deyling writes: "An evangelical pastor [*Pastor*] is obligated to instruct his listeners not only publicly but also privately at every opportunity that presents itself, to be concerned about the individual, and to apply to everyone who is entrusted to his faithfulness and supervision that which is necessary for his specific person, to work for his salvation, according to the diversity of personalities and circumstance. For the teachers of the Word are called shepherds (pastors) in Eph. 4:11. Therefore they must be concerned not only for the whole flock but also for each individual sheep. So if one of them has strayed from the path, the shepherd seeks him without delay, leads him back to the flock, strengthens him, and heals the sick.

"Further a minister of the Word is appointed by God to be a watchman over the church, according to the examples of Ezekiel, Isaiah, and Jeremiah (Ezek. 3:17; 33:7-8; Is. 52:8; Jer. 6:17; see Heb. 13:17). But how would he correctly keep watch if he did not carry out his watchman's office toward every individual part, toward every member of the congregation? Further the pastor [*Pastor*] must give account for every listener of the whole congregation that is entrusted to him. Therefore he must carefully explore the life of each one and instruct him not only publicly but also privately.

"The pastors [*Pastoren*] are further called bishops, that is overseers, and in Acts 20:28 and 1 Pet. 5:2 they are commanded to *episcopein,* to pay attention and oversee, privately as well as publicly. So they are also called God's co-workers in 1 Cor. 3:9. But as God is concerned not only generally but also specifically for the salvation of every individual person, the minister of the Word, as God's co-worker, is obligated to do the same.

"The Persian King Cyrus, if we can grant credence to the old documents, is considered worthy of praise because he knew the name of every individual soldier in his large army. Cowherds and shepherds know each of their animals individually and care about each one. Why should not a shepherd of souls [have the same care] for the souls purchased by Christ's precious blood?

"So the Apostle Paul did not omit to teach each one (*hena hekaston*) individually, from house to house, as well as publicly (*demousia kai kat' oikous*) (Acts 20:20, 31; 1 Thess. 2:10[-11]). So every minister of the church is obligated to undertake the same home visitation and private teaching. This point was made very sharp by John Chrysostom in his thirty-fourth homily on the Epistle to the Hebrews, where he says: 'You must give account of each and every individual committed to your care: women, men, and children. Consider the danger in which you stand. It is amazing if a priest is saved.'" (*Institut. prudentiae pastoral.* P. III, c. 2, sec. 34, pp. 338f.).

[Footnote: We have a remarkable example of the individual application of God's Word to individual persons in the speech reported in Acts 24:24-25. Paul's listeners were his unjust judge Felix and his [Felix'] unchaste wife Drusilla. But the topic of his speech was: "righteousness, temperance, and judgment to come"! Therefore it says also: "Felix trembled, and answered, Go thy way for this time; when I have a convenient season, I will call for thee."]

**Comment 2.**

About the correct nature of private pastoral care [*Privatseelsorge]* in general and home visits in particular, Dr. Mich. Foertsch (professor at Jena, d. 1724) writes: "It is clear from what has been said that a minister of the church must be concerned with all diligence that he does not, by private activities, make himself unfit

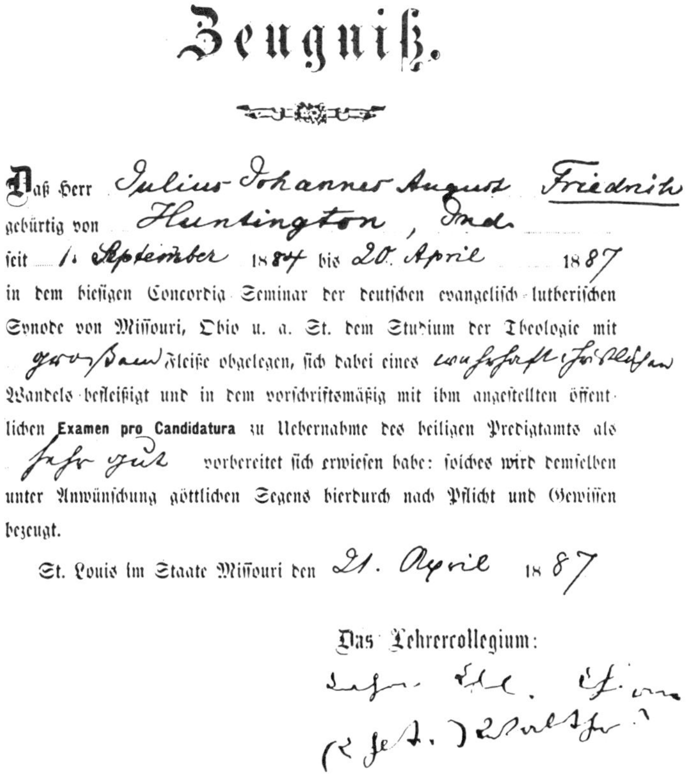

Zeugniß.

Daß Herr Julius Johannes August Friedrich
gebürtig von Huntington, Ind.
seit 1. September 1884 bis 20. April 1887
in dem hiesigen Concordia Seminar der deutschen evangelisch-lutherischen Synode von Missouri, Ohio u. a. St. dem Studium der Theologie mit großem Fleiße obgelegen, sich dabei eines wahrhaft christlichen Wandels befleißigt und in dem vorschriftsmäßig mit ihm angestellten öffentlichen Examen pro Candidatura zu Uebernahme des heiligen Predigtamts als sehr gut vorbereitet sich erwiesen habe: solches wird demselben unter Anwünschung göttlichen Segens hierdurch nach Pflicht und Gewissen bezeugt.

St. Louis im Staate Missouri den 21. April 1887

Das Lehrercollegium:

**Fig. 12: Last diploma signed by Walther, April 21, 1887, a testimony that Julius Johannes August Friedrich has shown himself to be "very well prepared" for the holy preaching office.**

**Courtesy of Concordia Historical Institute.**

for the public ones, which happens, for example, if he spends his time with inopportune visits or, in order to speak the truth more clearly, with running around while claiming to carry out his office with respect toward individual souls, and gets into the pulpit without meditation and proper study, to deliver extemporaneous and unprepared sermons; . . ." (*Dissertation de privata fidelium instututione* (1691); see Pfeiffer's *Miscellanea*, p. 695).

Every preacher, especially young and unmarried preachers, should carefully guard against too great an intimacy with the women and daughters in the families he visits at home. When the apostle speaks about the exercise of private pastoral care [*Privatseelsorge*] for old and young, he writes that the young women are to be admonished "as sisters, and with all purity" (1 Tim. 5:1-2). Of the errorists of the latter days it is said: "For of this sort are they which creep into houses, and lead captive silly women laden with sins, led away with diverse lusts" (2 Tim. 3:6). Not only must the preacher avoid the appearance of evil (1 Thess. 5:22) and act honorably in the sight of God and of people (2 Cor. 8:21), but the preacher must also beware of himself and consider that Satan pursues him everywhere to dash him, with the help of his flesh, into sin and shame, God's wrath and anger, death and damnation, and through him to cause fatal offense to whole groups of weak Christians while hardening the world.

In his official home visits, a preacher must also avoid the appearance of preferring to visit those homes where he will find enjoyment. About the words, "And into whatsoever city or town ye shall enter, enquire who in it is worthy; and there abide till ye go hence" (Matt. 10:11), Flacius comments in his *Glossa N. T.*: *Prohibet, ne subinde lautior hospitia quaerant*, that is "He [Christ] forbids them then to seek better lodging."

It probably does not need any thorough proof that the preacher should direct his private pastoral care [*Privatseelsorge*] primarily to those who have fallen. About Luke 15:4, Osiander makes the comment: "The human heart has such an attitude that it sorrows more about something that has been lost than it rejoices about things which it still possesses. So also Christ, the Son of God, is more concerned about the conversion of a sinner than about those who are already in God's sheepfold although he also bears the most zealous care for the latter, too (Ezek. 34). So we, too, namely we ministers of the church, must also be concerned with the greatest diligence to call sinners to repentance" (*Biblia as 1. c.*).

# 31

## The Pastoral Care of the Sick

Care for the sick and dying, primarily for their spiritual needs, is an extremely important obligation of a Christian preacher. The preacher should instruct his congregation that, as soon as a member of the family gets sick, the family members or whoever learns of it should promptly let him know about it (James 5:14-15). The preacher himself should also diligently inquire whether a member of the congregation has gotten sick and, as soon as he learns in any way that that is the case, not wait for an invitation but visit the sick person right away and continue his visits until the recovery or death of the patient (Ezek. 34:1-16; Is. 38:1; Sirach 7:39; Matt. 25:36ff.).

**Comment 1.**
How highly our church has always held the duty of a preacher to visit the sick and the dying within his congregation may be proven by the following excerpts.

The Saxon "General Articles," which were first drafted on the basis of the experiences of the church visitation in 1555 and were later expanded and amended and published in their present form in 1580, say under No. XIV: "The pastors [*Pfarrer*] and ministers of the church should visit and comfort the sick, troubled, and anxious Christians often but especially when they are close to death, and administer to them at their request the most worthy Sacrament of the body and blood of Christ. They should be willing and untiring in doing so, not omit such duty out of negligence nor out of vengefulness or antipathy toward any person, and also be just as willing to serve the poor as the rich in such cases.

"For this reason, when a parishioner among his listeners has fallen into severe illness, to whom the pastor has something good to speak for his soul's salvation, the pastor should not put it off until the end but should go to the sick person voluntarily, even without being called, to remind him properly [of God's Word] with all Christian gentleness and modesty, with comfort and admonition, because the sick person can still grasp it and can still take a Christian attitude toward his dying.

"The pastors and deacons should also frequently visit the sick in the hospital, where they [the hospitals] exist, give them the holy Sacrament, comfort them with God's Word, etc." (*Des Durchlauchtigsten Herzog Augusten . . . Ordnung, wie es in seiner Churf. G. Landen bei den Kirchen . . . gehalten werden soll* (Leipzig, 1580), fol. 318f.).

The Wuertemberg Church Order of 1582 says: "The almighty, merciful God cares so graciously about those who are suffering and troubled and call on His name with true trust, that He not only promises them all fatherly protection and help but also bears as a surname of His majesty primarily this title that He is a Refuge to those in suffering, a Savior of those whose hearts are broken, and has often preferred to alter the natural course of heaven and earth than to abandon the suffering in their trouble. In addition, the Son of God also calls all the troubled to Himself and promises to help them. 'Come unto Me,' He says, 'all ye that labour and are heavy laden, and I will give you rest' [Matt. 11:28].

"Now the sick are not the least among those who labor and are heavy laden, as those who have great, severe anxiety and temptation not only because of their bodily illness but also because of sin, death, and damnation, of which the illness reminds them. So the ministers of the church should also care with all seriousness and diligence about the sick who desire their ministration, and they should show them Christian comfort by virtue of their calling.

"It also seems good to us, for all sorts of important reasons, that the ministers of the church demonstrate their good will and offer their ministration also to the sick who do not want [to see] them, either on their own or through their [the sick persons'] friends and relatives" (*Von Gottes Gn. unser, Ludwigs, Herzogen zu Wuertemberg, . . . summarischer und einfaeltiger Begriff, wie es . . . in den Kirchen unseres Fuerstenthums . . . gehalten und vollzogen werden solle* (Tuewingen [sic; Tuebingen], 1582), fol. 146f.).

The [church] order for Ernestine Saxony says: "If the preacher hears that one of his listeners has become dangerously ill or has become anxious through some painful situation, he should willingly and gladly attend him, not only if he has been asked, but also if he has not been asked, but [in the latter case] after first announcing, visit him, and carry out his office with him according to his need with comfort and other discussion. Unless it would be that one was a malicious despiser of the divine Word and the holy Sacraments and gave evidence of his persistent impenitence also by not having the pastor called; in which case a pastor is not obligated to come right away on his own without being called; although also here [he is] to exercise great caution that not a single opportunity be missed to convert the impenitent and to tear a poor soul from the devil's jaws" (*Fuerstlich-Saechsische Verordnungen, das Kirchen-und Schulwesen betreffend* (Gotha, 1720), p. 106.).

[In a footnote, Walther says the preacher should, when asked, also visit patients who do not belong to his congregation, as long as they do not belong to another congregation, in which case he would be interfering in another pastor's ministry. In a later footnote, Walther says that a preacher should absolutely not accept any gifts in return for visiting the sick.]

Ludwig Hartmann writes: "It is not subject to doubt that visiting the sick and the bed-ridden in their homes, in order to comfort them, is thoroughly necessary work and is not to be omitted because it is burdensome or because there is the danger of contagion. Since, because of their illness, it is not granted to them to be present at the public worship service, it is necessary for their souls that they be privately refreshed so that in such troubles they do not helplessly fall victim since Satan is shooting his fiery arrows at them so cunningly" (*Pastoral ev.*, p. 1287).

Johann Fecht writes: "If every Christian owes the other the duty of visiting him in illness, how much more the minister of the church [owes it to] his sheep! Therefore it is also explicitly commanded in some church orders that the pastor visit the sick, even without waiting for an invitation" (*Instruct. pastor.* c. 10. sec. 2, p. 90).

**Comment 2.**

No matter how loathsome and contagious the illnesses are, the preacher must never allow himself to be moved by that to omit visiting the sick. So the theological student should already harden himself, by visiting hospitals, to the impressions of loathsome diseases. But in such cases the pastor, before he visits the sick, should not only seek to occupy himself with the Word of God and prayer but should also not go on an empty stomach to visit someone who has a contagious disease. [In a footnote, Walther recommends Luther's writing *Ob man vor dem Sterben fliehen moege* ["Whether One May Flee From Death"] (X, 2321-49).]

Only where several preachers work in the same congregation can, in a time of the plague or other epidemic diseases, one or the other, who is most courageous in God, be singled out for visiting the sick. Where there is only one preacher, he cannot, without becoming a hireling, absolve himself of the responsibility of diligently visiting also those who have contagious diseases.

When Luther wants to picture the correct preacher, he writes in that remarkable letter, *Vermahnung an einen Pfarrherrn, dass er zu unbilligem Absetzen eines Predigers nicht stille schweigen solle* ["Admonition to a Pastor That He Should Not Be Silent About the Improper Deposing of a Pastor"] (1531): "You know that you are the correctly called . . . pastors and soul-carers [*Seelsorger*] of the church at . . ., so that you will have to give account on that day for the same church which has been committed to you, and you are obligated, as long as you live, to provide it with the pure doctrine, to pray, care, watch for it earnestly, and to risk and abandon your life in all kinds of trouble and danger that may occur, such as the plague and other illnesses, whatever they may be called, and to stand at the front against the gates of hell and everything that a devout, faithful pastor and soul-carer should do, suffer, and endure for the sake of this office. All of which are severe, great, indeed, divine works" (X, 1892).

# 32a

## The First Visit to the Patient

The most important rules for pastoral sick calls are, according to our most experienced theologians: "First, so that a minister of the church who is called to [visit] a sick person, does not take up the function with unwashed hands (as one says) or clumsily, he can most properly begin with the patient by using the passage that the hairs on our heads are all numbered, etc., (Matt. 10:30), and then tell the sick person that this sickness or whatever condition it may be has not come upon him by chance or without our God's foreknowledge but rather that everything happens according to God's counsel and will, which he should also receive and accept and not doubt at all that, whether this sickness is for life or for death, it will turn out to be the best for him; now he should take the correct attitude toward it. Then follows a further statement of the cause for which God usually burdens us with sickness or similar conditions" (Felix Bidembach, court preacher in Stuttgart, *Manuale ministrorum ecclesiae*, "Handbook for Young, Beginning Ministers of the Church," (1603), p. 647).

**Comment**

On the first visit to a sick person, the preacher should naturally turn first to the members of the family who welcome him and, after assuring them of his sympathy, speak a brief word of encouragement and, depending on circumstances, comfort. When the preacher then approaches the sick person, he naturally begins the discussion with him with a greeting, with the assurance of sympathy, and with an interested question about the condition of the patient.

# 32b

## The Condition of the Patient

A second important rule is that the preacher, in order to determine the best pastoral care for the patient, start an exploration, depending on how well he knows the condition of the patient.

**Comment 1.**
Seidel correctly remarks: "The distinction between the external and primarily the internal condition of the patient requires that a teacher inquire particularly into the nature of the patient and carry out his office toward him with proper wisdom. It is easy to see that it is not fitting to approach every patient in the same way and that it is not enough to read something aloud from the church order as happens in many places. The preacher must rather show himself to be a physician who recognizes the illness of each person and knows how to apply to him the medicine that will be useful against it" (*Pastoraltheologie.* I, 13, 2, pp. 212f.).

**Comment 2.**
Olearius gives the advice that in his exploration the preacher especially ask about the following six points:
"1. Whether or not the patient has acquired a sufficient knowledge of the way of salvation.
"2. Whether he has also gone through life in his practice according to this way or impenitently in manifest sins to the point of being on his sick-bed or death-bed; or whether he has lived in external blamelessness, on the basis of which, however, one cannot be assured that it has been done out of faith with true sanctification.
"3. In which particular profession he has been and to which temptations he may especially have been subjected; also what kind of divine leadings and judgements of grace or wrath he may have

## The Condition of the Patient

experienced or can have observed in his condition.

"4. What the nature of his illness may be; whether it will permit such speaking, questioning, and answering; whether the patient may soon die or may be granted some time to be concerned for himself and to set his house in order; whether or not his mind is left clear and unconfused or whether his speech and gestures originate from his illness or from rational processes (which consideration is especially to be taken into account in illnesses involving fever).

"5. The particular (natural) attitudes of the patient are certainly to be taken into account (temperament and mental capacity).

"6. One must especially notice what the horror of death may awaken in the same [the patient]" (*Collegium pastorale*, pp. 809ff.).

About No. 2, it should yet be said that the preacher should also investigate whether the patient, if he bears in himself the signs of one who is not yet converted, is self-righteous or is stuck in carnal security, or whether he stands in servile fear. If he has the signs of a truly believing Christian, [the preacher should investigate] whether he is strong or weak or under assault in his faith. It is especially important in our days that the preacher inquire whether the patient may be in doubt about the truth of the divine Word or about certain fundamental articles of the divine faith.

## Comment 3

It is self-understood that the examination of the condition of the patient must not take place in an inquisitorial manner. It should happen in such a way that one concludes part of what he needs to know from the behavior of the patient and also brings them to reveal his condition voluntarily. Bidembach writes: "The minister of the church should also diligently pay attention to the words, gestures, and all the behavior of the sick person, from which he can be best informed and have opportunity to converse with him" (*op. cit.*, p. 648).

# 32c

## The Primary Need of the Patient

A third rule is that the preacher be concerned first for what is most necessary for the patient, according to his condition; otherwise everything else would be fruitless.

**Comment**

This rule, which is as simple as it is important, is stated by Olearius: "The general rule remains that one take up first that which is most important, that without which any other actions would be fruitless, and try primarily to do justice to it. For example, if the patient is very impatient and inattentive . . . because of his illness, one should first bring him to quiet, calmness, and attentiveness because otherwise all other talking and preaching would be in vain. If it is noticed that the necessary instruction that pertains to repentance, faith, and sanctification, is lacking, one should first strive to impart thorough instruction.

"If doubts arise, perhaps pertaining to essential elements of religion, one should primarily try to remove them (as the correct certainty that Scripture is God's Word is lacking in many, indeed, sadly in most people, for the opinion that they have of it is not a firm, inward conviction; therefore the divine origin and respect of Scripture should be treated more often [in regular sermons] than is probably done). If the knowledge is good in theory but is still lacking in practice or in self-knowledge or in upright repentance, one should begin here. If, for this or that reason, doubts occur about the grace of God in Christ, this matter should first be taken up" (*op. cit.*, pp. 848f.)

# 32d

## The Approach to the Patient

A fourth rule is that the preacher give the patient the necessary spiritual nourishment in a conversational, not a sermonic, way; especially that he not preach much to the severely ill, and, if they are in great pain, that he impress on them only passages of holy Scripture with short applications and suitable hymn verses, pausing from time to time, and praying with short, heartfelt sighs. In severe illnesses or when great spiritual distress is connected with the illness, the preacher should not only urge the patient to pray but should also help him pray according to his condition or make fervent intercession for him at his bedside.

**Comment 1.**

Bidembach writes: "The great pains of the sick person should also be considered as they do not always permit much speaking. So one must leave them with less discussion so that they are not made unwilling or too tired. And then it is especially necessary that one practice brevity. . . . In expressing comfort and other matters it is not necessary, also not beneficial, to bring together and *coacervire* (heap up) too many *dicta Scripturae* (Bible passages) at one time. For otherwise the weak cannot retain it and later remember them and refresh themselves with them. So the most nurturing thing is to present one *dictum Scripturae* (of which one may have a selection), three or four [at the most], those that are strongest and most easily grasped, or on occasion to explain them a little and apply them to the person . . . so that one can spend a little time with them and impress them on a person until another time" (*Manual.*, pp. 648f.).

It is self-understood that, when the patient's condition permits it, especially in chronic illnesses, the preacher can and should speak at greater length to the sick person, read and explain longer sections of holy Scripture to him (for example, John 5:1-16; Is. 38:1-22; Job 33:15-30; Luke 15:11-32; whole psalms, especially the penitential psalms, the seven letters of the Lord to the churches in Asia Minor, Rev. 2 and 3; etc.), share the content of the last sermon presented in public worship, or even read it to him in its entirety, etc.

With chronic illnesses, if they permit longer [periods of] mental activity, the pastor should also be concerned that the patient receive suitable reading material. [Walther recommends the Bible, the Catechism, the Book of Concord, Luther's writings, etc.]

## Comment 2.

So that a preacher is not lacking the necessary material, even when he is called on to visit a sick person quickly and unexpectedly, it is necessary for him to memorize a collection of refreshing and comforting [Bible] passages and hymn verses for all types of spiritual conditions. When he wants to make a sick call, he should run through them briefly either on the way or before he sets out. Also a supply of especially refreshing or comforting stories can sometimes accomplish excellent services at the sick bed.

## Comment 3.

Even if the preacher perceives in the patient the greatest ignorance and blindness about himself, the greatest self-righteousness and impenitence, he should not despair of the possibility of still helping the sick person. He should not deal with him in a scolding manner. Rather, in order to bring about true repentance in the sick person, he must then show him the spirituality of the Law in calm earnestness, describe to him how serious God is about it, and specifically present to the patient that from the divine Law in which he will find a mirror of his heart and life.

The preacher should never forget that there are many who appear to be living securely in coarse sins, who do not want to confess that they are sinners, who continue to sin and express a coarse self-righteousness only because they are stuck in secret despair and so think that they cannot be helped, that they are lost beyond salvation. But in spite of the excess of their sins, the whole wealth of God's free grace in Christ is to be shown them according to Rom. 5:20.

The same is the case for those who have some terrible crime (perjury, murder, adultery, incest, and the like), without anyone

## The Approach to the Patient

knowing it, and so cannot come to any peace. If the preacher notices that the patient remains closed to all comfort, he should suspect that the cause for it lies in this that, contrary to the urging of the Holy Spirit, the patient does not at all want to confess a deed that lies on his conscience. He [the preacher] should encourage him to lighten his burdened conscience through an upright confession (Psalm 32:3-5). In this case the preacher must naturally be concerned that he be left alone with the patient.

# 32e

## The Critically Ill Patient

The fifth rule for visiting the sick is given by Bidembach in the following words: "With patients for whom life and death are still very uncertain, it is not advisable either to make them too dejected and right away tell them that they are certainly not going to live or to make them too comfortable and tell them that death is still very remote. Rather since our life and death stand in God's hands, it is best to leave them *in suspenso* (undecided), to place everything in God's will. But it is not unnecessary, in uncertain cases, always to incline somewhat more toward [the possibility of] dying so that the patient may prepare himself that much more for it. For otherwise many think only of the hope of living longer, and only with difficulty can one accustom them to thinking about dying" (*op. cit.,* pp. 549f.).

**Comment 1.**
One should remind the patient that every bodily illness is a messenger of death, even if it [death] does not follow (Is. 38:1ff.), and that the more seriously one prepares for death, the more greatly he will benefit from it [the preparation] even if he remains alive.

**Comment 2.**
Seidel remarks: "There is a common opinion among preachers that, if they find the least appearance of recovery in a patient, they are no longer obligated to visit him. A conscientious teacher will observe the following with those who begin to recover: 1. one testifies to them with as much love as earnestness that the lengthening of their life is of brief duration, that God may have thereby the infallible intention to purify them yet more from the adhering impurities, and that they should bend every effort for this purpose; 2. one has them promise (that is, if they were not

previously living properly) that they want to give up whatever sinful custom has previously been noticed in them," etc. (*op. cit.*, p. 223).

**Comment 3.**

As a rule, the preacher takes leave of the patient with a heartfelt wish and with a promise to return soon if possible. Olearius remarks: "Then, depending on the patient's condition, a special, brief memory passage may be recommended to him which can encourage him to continue to meditate on what has been presented [by the preacher]" (*op. cit.*, p. 846).

# 33

## The Patient to Be Communed

If sick persons desire the holy Supper, the question whether to administer it to them is to be decided according to what has already been said in Chapter 18.

**Comment 1.**
For communing the sick, the preacher should provide himself with the elements; see that it [Communion] is preceded by confession and Absolution with the laying on of the hands [a Lutheran custom in individual Absolution]; neatly arrange the table on which the consecration will take place; read aloud, depending on conditions, the admonition to the communicants contained in the agenda; read a suitable antiphon and collect for the consecration and after the distribution; and conclude with the benediction and the Our Father and finally with an admonition or a wish [for blessing, recovery].

Bidembach remarks: "It is proper to stay with this that, where the need and sickness are so great that so long a delay cannot be permitted, the admonition, the prayer (after confession and Absolution), and Christ's Words of Institution should never be omitted. If the sick person wants to make confession in the way in which he is accustomed to it, that is also to be permitted him, or the customary form should be spoken to him.

"Before the Absolution follows, the sick person should be reminded in a few words [to consider] whether he has any other secret concern in his heart or some other burden on his conscience that is oppressing him. If he finds himself burdened, he should clear his heart and indicate it (in general or in specific) to the ordained minister of the church so that it can further be reported [if necessary, as for a reconciliation]. Again, he should be reminded that he should retain no enmity, jealousy, or hatred in his heart

## The Patient to Be Communed

but should by all means give it up according to Christ's admonition in Matt. 5:23, and as he desires to be forgiven, he should also have the same attitude toward his neighbors. If the sick person declares himself correct [in these respects], the Absolution should follow.

"Before leaving, the minister of the church should remind the sick person briefly about the special, glorious comfort which the sick person may have from this food and especially about the presence of the true body and blood of Christ, namely so that he may most especially be certain of the forgiveness of his sins since he has received in the Supper that body and that blood which Christ gave and sacrificed for him. Again, [he should be reminded] that he has received the true viaticum and nourishment for the journey to eternal life if indeed God should desire to take him to Himself this time. And since now his Lord Christ is with him, he has nothing to fear but should say with Psalm 23[:4]: 'Yea, though I walk through. . . .'" (*Manuale,* pp. 655ff.).

### Comment 2.

In carrying out private Communion, the preacher should wear at least the *Beffchen* (*Ueberschlegel*) and use his own Communion ware. [Walther is recommending that the pastor be dressed in a way that indicates his office, not necessarily in full vestments, for private Communion.]

# 34

## The Pastoral Care of the Troubled

It is a preacher's duty to visit those members of his congregation who, while not physically ill, have been visited by some other severe misfortune or find themselves in special spiritual danger and distress; who are in danger of falling away to a false religion; who stand in severe temptations by their own hearts, the world, and the devil (with doubts about divine truth, with despair, with blasphemous and suicidal thoughts); who are involved in dangerous trials; who come to be seriously suspected of a severe crime or have already been thrown into prison; who have fallen into melancholy [depression], insanity, etc.; who are physically possessed by Satan; and the like.

**Comment 1.**
[Walther suggests good reading in this matter, but the books he mentions are not available in English if they are available at all: Olearius, *Seelencur;* Nic. Haas, *Treuer Seelenhirt;* Lassenius, *Betruebter und Getroesteter Ephraim.*]

**Comment 2.**
As far as bodily possession by the devil is concerned, the preacher must know that physical possession can be imposed by God even on devout children of God. J.W. Baier writes: "Satan's works include also physical possession, by virtue of which Satan dwells essentially in the bodies not only of godless persons but sometimes even of devout persons, and works in them by divine permission. Namely when God either directly or indirectly (that is, through people, either through good ones, for example, ministers of the church when they exclude coarse sinners by excommunication (1 Cor. 5:5; 1 Tim. 1:20), or through evil ones who intend to harm others, for example, by means of spells and curses) permits people

to be subjected to Satan.

"For although the purpose of this possession from Satan's side is harm and corruption, in part to the person himself, in part to other people; yet from God's side, Who permits it and is thereby either visiting severe sins (despising God's Word, carnal security, blasphemies, conspiracy with the devil) with His serious judgement or is rebuking and testing devout persons through physical chastening, the purpose is the revelation of His power, righteousness, and goodness, and the repentance, faith, and salvation of people, if not of the possessed person himself, at least of others, namely the eye and ear witnesses" (*Compend. th. posit.* P. I. c. 3, sec. 51).

Quenstedt writes: "The proper marks of physical possession are:

"1. The knowledge of foreign languages as well as arts and sciences which the possessed persons have never before learned and, if they are freed, no longer know;

"2. Knowing and stating things which are hidden, which have happened elsewhere, in very distant regions, or which are in the future;

"3. Superhuman or supernatural power and strength;

"4. The exact reproduction of the voices of birds, sheep, cattle, etc., without the disposition of the [speech] organs necessary for it.

"To this are to be added yet:

"5. Obscenity in speech;

"6. Monstrosity in gestures;

"7. Horrifying screaming (Mark 5:5);

"8. Blasphemy toward God and scorn for the neighbor;

"9. Fury and violence against one's own body and against the others watching (Matt. 8:26; 17:15; Mark 5:5; Acts 19:16).

"Physical possession can be recognized from these and similar signs, which, however, do not all occur at the same time in every possessed person but sometimes more, sometimes less. But a special caution is required so that those who are severely ill are not considered possessed" (*Theolog. didactico-polem.* P. I. c. 11. s. 1. fol. 652).

About the correct treatment of those who are physically possessed, Luther writes: "We cannot now and also should not drive out the devils with certain ceremonies and words as previously the prophets, Christ, and the apostles did. We should pray in the name of Jesus Christ and seriously admonish the church to pray that the dear God and Father of our Lord Jesus Christ will free the possessed person through His mercy. If only such prayer is made with faith in Christ's promise in John 16:23, then it is strong and powerful so that the devil must retreat from the person, as I could relate some examples. Otherwise we cannot drive out evil spirits and also do not have the power to do it.

"The poor people possessed by the devil under the Papacy were not freed from their evil, burdening spirits by the art, words, and gestures from which the exorcists used. He does not let himself be driven out with mere words such as: Depart, you impure spirit! The exorcists also did not seriously mean it that way. The power of God must do it, and one must risk his life, for the devil will make it terrifying enough for him. . . .

"But that the devil departed through exorcism by Papistic monks and priests and left behind a sign, perhaps pushing out a pane of glass or a window or tearing out a part of the wall, he did

**Fig. 13: In his later years, Walther's congregation provided him with a carriage to make it easier for him to get around St. Louis.**
Courtesy of Concordia Historical Institute.

that to mock the people, who would otherwise not have known that he had departed [merely] because he no longer plagued the possessed person; [he did that] all with the intention that later, through such a sham, he might possess the people in another way, namely spiritually, and strengthen them in their superstition.

"So it happened in St. Ciliax in the cloister at Weimelburg, not far distant from Eisleben, to which there was a great pilgrimage and concurrence, that a monk, a good drinking buddy, commanded a possessed monk to open his mouth, let him put two fingers into it, and still not bite him, and it happened so. He also commanded the devil to depart when the bell of St. Ciliax would be rung. The rascal did that also so that he would strengthen the people in their deception and error that the bell was so holy that the devil had to depart when it rang, and so totally wiped out faith in Christ" (XXI, 1104ff.).

One should also see Luther's 1545 letter to Pastor Schulze in Belgern, in which there is the form of a prayer which the pastor should repeat over the possessed person in addition to the Creed and the Our Father with the laying on of the hands (XXI, 1343ff.).

As sad as it is when even pastors think that physical medicines are the only help for those "possessed" persons because they consider it to be only melancholy [depression], it is nevertheless not to be denied that it is often very important to use physical medicines against possession as well as prayer and [God's] Word.

Balduin states that, *caeteris paribus* [other things being equal, that is, if the person is otherwise qualified], the holy Supper can be administered also to a possessed person in lucid intervals (*Tractat. de cas. consc.*, p. 630 s.). Fecht also points out that the possessed person, if he is a believer, is to be told in lucid hours that the blasphemies which rush out of him when he is convulsed by Satan are not reckoned against him (*Instruct. pastoral.*, p. 93).

# 35

## The Welfare of the Congregation's Needy

Although the preacher should be concerned above all for the spiritual needs of the members of his congregation, the area of his official duties includes concern for physical welfare, especially for the necessary needs for [this] life of the poor, the sick, widows, orphans, the infirm, the needy, those weak with age, etc. (Gal. 2:9-10; see Acts 6:1ff.; 11:30; 12:25; 24:17; Rom. 12:8, 13; James 1:27; 1 Tim. 5:10; 1 Thess. 4:11-12).

**Comment 1.**
This is an extremely important point in this country. The secret societies are eating like a terrible cancer at the body of the church. Thousands and thousands join them at first mostly to insure themselves support and help in time of poverty, illness, or other trouble. But the result is that they are finally estranged from the church and consider their secret society a better representative of the true—because it is active—religion than the church.

The fundamental reason for that is unbelief and the lack of Christian knowledge. But another major reason is that the Christian congregations do not do what they are obligated to do with respect to their members who are in physical need [trouble]. The people know that, even if they are members of a Christian congregation, they are still abandoned in poverty, illness, and other troubles. So then, unawakened as they are, they join societies which give them the prospect of certain help in time of need. It is inexpressible how much that serves to dishonor the church and the Word of God.

The apostle writes to the Christians at Thessalonica: "And that ye study to be quiet, to do your own business, and to work with your own hands, as we commended you; that ye may walk honestly toward them that are without and that ye may have lack of nothing"

## The Welfare of the Congregation's Needy

(1 Thess. 4:11-12). So God's Word says that Christians should try to get into a situation in which they will not be dependent on the generosity of "them that are without [outside the church]."

On the words, "that ye may have lack of nothing," Hedinger comments: "Paul wants them to work for themselves in blessing so that they do not have to look into the hands of the godless, which would serve as a mockery to them, an offense to their faith, and a misleading of their souls through the association" [no reference given].

But it is clear that if Christians want to work and to eat their own bread, but cannot do so and find it necessary to appeal to the generosity of unbelievers, then they are not guilty. But the congregation whose members they are is guilty for the offense given to the world and for the dishonor which comes upon the Gospel. The zeal of a congregation against the secret societies is obviously Pharisaical if it is not connected with a zeal to provide sufficiently for its poor and suffering [members].

A Christian congregation must not appeal to the fact that there are governmental relief funds and poor-houses, which they also support. No Christian congregation should care for its poor in this way. The state should rather perceive that it need not forcibly impose taxes for the poor, in order to support the poor Christians, but only [to support] people who would otherwise be abandoned by all the world. The Christian congregation should consider it a disgrace to see its poor cared for by the worldly government.

It was a different matter in the so-called state churches, in which a merging of church and state took place. There the state poor institutions were really those of the church. Here, where the church and state are strictly separated, the church should not let the exclusive care for its own poor be taken away from it. If God called already to the church of the Old Testament: "There should certainly be no beggar among you" (Deut. 15:4 [Luther's translation]), how much more is that true for the church of the New Testament! If it dishonors God when Christians must go begging among Christians because they are not given what they need—so that Christ must go begging in them—what an insult it must be to the Christian name if Christians must go begging to the loveless world because their brothers close their hearts to them!

Luther writes about the history of setting up a special office of almoner [*Almosenpfleger*] in the apostolic congregation at

Jerusalem (Acts 6:1): "In this history you see first how a Christian congregation should be organized; then you see a correct picture of spiritual administration [*Regiment*], which the apostles conduct here. They provide for the souls, are occupied with preaching and praying, but also bring it about that the body is provided for, set up some men who distribute the goods as you have heard. So Christian administration provides for the people, both body and soul, that none of them has any lack and all are abundantly nourished and well provided for both in body and in soul" (*Kirchenpost.* XI, 2754ff.).

**Comment 2.**

It is clear from Gal. 2:9-10 and Acts 6:1ff. that caring for the poor belongs to the specific official duties of the preacher. Whenever our old theologians enumerate the official functions of a preacher, they also include caring for the poor.

**Fig. 14: C.F.W. Walther's House on his death, near the location of Concordia Seminary at that time, on South Jefferson Street in St. Louis.**
Courtesy of Concordia Historical Institute.

## The Welfare of the Congregation's Needy

Gerhard writes: "There are in general seven functions or duties of the ministers of the church, in which the others can easily be fitted: 1. the proclamation of the divine Word; 2. the administration of the Sacraments; 3. prayer for the flock entrusted to them; 4. an honorable way of life; 5. dealing with church discipline; 6. the preservation of church customs; 7. caring for the poor and visiting the sick" (*Loc. th. de minister. ecclesiast.*, sec. 265).

Luther comments on Gal. 2:9-10: "When a faithful shepherd or pastor [*Seelsorger*] has provided his little flock with the preaching of the Gospel above all things, then he should be more diligently concerned about nothing else than that the poor may be nourished and preserved. For it never fails, where a church or congregation of God is, that there must also be poor people, who are commonly alone the upright students or disciples of the Gospel; as Christ Himself testified in Matt. 11:5: 'The poor have the Gospel preached to them'; and 1 Cor. 1:27-28: 'The foolish things of the world.' etc. For evil people and the devil persecute the church and congregation of God and make many poor people, who are then afterwards so abandoned that no one wants to care about them or give them anything" (VIII, 1762).

L. Hartmann writes: "As in the flock the suffering sheep need greater and more abundant help on the part of their shepherd (Ezek. 34:4), so in the parishes suffering persons such as the poor, especially if they are sick, widows, orphans, and other people who have been abandoned by all help and oppressed by others, need the special help and care of their pastors and have a full right to expect it from them. For although Christian love demands this duty also from others, it is still the duty of the pastor, above all others, to have a paternal concern for suffering persons, and he must not convince himself that it is enough that they receive support from the administrators of the poor chest [literally: God's chest]. Rather in soul and conscience he must consider the poor so that they do not fall away from the Gospel because they lack the necessities of life and move elsewhere or envy the rich. So according to Paul's example, the pastor must also make frequent admonitions to make collections for the poor (Gal. 2:10).

"So primarily the pastor should diligently seek to find out who among his people are in misery, who deserve it that others should be merciful to them. . . . For this purpose the pastor must have a list of the poor, prepared by himself and the [congregational] officers [*Vorsteher*], and actively check whether anyone has been impoverished by occurring illnesses, shortages of food, or through other misfortunes, in order to support them from the congregational poor chest and from his own means" (*Pastoral. ev.* III, 54, p. 1023 sqq.).

**Comment 3.**

The preacher should be concerned that in his congregation, especially if it is numerous, assistance for the poor is properly organized and that specific almoners are appointed to administer it properly, according to the example of the congregation at Jerusalem (Acts 6:1ff.), and that they are provided with a suitable job description. Luther writes about the passage already cited: "That is a very fine picture and example, and it would be good for one still to begin in that way, if there were people behind it, for a city as this one here to be divided into four or five parts, and for each part to be given a preacher and some deacons, who provided that part with preaching, distributed the goods, visited the sick, and saw to it that no one suffered any lack. We do not have the people for it; therefore I do not dare to begin it until our Lord God makes Christians" (XL, 2755). Later there will be opportunity to deal in greater detail with the churchly offices alongside the office of the Word.

**Comment 4.**

About the people who are to be supported by the congregation, and about the nature of the support, we cite the following testimonies: [helping the poor who are honestly poor; no one should starve or freeze; but also wisely applying 2 Thess. 3:10].

**Comment 5.**

With respect to the sick, it is the preacher's duty to be concerned not only that they receive the necessary means of support if they are poor, but also that they receive the necessary medical treatment and care. [It could be organized in the church in the same way as general care for the poor is organized.]

# 36

## The Pastoral Care of the Dying

If the preacher is called to [visit] a dying person, he should indeed remind him of his sins but above all (however he may have lived) point him to Christ and present to him well-known [Bible] passages and speak hymn verses and heartfelt sighs to draw [him] to Christ as the only certain Savior from sin, death, devil, and hell. He should ask him whether he recognized himself to be a poor sinner, lost by nature, and whether he places his confidence in Christ alone and so is ready to die with faith in Him. If he affirms that, the preacher should strengthen him in it with comfort. If he loses consciousness, the preacher joins with those present in prayer on the knees. If death follows, he blesses the one who has fallen asleep with the laying on of hands (according to Seidel's instructions) with words such as the following: "Lord God, I commend into Thy faithful hands what Thou, the Father, hast created; what Thou, the Son, hast redeemed; what Thou, the Holy Spirit, has sanctified. Amen!" In conclusion the Our Father may be spoken.

**Comment 1.**
See Chapter 18, Comment 2, about the administration of the holy Supper to people on their deathbeds.

**Comment 2.**
The blessed Mathesius writes: "If someone postpones it (the holy Supper) to that point (until the little hour of death), I do not tell him to despair. For the thief still came correctly [to repentance], before the door was closed, even though he came late (Luke 23[:39-43]).... Augustine says; *Poenitentia vera numquam est sera, sed sera raro est,* that is: True repentance is never too late, but a late one is seldom a true one" (*Postille* (Nuremberg, 1565), fol. 135).

It is true that repentance is not such a minor work that it consists in nothing more than confessing with the lips: "God be merciful to me a sinner!" [Luke 18:13]. True faith does not arise in a heart through the Gospel unless the Law has first done its work, revealed the heart's inexpressible corruption, broken it, softened it, and made it hunger and thirst for grace. But if one has to do it with someone near death, it is impossible to start a thorough exploration. So nothing is left but, after briefly holding before him the mirror of the Law, to show him the Lamb of God Who takes away the sin of the world [John 1:29]. If the dying person is still to be saved, it can only be done through the latter. The servant of Christ cannot omit it, no matter what his [the dying person's] previous condition has been.

This knowledge was always present in Christendom, even in its darkest times. Well-known is the conversation which Anselm of Canterbury (d. 1109) prepared for visits at the sickbed:

"Brother, are you glad that you will die in the faith?—Yes.

"Do you confess that you have not lived as you should have?—Yes.

"Do you want to believe that the Lord Jesus Christ, the Son of God, died for you?—Yes.

"Do you believe that you can be saved only through His death?—Yes.

"Do you thank Him for it from your heart?—Yes.

"Then thank Him always, as long as your soul is in you, and set your whole trust in this death. Rely entirely on this death; cover yourself entirely with this death and wrap yourself in it.

"And if the Lord would want to judge you, then say: Lord, I throw the death of our Lord Jesus Christ between me and Thee and Thy judgment; I will not contend with Thee in any other way.

"If He would say that you have earned damnation, then say: I throw the death of our Lord Jesus Christ between me and whatever evil I have deserved; the merit of His very precious suffering instead of the merit which I should have had and oh! do not have.

"Let him say further: I lay the death of our Lord Jesus Christ between me and Thy wrath. Finally let him say three times: Lord, into Thy hands I commend my spirit.

"And those from his convent who are standing by may say: Lord, into Thy hands we commend his spirit. So he will die in peace and will not see death eternally." (See M. Chemnitz, *Examen Concil. Trid.* (Berlin, 1861), p. 164.)

Truly evangelical directions for a blessed death are found in Luther's *Sermon von Bereitung zum Sterben* ["Sermon on the Preparation for Death"] of 1519 (X, 2292-2313; Erlangen, XXI, 253ff.).

One should certainly observe what Quenstedt writes: "The preacher should also not mix into the disposition of the temporal goods of the sick" (*Ethica pastoralis*, pp. 312 s.).

**Comment 3.**

About preparing people for death who have been sentenced to death because of their crime, see Porta's *Pastorale Lutheri*, Cap. 18, sec. 10; Felix Bidembach's *Manuale ministrorum ecclesiae*, pp. 744-766: L. Hartmann's *Pastorale evangel.*, pp. 1320-1332; Seidel's *Pastoraltheologie,* Th. I, Cap. 14, pp. 230-244. Especially the last-named book contains excellent practical indications, to which F.E. Rambach, the editor of the 1769 edition, has made some very valuable additions.

Seidel presents the following rules [about a pastor visiting a criminal sentenced to death]:

1. "On the first visit to the criminal the preacher must see to it that he brings to him a good opinion of his person." So he should guard against asking the prisoner about the reason for his imprisonment. [Footnote: Other theologians, such as Bidembach, recommend the opposite, advising the preacher to ask this question in order to reveal, through the answer, the spiritual condition of the prisoner.]

2. "He is obligated to present to the criminal sufficient knowledge of the way of salvation."

3. "A preacher is obligated to present to the one sentenced to death the reason which can move him to endure with joy a forceful death which the world considers shameful." [Footnote: Rambach correctly warns against encouraging one who is dying because of his crime to have a martyr's joy of death and then to want to make a show of his repentance.]

4. "A preacher is finally obligated to accompany the one sentenced to death to the place of execution and to stand by him and speak to him up to the last moment." [No further references given.]

# 37

## The Christian Funeral and Burial

The duties of a preacher toward the individual members of his congregation include the concern that those who have fallen asleep in the Lord receive an orderly, honorable, and Christian burial (see Matt. 14:12; Acts 8:2; Matt. 26:12-13; Tobit 1:19-21; Is. 53:9; Jer. 22:18-19).

**Comment 1.**
An honorable, orderly funeral in Christian solemnity is: during the day, with the ringing of the [church] bells (by which the Christian funeral procession is called together), hymns, prayers, the preaching of God's Word (at the grave, at the altar, from the pulpit, perhaps also the reading of the obituary), the benediction, a Christian procession (perhaps with the school children and their teacher, following the crucifix), etc. Here the preacher will be guided by custom and tradition. Deyling writes: "The funeral procession is undertaken according to the custom of each locality, with hymns, the ringing of bells, and other customary ceremonies, which the preacher may not arbitrarily alter" (*Institut. prud. past.* III, 11, 20).

**Comment 2.**
About the distinction of persons which should be observed in funerals, Deyling writes: "Although the burial of the human corpse pertains neither to sacred or religious things, nor to the worship of God; nevertheless among the Christians the nature and manner of the burial constitute a part of the liturgy and public worship, being done usually, for the most part, with hymns, preaching, and prayer in a public church assembly.

"The manner of treating corpses was once very diverse, depending on the diverse customs of civilized and uncivilized peoples. It was indeed customary at one time among the Greeks as well as the Romans to bury the corpses, but that was done more rarely. It was much more the custom to cremate them. The ancient Christians followed the very ancient custom, agreeing with Scripture, of burying the corpses and had a great abhorrence of cremating them. Our church is right in following this custom of burial. For the body, having been formed from a lump of earth, should become earth again after it has fallen (Gen. 3:19). So it is by no means necessary or useful to embalm the corpse, which has very frequently been the custom among Jews and Christians.

"There is a distinction between honorable and dishonorable burial. The former is either solemn or less solemn. The first is done publicly, during the day, with the customary ceremonies. The second is done without the usual solemnity in that it [ceremony] is sometimes omitted entirely or is sometimes minimized either because of poverty, or because of pestilential air and the danger of infection, or because of suicide committed out of melancholy. But the last will of the deceased alone is not enough for the pastor to omit the customary and solemn funeral ceremonies.

"The pastor should by all means be concerned that the old, godly funeral ceremonies are not done away with so that corpses are buried at night without the usual customs; rather [he should be concerned] that the burials are completed in good order in the traditional manner, and in the villages that someone from each house join the funeral procession. [In a small village a procession would be possible only with rather full participation.]

"No one is to be denied an honorable burial because of poverty. Much rather it is proper that the poor have a public funeral the same as the rich, with the honorable and customary ceremonies. This institution of humanity is counted among the works of love and is praised by Christ Himself (Matt. 26:12). On the contrary, the denial of an honorable burial is in the nature of the punishment, which must not at all be done to an innocent person. So the ministers of the church should be concerned that the poor, if they have departed from the world with a commendation for piety, receive an honorable burial as the members of Christ through the generosity of others. So the preacher and the schoolmaster must accompany the corpses of the poor [join the funeral procession] without remuneration.

"An honorable burial is not to be denied either to children who died without Baptism, nor to women who died in the six-weeks [confinement connected with childbirth], nor to those who died accidentally or were murdered, nor to those who were found [dead] on a public street or elsewhere. In doubtful cases, where clear indications do not make it apparent that the deceased has committed suicide, one assumes the more favorable case [that it was not suicide].

[In a footnote, Walther presents a quotation from the 1580 Church Order of Electoral Saxony to the effect that a full Christian burial is to be carried out for stillborn children and other children who died before they could be baptized, and their salvation is not to be doubted based on a passage such as Gen. 17:7 and on the

**Fig. 15: Walther's Tomb.**
Courtesy of Concordia Historical Institute.

## The Christian Funeral and Burial

fact that many Old Testament children died before circumcision on the eighth day; Baptism is not absolutley necessary for salvation.]

[The Deyling quotation continues:] "A dishonorable burial is either a human burial or a donkey's burial (Jer. 22:18-19). The former is when a human corpse is buried either outside of God's field [*Gottesacker*] or at a separate place within it by the regular grave-digger. But the latter is done by the executioner at an infamous place which is set aside for the corpses of animals and criminals, in the animal graveyard or under the gallows. Such a dishonorable donkey-burial is usually allotted not only to malicious suicides... but also to those who have been convicted of a capital crime or have confessed it but have died or committed suicide in prison, impenitent and loaded with guilt, before the punishment was suffered.

"A dishonorable but human burial... is allotted to heretics. So the corpses of Pagans, Turks, Jews, also those of Socinians [Unitarians], who are not counted among the Christians, are not to be admitted to our [church] cemeteries [Gottesaecker], which represent the fellowship of true Christians even after death. Those who belong to the Papist or Reformed religion must not be treated that way nor excluded from the public [church] cemeteries and honorable burial.... For in Electoral Saxony, the Roman Catholics and Calvinists are buried in our [church] cemeteries, but in silence, with the ceremonies omitted. The same, less honorable burial is allotted to the excommunicated who have departed this life without repentance.... In this category are reckoned also the manifest despisers of God's Word and the Sacraments, who are also considered unworthy of an honorable, churchly burial, .... The same punishment is imposed on those guilty of capital crime if they have died in prison with irrefutable evidence of their guilt, as well as those who have died in a duel" (*Institut. prud. past.*, III, 10, sec. 1-13).

Some preachers think that they must in every case accept the request to deliver a funeral sermon for one who has died since thereby an opportunity is granted to preach God's Word. But they do not consider that a burial with Christian ceremonies is a privilege only for those about whom one can lovingly believe that they have fallen asleep in the Lord, and that despisers of God's Word, who have remained the same until their death, are, according to God's Word, not to be granted this final honor. See Jer. 22:18-

19; Matt. 8:22. Some indeed believe that they are satisfying their consciences by mentioning the deceased in their sermon either not at all or as a non-Christian. But they are thereby not only contradicting themselves but also, as a rule, not achieving their purpose but rather the opposite. Instead of people being awakened to repentance, they are only embittered, or the people's minds are so dull that they are satisfied that they have gotten an honorable, Christian burial for one who has died as a non-Christian.

**Comment 3.**

In the funeral sermons, the preacher should use the example of true godliness, which shone manifestly in the deceased, or the case of a clear conversion in the final hours. But he should guard against making others suspect him of flattery, partiality, untruthfulness, or even of bribery, or producing in people the thought that now in death one should accept as good everything that caused spiritual harm.

**Comment 4.**

The preacher should work toward this goal that the congregation acquire its own cemetery [*Gottesacker*], arrange it according to its purpose, and have it well kept up. The greater the barbarism of which people are here [in America] guilty with respect to burial places, the more zealous Christian congregations should be here in keeping holy those places in which the bones of those who have fallen asleep in Christ are resting and awaiting a future resurrection in glory (2 Kings 23:18).

The preacher with the congregation should also see to it that the epitaphs contain nothing unscriptural, and no one should be permitted to have one made unless it has been checked and approved by suitable persons.

**Comment 5.**

Seidel makes the remark, which should also be observed here: "Because there are examples that some person have lain in deep comas and have been considered dead but have later come out of it, it is also thoroughly indecent to proceed all too quickly with the burial. So the preacher is obligated to see to it that sufficient time is taken into consideration between the death and the burial" (*Pastoraltheologie*, I, 23, 5).

# 38

## The Members of Another Parish

The preacher should guard against carrying out official functions for those who belong to another parish without the knowledge and consent of the pastor concerned, whether he is orthodox or erring (1 Pet. 5:2; 4:15; 2 Cor. 10:15-16; Acts 20:28; Rom. 10:15), especially [not] for those who have been justly excommunicated (Matt. 18:17-18). But if Christians have already renounced their preachers and congregations because of false doctrine or tyrannical practice, the preacher cannot reject them, even if they are under an unjust excommunication (John 6:37; Matt. 11:28; John 16:2-3; 3 John 10; John 12:42-43; 9:34-37). That holds true for travellers, especially in an emergency.

**Comment 1.**
In Luther's writings there are many earnest testimonies against carrying out official functions toward persons who already have a regularly called pastor [*Seelsorger*]. He writes: "That the apostles also went first into strange houses and preached, they had the command to do so and were called and sent for this that they should preach at all places, as Christ said, 'Go ye into all the world and preach the Gospel to every creature' (Mark 16:15). But afterwards no one has such a common apostolic command any more. Rather each bishop or pastor [*Pfarrherr*] has his definite church territory or parish [*Pfarre*], which St. Peter in 1 Pet. 5:3 also calls *cleros*, that is, 'part,' so that to each one his own part of the people is committed, as St. Paul also writes to Titus (Titus 1:5)..

"In it no one else, no stranger, should undertake to instruct his parishoners, either publicly or privately, without his knowledge and permission. And, body and soul, no one should listen to him [the interloper] but rather report and inform his pastor or the government. And so this should also be firmly held that no preacher, no matter how devout and upright he may be, should preach to the people of a Papist or heretical pastor or undertake to teach them privately without the knowledge and permission of the same pastor. For it has not been commanded to him. But one should leave alone what is not commanded. We have enough to do if we want to carry out what had been commanded" (Exposition of Psalm 82, 1530, V, 1060f.).

Right before that Luther had said, "Those are thieves and murderers, of whom Christ says in John 10:8 that they fall into another's parish and reach into another office, which is not commanded but rather forbidden to them" (p. 1059). Compare the comment on Section 4.

[Footnote: Therefore St. Peter, in 1 Pet. 4:15, includes one who "reaches into another's office" [Luther's translation] in the same category as the murderer, the thief, and the evildoer. See chapter 5 to the effect that the true office [of the ministry] is still present even in heterodox [*falschglaeubig*, falsehood-believing] fellowships and that even "heretical pastors" hold it by virtue of the call they have received. [See Luther's translation of 1 Pet. 4:15; in English that verse seems to pertain to a general "busybody," not to a pastor who interferes in another's ministry, but the Greek word is *allotrioepiscopos!*]]

**Comment 2.**

On the point that a preacher should especially guard against receiving and so actually absolving those who have been justly excommunicated in other congregations, L. Hartmann writes: "One who has been excommunicated by a local congregation can by no means be received by another as a member of the congregation unless the congregation that has excommunicated him is reconciled and agrees to it. For the acceptance again pertains to the same one to which the exclusion pertained. And those who had to deny fellowship have to decide about the reason to deny exclusion. And a sentence which is not pronounced by one's own judge has no validity. This pertains to the seriousness of church discipline so that for the stiff-necked every way is cut off in which they would try to withdraw their necks from salutary discipline" (*Pastoral. ev.*, pp. 873 s.).

It is a very severe sin to accept those who have been justly excommunicated by another congregation until they have been properly absolved by the same. In addition to reaching into another's office, they are trampling on the divine binding key; despising God's congregation and its holy office; causing a great offense and church schism; hardening an impenitent sinner and participating in his sins; hindering and destroying all church discipline and order; and misusing the means of grace in that, contrary to Christ's prohibition, they are giving that which is holy to dogs and casting their pearls before swine. Woe to them eternally if they do not repent for it in time!

**Comment 3.**

About cases in which strangers coming from another congregation are not to be rejected by preachers, we present the following testimonies from our theologians.

[By a series of quotations, Walther shows that preachers may administer the means of grace to those who belong to another parish if they are absent from their own congregation because of business, military service, etc.; if they have turned away from a pastor who cannot or will not preach God's Word correctly; or if they have been unjustly excommunicated; but not if they have despised their orthodox and upright pastor.]

# 39

## The Administration of Christian Discipline

It is the preacher's duty to administer the means of grace to his congregation not only as a teacher but also as a watchman, bishop, shepherd, leader, etc., of the congregation; to see to it that God's Word is followed there in every way and that the Christian discipline commanded in God's Word is practiced (Matt. 18:15-17; 7:6; Rev. 2:2, 14-15, 20; 1 Tim. 1:20; 3:5; 5:20; 1 Cor. 5:1-5, 9-13; 2 Cor. 2:6-11; 2 Thess. 3:14-15).

**Comment 1.**
Church discipline with respect to life can sometimes fall into decline, even in an orthodox church, without it ceasing to be orthodox, because the wicked have the upper hand in it (1 Cor. 5:1-2). Circumstances can even occur in which the well-being of the church requires that a well-deserved excommunication not be carried out. The thorough practice of church discipline is not a necessary sign of the true church, according to the "it is enough" of Article VII of the Augsburg Confession.

The Formula of Concord correctly rejects as an error of the Schwenkfeldians the theses: "That there is no true Christian congregation where no public exclusion or orderly process of excommunication is held" (Epitome, Article XII).

Although he complains bitterly about the decline of church discipline, Ludwig Hartmann nevertheless writes: "Those who cannot be separated without an uproar are not to be excommunicated. . . . [Hartmann gives several quotations from Augustine.] So also, if there is not a suitable board of elders [*Presbyterium*] or the people do not agree to a just excommunication, the formal trial can be completely omitted. But in the meantime a faithful minister of the church must work for this purpose and together with other devout believers see that public offense is rebuked and that that

## The Administration of Christian Discipline

which is holy is not cast to the dogs and sows" (*Pastoral. ev.*, p. 474).

As late as 1533, Luther, Jonas, Bugenhagen, and Melanchthon stated that, because of the circumstances at that time, they could exercise church discipline only through confessional announcements and suspension from the holy Supper. They write about the church order to be set up in Ansbach and Nuremberg: "Yet at this time we have set up no other excommunication [*Bann*] than that those who live in manifest vices and will not give them up are not admitted to the Sacrament of the body and blood of Christ. And that can be preserved in this way that among us the Sacrament is administered to no one unless he has first been heard by a pastor or deacon. We also cannot see how another excommunication can be set up at this time. For many matters occur which require a *cognitio* (investigation and decision by a formal court). We cannot now see how the *cognitio* should be arranged and organized" (Letters, ed. de Wette (Berlin, 1827), IV, 388).

After an explicit order for excommunication had been drafted for Hesse at a synod [convention] in Homburg and had been sent to Luther, he wrote to the Hessian theologians on June 26, 1533: "I have viewed your zeal for Christ and Christian discipline with great joy. But in this time of such unrest, which is not yet suited for the acceptance of discipline, I would not dare to recommend such a sudden innovation. . . . In the meantime I would like to recommend this that one begin gradually, as we are doing here, and that those who are recognized as worthy of excommunication first be turned away from Communion (what is called the minor excommunication is also the true excommunication); and then that they not be permitted to be sponsors at the Baptism of children" (*op. cit.*, p. 462).

So it would certainly not be according to the mind of our church to want to introduce the formal excommunication procedure right away in a new, unrefined congregation. Here, too, the preacher must let himself be guided by the principle: *Salus populi suprema lex esto*, that is, let the salvation [or: welfare, *Heil*] of the people be the highest law. To want to require a congregation to practice it before being thoroughly instructed in the nature of correct church discipline means wanting to harvest before planting. And would it not be a great foolishness to risk the life of a congregation and to prefer to see it lose the pure Gospel than to omit something which belongs not to the essence but to the well-being of a correct congregation?

[Footnote to *salus populi suprema lex esto*: On the basis of the moral canon: *Praecepta negativa semper et ad semper, affirmative semper, sed non ad semper obligant* (Balduin, *Cas.*, p. 78; Dannhauer, *Liber Consc.*, II, 317; Musaeus, *tr. de eccl.* I, 367 s.). ["Negative precepts are binding always and constantly; affirmative precepts are binding always but not constantly." A prohibition applies at all times, but a command may apply only at specific, appropriate times.]]

## Comment 2.

But those who suppose on the basis of what has been said that the Lutheran Church considers church discipline something indifferent are erring greatly. The fact that church discipline was hardly practiced at all at so many places in the state churches [in Europe], especially as pertains to the way of life, did not result from people holding in principle that church discipline was not necessary for the church to be in its proper condition. Rather [it resulted] from temporary circumstances which hindered it.

Johann Fecht, who is quite incorrectly considered an opponent of pure doctrine who did not care about life and discipline, writes instead: "The whole building of the church of Christ rests on two supports, on the presentation of sound doctrine and on the practice of church discipline. As the former at the same time brings about the internal life of the church, so the latter regulates the external [life]. . . .

"The more strenuous the ancients were in the latter, the more negligent we have become in it in our time, the last of the world. And this lack of discipline began already with our Reformation. For because the clergy previously exercised it alone, often tyrannically, to the exclusion of the other estates, and indeed according to their pleasure, mostly also in their own interest, we in the Reformation have fallen into the other extreme and have committed only the preaching of the Word to the preachers and what pertains to church discipline only to the government. So the latter thought they were losing some of their rights if ecclesiastical persons exercised any censure, either in the consistories or in any other way.

"But where a shadow of discipline still remained, there the hands of ecclesiastical persons, even in the consistories, were tied by the political lords so that eventually no discipline at all could be exercised. Upright theologians of our church have continually complained about this lack and have desired the reintroduction of more strenuous discipline." [Fecht lists theologians such as Joh. Gerhard and J. Valent. Andreae.] (*Instruct. pastoral.*, pp. 164 sqq.).

All that is the pure, incontestable truth. The Apology of the Augsburg Confession says: "So in addition it is also always announced by our preachers that those are to be excommunicated and excluded who live in manifest vices, fornication, adultery, etc., also those who despise the holy Sacraments" (Art. XI, Of Confession).

The Smalcald Articles say: "The major excommunication [*Bann*], as the Pope calls it, we consider a purely worldly punishment, and it does not concern us ministers of the church. But the minor excommunication is the true Christian one, that one should not admit manifest, stiff-necked sinners to the Sacrament or other fellowship of the church until they amend their lives and avoid the sin" (Part III, Art. IX).

Luther writes: "But if we cannot excommunicate [because of] sin in life [because people would not tolerate it], yet we excommunicate [because of] sin in doctrine. We have nevertheless retained this excommunication that we say: one should not hear Anabaptists, Sacramentarians, and other heretics but [should] excommunicate and separate them from us. That is the most important part. For where the doctrine is false, the life cannot be improved. But where the doctrine remains pure and is retained, there one can give sinners good advice about life. For there one has Absolution and forgiveness when it comes to doctrine. But if the doctrine is gone, one will go astray and find neither binding nor loosing. For then it is all lost" (On Matt. 18:18; Erlangen, XLIV, 94f.).

Although Luther did not see himself in a position to introduce complete church discipline, also with respect to life, he still wished for it from his heart and expressed that also in uncounted passages. So it would be a wicked error to suppose that one should not be intent on reinstituting church discipline because the Reformation did not put it into full swing.

# 40

## The Order of Fraternal Discipline

The necessary basis of true Christian church discipline is that the order of brotherly admonition prescribed by Christ in Matt. 18:15-17 be followed in every way, not only by the individual members of the congregation and by the congregation as a whole, but also by the preacher himself.

**Comment 1.**
Luther writes: "What hinders excommunication now at our time? Nothing but that in this matter no one does what is right for a Christian. You have a neighbor whose life and walk are well known to you but are either not at all known or not so well known to your pastor. For how can he know everyone's life in detail, how it is? So if you see that your neighbor is getting rich by unrighteous business or trade; see that he is practicing immorality or adultery or that he is lazy and negligent in raising and governing his household; you should first admonish and warn him in a Christian way so that he would pay attention to his salvation and avoid offense. And, oh, what a very good and blessed work you have done if you gain him in this way!

"But, dear fellow, who does it? For, in the first place, truth is a hostile thing. People get angry at anyone who speaks the truth. So you prefer to retain your neighbor's friendship and favor, especially if he is rich and powerful, rather than to anger him and make him your enemy. The same if the second, third, and fourth neighbor also do so, so that the second and third admonitions also fall into the well with the first one, through which the neighbor could have been brought to the right way again if only you had done your duty and obligation in admonishing" (On Joel 3:17; VI, 2494f.).

Our Confessions also testify that excommunication must be preceded by step-by-step, fraternal admonition. The Large

## The Order of Fraternal Discipline

Catechism says: "But that would be the right way if one would retain the order according to the Gospel, Matt. 18[:15], where Christ says: 'If thy brother shall trespass against thee, go and tell him his fault between thee and him alone.' There you have a fine and precious doctrine about governing the tongue, which is certainly to be observed against grievous misuse. Now be guided by it so that you do not right away gossip about your neighbor elsewhere and slander him. Rather admonish him privately to amend his life. The same also if another brings something to your ears which this one or that one has done; then instruct him also to go and admonish him himself if he has seen it; if not, [instruct him] that he should hold his tongue.... As Christ also teaches: 'If he shall hear thee, thou hast gained thy brother'[Matt. 18:15]. You have done a great, excellent work; for do you think that it is a minor thing to gain a brother?" (Large Catechism, Exposition of the Eighth Commandment).

So if a preacher wants to introduce Christian church discipline in his congregation according to Christ's prescription, he must begin with the introduction of Christian, fraternal admonition.

**Comment 2.**

The preacher must not accept complaints about the private sins of others which are presented to him if these sins have not already been fruitlessly admonished privately [literally: under four eyes, that is, between two people] and then also before witnesses. Rather he should reproach the complainant for revealing a sin which is still hidden and has not been rebuked and so transgressing the divine order and encourage him with all earnestness to observe the same. What Luther says in the above quotation holds true in an even greater degree for a pastor. Only those sins belong before the pastor, as a public person, which he himself has witnessed or which are in the third stage of fraternal admonition. It is shameful for a preacher to lend an open ear to gossip.

[Footnote: It is even more reprehensible if the preacher brings to the pulpit on Sunday what he has heard from gossip during the week. So Luther writes: "Whatever spirit does not retain this order (Matt. 18) intends nothing good" (XXI, 167).]

In the practice of church discipline, the preacher should primarily remember that he does not have the power in any case to excommunicate any person alone and without the preceding trial by and knowledge of the congregation. Valid here is the axiom: *Quicquid omnes tangit, maxime in re salutari, ab omnibus debet curari*, that is, whatever concerns all, especially in a matter of salvation, ought to be taken care of by all. It is against all reason and righteousness for one person to decide the relationship of one member to the whole and of the whole to one member, especially if it is a matter of fraternal fellowship in the faith. So in God's Word not only the preacher but rather the whole congregation is rebuked for omitting church discipline and is told: "Put away from among yourselves that wicked person" (1 Cor. 5:1-2, 13). For greater detail on this topic, see *The Voice of Our Church in the Question of Church and Ministry*, Part II, Thesis 9, C.

Val. Ernst Loescher writes: "In our church no one has ever said that excommunication and discipline pertain only to the clergy. Rather it is committed by Christ to the whole church. The latter recognizes and decrees it, and Christ's servants as *os ecclesiae*" (the mouth of the church) "proclaim it to sinners and have, according to Christ's ordinance, the *exercitium clavis ligantis*," that is, the exercise of the binding key. (*Fortgesetzte Sammlung von alten und neuen theologischen Sachen*, 1724 volume, p. 476).

**Comment 3.**

If the sin of a congregation member if so manifest that the whole congregation knows it and is offended by it, it is not necessary to retain the stages of admonition indicated in Matt. 18. For in this case the congregation is the one of whom the Lord says: "If thy brother shall sin against thee, go and tell him his fault between thee and him alone" (Matt, 18:15). So we read that, after Peter had given public offense Paul rebuked him, not in stages, but right away "before them all," publicly (Gal. 2:13-14). Paul writes explicitly about such a case: "Them that sin rebuke before all, that others also may fear" (1 Tim. 5:20).

[Footnote: Therefore Augustine writes: "If you [singular] alone know the sin, then he has sinned against you alone [singular]. But if he has done wrong before many persons, then he has sinned also against them" (*Serm. 16 de verbis D[omini]*.]

Christian Kortholt says: "A distinction is primarily to be observed between hidden sins and manifest sins. But we do not call those sins hidden which are known to no one at all, for God alone judges them (Rom. 2:16), but rather those which are known

# The Order of Fraternal Discipline

to a few and are not connected with an offense to many. But [we call those sins] manifest [*offenbar*] which are publicly [*oeffentlich*] known and are therefore connected with an offense to many. As far as hidden sins are concerned, the minister of the church, no less than every upright Christian, has to observe the Savior's rule in Matt. 18:15ff. But manifest sins are to be rebuked publicly. Augustine says: 'What has been committed before all is to be rebuked before all.' And this is the prescription of the Apostle himself, who therefore addresses his Timothy: 'Them that sin' (namely with public offense) 'rebuke before all, that others also may fear' (1 Tim. 5:20)" (*Pastor fidelis* (Hamburg 1696), pp. 92, 96f.).

There can even be cases in which it is not only not necessary to observe the various degrees of fraternal admonition but in which it is rather necessary not to observe them. [For example, if someone had committed murder, one would not observe the steps before having him arrested.]

As always, so here, too, love is the highest law. So if love for the one who has fallen requires that he first be admonished privately, the use of the right to rebuke him publicly right away would involve a severe wrong. [One would exercise patience, if possible, in order to avoid hardening the sinner's heart.]

**Comment 4.**

Hartmann sets up the following eighteen rules about the correct method of fraternal admonition:

"1. The admonition of the neighbor is to be practiced in such a way that it serves the glory of God and the salvation of the neighbor and that the neighbor is not exposed to scorn and mockery before the world for it; rather that the one doing the admonishing is not doing it out of malice, hatred, and vainglory.

"2. Every admonition must be based on certain knowledge of a sin that has been committed.

"3. The one doing the admonishing must in his admonition also keep an eye on general weakness and on his weakness and so also admonish himself.

"4. Anyone who reproaches his neighbor must guard himself, that he is not implicated in the same sin or a similar one.

"5. Hidden sins of those which are known only to a few are to be corrected not publicly but between you and the erring one alone.

"6. Therefore those who bring the hidden sins of their brothers before the congregation, without observing the steps prescribed by Christ for such fraternal dealings, are not to be heard but are rather to be rebuked and recalled to the laws of love.

"7. Even public sins, known to all, are not to be rebuked publicly right away, the first time." (See Comment 3.)

"8. The reproach made to the neighbor should be neither too cold and mild nor too hard and earnest but should be weighed and tempered so that the brother is led, by means of it, through recognizing his sins and considering God's wrath, with a contrite heart, to true repentance.

"9. So a middle road should be taken in admonition so that one mixes a mildness of spirit with the bitterness of the reproach.

"10. The one doing the admonishing will not reprimand the neighbor in a fruitful way if he does not consider the nature and the condition of the one he wants to reprimand.

"11. The reproach is to be guided according to the nature of the sin and is to be given distinctively according to it.

"12. In admonishing the neighbor, the time and place are to be taken into consideration (Prov. 25:11; Sirach 22:6; 1 Sam. 25:36-37).

"13. If the crime which the neighbor has committed serves to harm either the church or the state, or if danger also lies in delay; and also if one who knows of the crime and does not reveal it is considered to be implicated also in the crime; or if there is, finally, little hope if hindering it; then there should by no means be an insistence on private admonition; rather, either completely omitting it or applying it according to circumstances, the crime is to be made known publicly and reported at the proper place.

"14. If the crime to be committed is greater and more severe than the loss of the good reputation of the one who intends to carry out the wickedness, then the same is to be revealed without further ado, especially to those who can avert it through their authority and power (Acts 23:13-14).

"15. If the neighbor repents of his error or crime; or if he can be corrected right away without any reproach; or, finally, if others who should be taken into greater consideration would be rebuked through [rebuking] him, then he is to be reproached either not at all or only in a very mild way.

"16. If it is manifest beyond doubt that all rebuking is in vain

## The Order of Fraternal Discipline

and, as it is said, one is preaching to deaf ears, then one can be completely excused from rebuking and admonishing.

"17. The witnesses who are needed for the second stage of admonition must be well suited to winning the brother and at least not be hated by the one who is to be rebuked. For if one takes for it people who are contentious or who are otherwise hated by the one to be rebuked, or who do not keep confidences or whom he cannot tolerate, one will accomplish nothing. Rather the one rebuked will want to heal sin with sin, either out of shame or out of hatred, and will remain stiff-necked. . . .

"18. All steps of admonition are to be repeated several times if necessity requires, and the one to be converted should be dealt with until he is corrected or until his lasting stubbornness [literally: stiff-neckedness] becomes manifest. For in Matt. 18 Christ shows the order and steps of admonition, not how often they should happen. That each one of them is to be applied several times is already seen from v. 22 of the same chapter, where Christ teaches that one must forgive the sinning brother seventy-times-seven times. See Luke 17:4" (*Pastor ev.*, pp. 853-862).

If anyone thinks that he has satisfied Christ's rule in Matt. 18 as long as he can prove that the one who was sinned has been unsuccessfully reminded of his sin three times before his final exclusion, no matter how hurriedly, superficially, and inconsiderately it has been handled contrary to love, he is in a great error.

# 41

## The Case of Public Repentance

Those who show themselves repentant after a manifest fall into sin or error, either right away or after admonition by the congregation, are not to be excommunicated but are to remove the offense they have given, as much as possible, by a public apology or repentance to the church [*Kirchenbusee*] and so to the offended congregation (Matt. 18:15; 5:23-24; Luke 17:3-4).

**Comment 1.**
A manifest fall into sin is at the same time a sin against the whole congregation. So a public reconciliation is necessary. If one wants to bring his gift to the altar and there remembers that his brother, against whom he has sinned, has something against him, he must leave his gift before the altar and first go and be reconciled with this brother, according to Matt. 5:23-24; then such a reconciliation with a whole congregation is certainly just as necessary and obligatory.

This reconciliation with the whole congregation or public church repentance [*Kirchenbusse*] is necessary, not because a person must pay for his sins in the church as in the state by suffering a corresponding punishment, but partly to restore the trusting relationship to his brothers, which has been disturbed by the fall into sin, and partly to do away as much as possible with the offense which has been given publicly. If those members of the congregation who have manifestly sinned severely and have privately confessed their sin to God alone, were to be absolved and communed by the preacher and treated like other upright members, that could have only a destructive effect. Then the congregation would exist as a society of people in which the members can live in sin and shame without repentance and yet remain members.

As a public sinner is to be rebuked publicly according to God's

## The Case of Public Repentance

Word (1 Tim. 5:20), he must also make his repentance publicly known and publicly say, "I repent," as a necessary sign if he wants to be considered a repentant brother and have the forgiveness of the whole congregation (Luke 17:3-4).

That is not a punishment in the proper sense [of the term], even if the penitent had already been excommunicated. Nicholas Rebhahn, General Superintendent at Eisenach (d. 1626), writes in his booklet *Von der Kirchenbusse*: "If nothing more happens than a public repentance for their sins, apology to and reconciliation with the offended church, then it is properly not a punishment but a work of the Fifth Commandment in God's Law, an action and a virtue, not a suffering or a punishment. But it becomes somewhat like a punishment in that the one who must be reconciled suffers it that his Baptismal name and surname are named to the congregation and that his crime is publicly mentioned (that he has thereby caused offense and earned God's wrath and temporal and eternal punishment), which bites him in the heart and causes him pain and which some (though out of lack of understanding) consider a greater shame and harsher punishment than that he was previously denied the Absolution and the Sacrament" (quoted in Hartmann's *Pastoral ev.*, pp. 852ff.).

**Comment 2.**

[Not all sins require public repentance. If sins of weakness required it, it would become cumbersome, commonplace, and meaningless. It is only for open and manifest sins of malice that have caused public offense.]

**Comment 3.**

If one who has fallen shows himself penitent right away, not only no excommunication but also no suspension can take place. Hartmann writes: "In manifest, notorious crimes, the truly repentant sinner is to be accepted, but not to be suspended for any time. For here is the place for Paul's statement: 'Lest perhaps such a one should be swallowed up with overmuch sorrow' (2 Cor. 2:6 [*sic*, 7]). And so it is not advisable to delay the Absolution for a while either as a punishment or as a test for the repentant person, for the advantages which this delay seems to have can bring with them greater disadvantages. It also has no basis in Scripture. To suspend for some time the fallen who repent is rather a type of torture of the conscience. Nathan, at least, did not first suspend the repentant David for a long time; rather he immediately proclaimed the forgiveness of sins to him" (*L. c.,* p. 864).

In the case of a repeated fall into habitual drunkenness, mendacity, and the life, there might be first a temporary suspension to test the sincerity of the apparent repentance and to guard against a [more] severe offense (Acts 8:18-24).

## Comment 4.

[Public repentance would not be necessary at a place other than where the manifest sin was committed unless it became public knowledge also at a place where the sinner had moved.]

## Comment 5.

The form of an apology is determined by the severity of the offense, the nature of the one who has fallen, and the congregation's level of knowledge. Depending on circumstances, the apology can be made either personally in front of the altar by the one who has fallen himself, or through the preacher from the pulpit, or in a congregational assembly [voters' assembly], or before a committee (in the case of women), orally or in writing, etc.

Caution is necessary so that the one who has fallen not think that public repentance can replace true repentance of the heart. The former is only a public sign of the latter. Otherwise it is an empty fraud. As much as possible everything is to be carefully removed that could produce the thought that repentance before the church is a punishment that pays for the sin. [See Article XII of the Apology of the Augsburg Confession].

The Apology clearly says that renewing the strict penitential discipline of the ancient church was not only necessary but would also be dangerous and harmful. Heshusius writes: "For the office of the Gospel seeks no payment for sin but only amendment. If that is achieved, it is satisfied. And Christ says: 'if he shall hear thee, thou hast gained thy brother' [Matt. 18:15], and [Christ] does not want anything imposed on him [the brother], . . . as happened in the wicked Papacy" (*Vom Amt und Gewalt des Pfarrherren* (Erfurt, 1561), G. 1. 2. 3.).

# 42

## The Case of Excommunication

The only one who can be excommunicated is one who 1. is still alive and capable of giving an account; 2. calls himself or wants to be called a brother (sister) (1 Cor. 5:11); 3. is a communicant member of the congregation (1 Cor. 5:13); 4. has committed an open, offensive sin against God's commandment (1 Cor. 5:11) or holds a fundamental error and is clearly committed to it (Titus 3:10-11; Rom. 16:17; 2 John 9-11); 5. in spite of all admonition remains hardened in his sin or error and so has become manifest as an incorrigible non-Christian (Matt. 18:17; Titus 3:10-11); and finally 6. whom the congregation has unanimously declared worthy of excommunication (1 Cor. 5:1-5; Matt. 18:17). Therefore excommunication cannot be carried out in the cases of: 1. people who have already died or are not capable of giving an account (the insane, the feeble-minded, those physically possessed, etc.) or children (Eph. 6:4; Deut. 21:18-21); 2. who are not members of the congregation (1 Cor. 5:13); 3. who do not want to be brothers, who have left the congregation themselves and so have excommunicated themselves (1 John 2:19); 4. whose sin or error is not open or is not yet so manifest that it can be clearly proven to them and to the congregation (John 13:21ff.; Titus 3:10-11); 5. whose sin or error pertains only to the human frailty and weakness even of a Christian (Gal. 6:2; James 3:2); 6. whose sin is not a transgression of divine Law and whose error does not overthrow the foundation of the faith (Rom. 14:1ff.); 7. who have not yet been fruitlessly admonished according to the divine order and so have not yet been revealed as stiff-necked and incorrigible errorists or sinners (Matt. 18:15-17; 2 Thess. 3:14-15; see Titus 3:10-11); 8. about whom the congregation cannot agree that they deserves to be excommunicated (1 Cor. 5:13); and finally 9. whole congregations (Gal. 1:2; see 5:4; 2 Sam. 15:11).

## Comment 1.

To the question: "Who is to be conscientiously subjected to church discipline?" Dannhauer answers: "1. One who calls himself a brother (1 Cor. 5:11); 2. who is rational; 3. who is a member of the visible church; 4. who is still alive; 5. who is an unrepentant sinner. But the person himself who has sinned [is excommunicated]; it does not include his posterity (Ezek. 18:4; 'The soul that sinneth, it shall die.'). The brother, not the brotherhood, not a whole congregation, is subject to the last point of church discipline, namely excommunication. For that would mean throwing the fellowship out of the fellowship, which is impossible, and uprooting the wheat with the weeds, for there is no visible, particular church in which the invisible does not lie hidden" (*Liber conscientiae* I, 1127-38). See Chapter 40, Comment 2.

## Comment 2.

To the question: "Which sins are subject to church discipline?" Dannhauer answers: "One witness is no witness" (Num. 35:30): (*op. cit.*, pp. 1122-26). [The sin must be proven by the testimony of at least two witnesses. In a long quotation, Dannhauer lists some specific sins that are to be subject to church discipline, including: despising Word and Sacrament, heresy, sorcery, superstition, syncretism, fellowship with errorists, rebellion against government, prostitution, irreconcilable enmity, divorce without proper grounds, dueling, usury, greed, a sharp tongue, adultery, incest, homosexuality, carousing, etc.]

## Comment 3.

If it is clear from God's Word to the great majority of the congregation that a sinner is to be excommunicated, and if one protests against it but cannot give valid reasons for his refusal ([but refuses] from obviously despising God's Word and command, obvious favoritism for the sinner, or pure stubbornness), the protestor is to be put under discipline before the excommunication is carried out. The excommunication is not to be carried out until unanimity has been achieved by settling the objection (whether the protestor withdraws his protest or shows himself stiff-necked and must himself be excluded as a manifest non-Christian).

Since according to God's Word the excommunication is a matter for the whole congregation, it cannot be carried out by a mere majority of the members, no matter how large. Since Christ has commanded excommunication, and the Apostle earnestly rebuked the Corinthians for omitting it in an obvious case (1 Cor. 5:1-13), a person is committing a manifest sin against God's command if he stubbornly opposes excommunication in an obvious case in spite of all instruction, proof, and admonition. So he himself becomes subject to church discipline.

It is different if the congregation or some members of it cannot be convinced from God's Word that a sinner deserves excommunication. That impossibility is a proof that the case is not one that can be taken as far as excommunication. Neither the moral conviction of the preacher nor that of a majority of the members can decide this matter.

Whenever it is a matter of a sin which cannot ultimately result in the excommunication of the sinner, the preacher should guard against instituting a disciplinary procedure and absolutely demanding a penitent confession. For if the sinner refuses it, the preacher must give up the disciplinary procedure, and bad only becomes worse. In such cases it is enough for the preacher himself to admonish and rebuke the one of whose sin he is convinced. He should do that publicly if a public offense exists without urging or expecting a public confession by the one who has sinned. We find that while the apostles urged church discipline and excommunication in certain sinful cases (1 Cor. 5), they let it remain with a mere admonition and rebuke in other cases (1 Cor. 6:1-8; see 1 Tim. 5:20). This rule should not be overlooked. If it is not observed, church discipline may be overdone, and, contrary to the Gospel, the whole life of the congregation may be turned into a life under constant church discipline, [a life] under the Law.

## Comment 4.

If a case of church discipline is only somewhat unclear, or if, in a congregation which has otherwise never consciously opposed God's Word, the preacher cannot resolve a case which is thoroughly clear to him, conscience and caution call for involving other ministers. The answers in cases which are available in the collections of theological opinions, in which our church is so rich— I will mention only the Wittenberg Counsels or Dedekennus' *Thesaurus consiliorum*—show the custom in our church in its best times, that in problematical cases one turned to learned theologians before proceeding to church discipline.

It happens with some frequency that, when the congregation has assembled to carry out the final admonition of one under church discipline, the latter does not appear and later excuses himself, [claiming] that he did not know that he was supposed to appear. So the summons to the final admonition should always be in writing, and it should be handed to the one concerned by a specifically chosen person. The one summoned should be asked whether or not he will appear so that the congregation can act when it assembles. If the one summoned states that he will absolutely not appear, he is not to be excommunicated since the final admonition, which is necessary according to Matt. 18:17, cannot be carried out. He has also already excluded himself from the congregation. It should be stated publicly from the pulpit that he has excluded himself from the congregation and the brotherhood and is to be treated as one who is outside (1 John 2:19). [Walther cites Luther, *Tischreden*, XXII, 974f.; and Erlangen, LIV, pp. 317f.]

If one who said that he intended to appear does not appear, he is by no means to be considered self-excluded, not even on the basis of the suspicion that he had not really intended to come. Before further steps [are taken], the reason for his failure to appear should be investigated.

## Comment 5.

A resolution to excommunicate a person in a legitimate congregational assembly should take effect as a definite congregational resolution only after it has been confirmed in the next assembly so that no one is excluded from the fellowship of those present at one meeting, without the knowledge and consent of the absent members. If the latter happens, an injustice has been committed against those members of the congregation who have been deprived of the opportunity to vote for or against the excommunication. Since, according to God's Word, the power to exclude or excommunicate from the fellowship of the congregation is an authority of the whole congregation (Matt. 18:17; 1 Cor. 5:2, 4, 13), and excommunication which is not unanimous, [but is] resolved by a simple majority, with the exclusion of the minority, without even the tacit consent of all members, is illegitimate and invalid.

# The Case of Excommunication

**Comment 6.**

[Formulas for the public proclamation of an excommunication.]

**Comment 7.**

[Excommunication suspends spiritual fellowship with the one who has been excommunicated, but church members should pray for him and assure him that they desire his conversion. Outward, civil relationships, including business and marriage, are not suspended, but one should avoid giving the impression that he does not take the excommunication seriously.]

**Comment 8.**

Finally it may be noted that no congregational business calls for more exact records than that which deals with church discipline. The congregation should always be able to prove from its minutes the correctness of its procedure in every excommunication. Without this proof, other congregations are not able and obligated to respect the excommunication in all cases.

# 43

## The Readmission of the Excommunicated

If an excommunicated person asks the preacher to absolve him and receive him back into the congregation, the preacher should communicate that to the latter. If the congregation unanimously declares that it is satisfied by the repentant confession of the one returning and is reconciled to him, the preacher should receive him again by publicly announcing the return and reconciliation or by absolving and communing in public worship the one who had been under excommunication (2 Cor. 2:6-11).

**Comment 1.**
Martin Chemnitz proves from 2 Cor. 2:6-11 that it was done this way in the apostolic congregations: "If it was perceived from the fact itself that such excommunicated persons were troubled in a godly way, recognized the magnitude of the sin, feared God's wrath, and were seriously asking for forgiveness and reconciliation with God and the congregation so that they could be received into the fellowship of the church again; then the congregation, having seen that discipline had achieved its desired goal, applied such mildness that he who was already sorry in a godly way was not driven by overly severe strictness either to despair or to hardening . . . ." (*Examen Concil. Trident.*, Loc de indulgentiis, p. m. 75-78).

**Comment 2.**
[From the Saxon General Articles, Walther quotes a formula for accepting an excommunicated person who has repented.]

**Comment 3.**
[No punishment is to be imposed on the repentant person by the church. The church has nothing to do with punishments imposed by civil government.]

# The Readmission of the Excommunicated

**Comment 4.**
For dealing with excommunicated persons who are suddenly near death and call for the pastor, see Chapter 18, Comment 5. About burying one who dies under excommunication, see Chapter 37, Comment 2.

**Fig. 16: Walther's desk and study guides on display at Concordia Seminary, St. Louis, Mo.**
Courtesy of Concordia Historical Institute.

# 44

## The Congregation's Officers

Since the church in America is independent of the state, it is that much more the preacher's duty to bring it about in his congregation that the office of church officer [*Vorsteher*] be instituted for his assistance; for the better administration of church discipline; for the preservation of good order inside and outside of the public worship services and other assemblies; for the conscientious administration of the church property; for the supervision of the school; and the like; and [for the preacher to bring it about] that [the offices be] committed to godly men equipped with the necessary gifts and [be] correctly conducted by them (1 Tim. 5:17; Rom. 12:8; 1 Cor. 12:28).

**Comment 1.**

The Bible passages cited leave no doubt that there were such congregational officers or lay elders in the apostolic age. Their office was not originally instituted by God alongside the preaching office, but like the diaconate it was an auxiliary office that had been branched off from the preaching office in Christian freedom, and certain functions were assigned to it. That is the constant teaching of our church. [Walther presents testimonies about this office from Christian antiquity and Lutheran history.]

Martin Chemnitz gives an excellent discussion of that in his *Examen Concilii Tridentini*, P. II, Loc. 13, Sec. 2. de septem ordinibus f. m. 574 sqq., where he calls the lay presbytery an official level, not in the episcopalian sense, for he recognizes only one divinely instituted ecclesiastical order to be auxiliary to the office *kat' exochen*. This is the constant doctrine of the teachers of our church.

For example, John Gerhard writes: "In the apostolic and original church there were two types of presbyters, which are called *seniores* in Latin, as is concluded from 1 Tim. 5:17. For some administered the teaching office, or, as the apostle speaks there, worked in the Word and doctrine, who were called bishops, pastors, etc.; but others were set up for censuring morals and preserving church discipline, since the government was still pagan and did not support the teachers in the church in this matter; the latter were called rulers or governors, as is concluded from 1 Cor. 12:28; Rom. 12:8.. Ambrose writes about the first part of 1 Tim. 5: 'The synagogue also and later the church had *seniores*, without whose advice nothing was undertaken in the church, and I do not know from what negligence that has fallen into disuse, as perhaps through laziness or much rather through the pride of the teachers in that they alone wanted to count for something.' Both types bore in common the name of elders [*Vorsteher*] (1 Tim. 5:17) and rulers [*Vorgesetzte*] (Acts 15:22; Heb. 13:7, 17, 24). Both together constituted the college which Paul calls the presbytery (1 Tim. 4:14): 'Neglect not the gift that is in thee, which was given thee by prophecy, with the laying on of the hands of the presbytery'" (*Loc. de ministerio,* sec. 232). [The Greek word *presbyteros* and the Latin word *senior* both mean "elder."]

## Comment 2.

The qualifications for these officers are the same as for deacons (Acts 6:3; 1 Tim. 3:8-12). According to the procedure of the apostles, the preacher should present and explain them to the congregation before every election of officers, and he should work for the election of suitable men. Since such officers are not "separated" (Acts 13:2) but remain in their worldly vocation, they are not to be ordained but may be publicly installed in office by the preacher in the name of the congregation.

## Comment 3.

The preacher should be concerned that the congregation give the officers a written job description in which the extent and limits of their duties are exactly described. It should be taken into consideration that the officers not be tempted to stand in the way of the pastor in his office, nor to interfere with the office of the Word or the office of the house-father, nor to offend against the rules of fraternal admonition (Matt. 18:15-17).

**Comment 4.**
At least once a month all the officers should meet to consider the needs of the congregation. The pastor of the congregation should open the meetings with a prayer and, because he bears the office of the Word which sets the standard for all offices, it would be proper for him to preside. But the preacher should not insist on presiding. (More about that in the next section about congregational meetings.)

**Comment 5.**
The officers have to deal conscientiously with church property, and they should be obligated in their job descriptions to give a public account at specified times and to submit to an audit.

# 45

## The Congregational Meetings

Since, according to God's Word, the congregation is the highest court within its circle (Matt. 18:17; Col. 4:17), and the preacher has church authority only in common with the congregation (Matt. 20:25-26; 23:8; 1 Pet. 5:1-3; 2 Cor. 8:8), the preacher must be concerned that congregational assemblies, both regular and special ones as needed at times, be held in Christian order to consider and carry out what is necessary for its governing (Matt. 18:17; 1 Cor. 5:4; 2 Cor. 2:6; Acts 6:2; 15:1-4, 30; 21:17-22; 1 Tim. 5:20).

**Comment 1.**
[Walther gives various testimonies, which are contained in *The Voice of Our Church in the Question of Church and Ministry [Die Stimme unserer Kirche in der Frage von Kirche und Amt]*(Erlangen: A. Deichert, 1852; second edition, 1865), Part II, Thesis IX, B.]

**Comment 2.**
[Neither the German state church system nor any system that usurps the congregation's authority corresponds to Biblical, Lutheran doctrine.]

**Comment 3.**
All adult, male members of the congregation have the right to participate actively in the discussions, votes, and decisions of the congregation since that is a right of the whole congregation. See Matt. 18:17-18; Acts 1:15, 23-26; 15:5, 12-13, 22-23; 1 Cor. 5:2; 6:2; 10:15; 12:7; 2 Cor. 2:6-8; 2 Thess. 3:15. Excluded from the exercise of this right are the youth (1 Pet. 5:5) and the female members of the congregation (1 Cor. 14:34-35) [see also 1 Tim. 2:8-15].

Johann Gerhard writes: "From Acts 15:22 it is concluded that not only the apostles but also the presbyters were present in this church assembly, indeed, that the whole congregation had a decisive voice with the apostles and presbyters" (*Confess. cathol.* f. 683).

**Comment 4.**

The external conduct of the meeting naturally pertains to those who in general preside over the congregation or who are to administer the office of external government as an auxiliary office branched off from the preaching office (see Sec. 44) (Acts 15:6; 1 Tim. 5:17; Rom. 12:8; 1 Cor. 12:28). The director (moderator, president) of the meeting should specifically be concerned about the following:

1. No one should speak unless he is a voting member of the congregation or has been given permission to speak for the present occasion by a congregational resolution on the request of a member.

Only one should speak at a time, and no one should interrupt another (1 Cor. 14:30).

3. Everyone who speaks should stand up and always speak facing the president (except in carrying out the third stage of admonition).

4. On the one hand, no one should speak in anger or passion nor use personally offensive expressions (1 Cor. 11:16; Rom. 12:10), and on the other hand everyone should be encouraged to speak so that those who bring up something absurd only because they are inept are not scorned nor made objects of ridicule.

5. No one should unnecessarily leave the meeting before it is over nor walk out with a show of displeasure because it is not going according to his opinion.

6. Before a matter comes up for a vote, the congregation should first have the opportunity to discuss it.

7. If one member calls for a vote, the congregation should, as a rule, first be asked to decide whether it can and should be voted on.

8. The question should be precisely and definitely phrased so that it can be answered yes or no.

9. If the least doubt prevails whether those voting for it or those voting against it are in the majority, first those voting for it and then those voting against it should be asked to stand up, and the numerical relationship can be determined by counting.

# The Congregational Meetings

## Comment 5.

Matters of doctrine and conscience can be settled only with unanimity and according to God's Word and the confession of the church (Is. 8:20). If a vote is taken in matters of this nature, it must not be done in order to let the majority decide but rather to determine whether everyone has recognized what is right and agrees with it. A congregational member who will not yield and agree to what has been presented from God's Word and the confession of the church, forfeits his right to vote and becomes subject to church discipline.

All adiaphora (*res indifferentes*, middle things [matters neither commanded nor forbidden in God's Word]) are settled by a majority of votes. That does not mean that the decision of the majority in adiaphora are as binding for the conscience of every congregational member as that which is resolved with unanimity on the basis of God's Word. A congregation must place the observance of matters decided by a majority resolution within the good will of the minority or of individuals. If it is to be feared that recklessly carrying out a majority resolution would lead to disunity or division, the pastor should try to move the majority to give up its resolution for the sake of the minority.

If the votes are equal, it may not be advisable for the pastor or the president to decide the matter by his vote. Rather [it may be advisable that] the matter be discussed again so that votes are changed, or that the matter be given up if no majority can be achieved.

## Comment 6.

It pertains to the validity of a congregational meeting that it be publicly announced in advance in a way determined by the congregation and that the number of members required by the congregation for a quorum be present. Anyone who does not attend thereby gives up his right to vote in this case. Precisely for that reason a meeting time convenient for the largest possible number of members should be chosen. The time for beginning and ending the meeting should be determined and observed. If it seems necessary to extend the time of the meeting, that should be done only after the unanimous resolution of all present.

**Comment 7.**

For the sake of love and peace, it is advisable for important resolutions about matters that can be delayed to be given the validity of a congregational resolution only if they are confirmed in the next meeting by the fact that no one protests against them.

**Comment 8.**

The secretary should make a record of the substance of the meetings. It should be read aloud each time at the conclusion of the meeting, and a vote should be taken about its correctness. It should be corrected if necessary, and it should be read again at the beginning of the next meeting.

**Comment 9.**

Since public prayer is part of the public preaching office, the preacher opens and closes every meeting with a prayer. If he is absent, a specific person reads a prayer chosen for such cases. Balduin writes: "In the public prayers, the minister of the church in praying is the mouth of the church, in whose name he then speaks to God, just as in preaching he is the mouth of God, in Whose name he speaks to the people" (*Tract. de cas. consc.*, p. 247).

# 46

## The Admission of New Members

Just as it does not belong to the pastor alone to exclude a person from the congregation (see Chap. 40, Comment 2), it does not belong to him alone to accept new members. The decision about that belongs rather to the whole congregation, the preacher and the listeners. The certainty that the one to be received is a true, converted, regenerate Christian is not a prerequisite for reception, but rather [the certainty] that he does not show himself to be an errorist or non-Christian, either in doctrine or in life [is a prerequisite] (Acts 8:13ff.). [Footnote to Acts 8:13: Arcularius, Lenaeus, the Weimar Bible, and others maintain, not without justification, that the conversion and faith of Simon Magus were not sincere.]

**Comment 1.**
For someone to be accepted into the congregation, the following are primarily required:
 1. That he have been baptized (Eph. 5:25-26; 1 Cor. 12:13);
 2. That, if he is an adult, he confess the faith that holy Scripture is God's Word and that the teaching contained in the Lutheran Confessions (namely in Luther's Small Catechism and the Unaltered Augsburg Confession—or at least the Catechism) is the pure Christian teaching (Gal. 2:4-5; Eph. 4:3-6; 2 Cor. 6:14-18; 2 John 10-11);
 3. That he wants to be a member of the Evangelical Lutheran Church (Matt. 10:32-33; 2 Tim. 1:8);
 4. That he is leading a Christian life without offense (1 Cor. 5:9-13; Matt. 7:6); and
 5. That he is not under a just excommunication by another congregation (Matt. 18:17-18; 2 Tim. 4:14-15).

## Comment 2.

Concerning the procedure to be observed in the reception of new congregational members, those who desire to be accepted should report to an elder [*Vorsteher*] as well as to the pastor. The former should investigate the external conditions and the external life of the applicant and also make that person familiar with the external order of the congregation (perhaps by the written congregational constitution if there is one). The latter should examine the person in his Christianity, faith, and confession. In properly ordered congregations, all unknown or uninstructed persons should take a course from the pastor in the chief parts of the pure doctrine before they are received, and only after this has been done should the congregation be asked to consult and decide about the reception of the person. But if the person entering is qualified to vote, the reception should finally be carried out when he signs his name to the constitution in a public meeting, in connection with an address by the pastor. The names of those who are not being received as voting members, of women and of those not yet of age, are to be entered into the congregational membership list by one who has been commissioned to do so, after their reception has been resolved by the congregation. If the applicant was already previously a member of congregation recognized as orthodox, a testimony of dismissal should be requested from him, but if that is a recommending [letter], he should be received on that basis without foregoing instruction. See 3 John 8-10; Acts 18:27.

## Comment 3.

If previous members of false churches and religions apply to enter the congregation, then the pastor must indeed approach them with all love and friendliness. But hereby the purity of their intention should first be investigated as much as possible but also with all caution, and they are then to be thoroughly instructed in the pure doctrine of our church. It is absolutely necessary that such converts first be shown, from the accepted writings of their erring fellowships, the coarse errors of the same and how these errors overthrow the basis of justifying, saving faith, and that secondly the contrary proofs from God's Word be so impressed upon them that they themselves learn to refute those errors from Scripture and to establish and defend the truth.

## Comment 4.

Under certain circumstances it can indeed be very beneficial if those who come over from the Papacy publicly renounce the Antichrist, his synagogue, and its atrocities, and confess the pure Evangelical Lutheran faith, and then be formally received by the pastor. But that is not to be required as a *sine qua non* of reception. In any case, it is sufficient if the one coming over appears in the congregational meeting and makes his confession there, and if perhaps on the Sunday on which he first communes as a Lutheran that be announced from the pulpit and the congregation be asked for its intercession. Those coming from other erring fellowships can, if special circumstances do not require otherwise, enter [the congregation] as all others.

# 47

## The Constitution of the Congregation

The preacher should not make it his job to have a new congregation immediately draft, subscribe, and observe as complete a congregational constitution as possible. At the beginning it should contain only what is most important, and there may be added from time to time that which has proven itself in practice and by which it may conform to what is found in congregations in larger ecclesiastical associations. Nothing determined in it about anything that is neither commanded nor forbidden in God's Word should be unalterable but should be able to be amended or abolished at any time by a larger majority of votes or at least by a unanimous resolution.

**Comment 1.**
[Walther shows that Luther advised against doing much organizing quickly.]

**Comment 2.**
The basis for a congregational constitution has already been indicated in Chapter 6, Comment 9. The following may yet be remarked here. It may be appropriate to accept in the constitution the provision that, in case any divisions arise, the church property should remain with those who not only retain the Lutheran name but actually retain the Lutheran confession, even if the latter were only two, but also that they are authorized to use the church property only for church purposes.

It also belongs in the constitution that the congregation in its own circle is the final and highest court according to Matt. 18:17. Therefore all its officers are responsible to it and may be removed from office in Christian order. But also all decisions and resolutions of the congregation which are contrary to God's Word or the

## The Constitution of the Congregation

[congregation's] confession are to be declared in advance null and void.

**Comment 3.**

A preacher should obtain not only some of the best, old-Lutheran church orders but also some good, proven constitutions for orthodox, independent congregations in America, from which is suitable for his congregation may be drawn and suggested.

# 48

## The Personal Life of the Pastor

According to God's Word, an upright preacher should take heed, not only to the flock entrusted to him and to doctrine, but also to himself (Acts 20:28; 1 Tim. 4:16). He should be blameless and irreproachable in his public and private life (1 Tim. 3:2; Titus 1:7) and an example to the flock in everything (1 Pet. 5:1-4). He should not give offense to anyone so that his office is not blamed (2 Cor. 6:3) and should adorn the doctrine in all respects (1 Tim. 3:1-10; Titus 1:6-9; 2:7-8), shine forth in him and that his whole household present the model of a Christian family (1 Tim. 3:4-5 (see 1 Sam. 2); Ps. 101:6-7). He should consider this important requirement for a minister of Jesus Christ in the choice of a spouse.

**Comment 1.**
What the apostle means by the words "blameless" and "irreproachable" [see Luther's translation of 1 Tim. 3:2 and Titus 1:7], he himself indicated with the listing of the virtues with which a bishop should be adorned and with the statement of the sins from which he should be free. It is obvious that those words do not say that one is unqualified to be a bishop unless he is free from all sins, even sins of weakness; nor that he may not be one who, before being enlightened, had fought against God's Word and church like Saul [Paul] or had thought to serve God with works that are against God's Word, in confusion of conscience, like Luther; rather only that one who has lived shamefully before the world in vices such as drunkenness, thievery, sexual immorality, and the like, should not be put into the office nor tolerated in it.

Luther correctly glories that God often makes such persons preachers of the Gospel who, although blameless before the world, have still lived without God from their childhood, who have indeed been the greatest sinners before God and have been converted only

## The Personal Life of the Pastor

later. He writes: "So God also acts in such a way that He chooses such poor sinners for it, as St. Paul and we have been, for this reason that He may fend off the arrogance and thinking of clever people. For He does not want to have such secure, arrogant spirits for it, but rather such people who have been through the mill, have been tested and broken, and such must know and confess that they have been wicked fellows, as St. Paul was, and have been burdened with such sins, which are called very great sins before God, as the enemies of God and the Lord Christ, so that they may remain humble and cannot be presumptuous or boast (as those untested spirits do), that they have been so pious, holy, and learned that God has chosen them for it; but that He always retains the glory and power, so that He could say to them if they did want to become proud: Friend, what do you have to brag about? Or against whom do you want to be so proud? Do you not know what kind of people you have been and what you have done against Me and Christendom and have loaded the blood of many people on your neck? Or do you want to forget what grace and mercy I have shown you? So He wants to have the cudgel bound around the dog's neck so that everyone will look behind himself and think in what stink and filth he is stuck so that he will well forget pride and arrogance" (VIII, 1191f.).

**Comment 2.**

The following testimonies show how important our faithful fathers considered the blameless life of a preacher, in addition to pure doctrine, for the blessed conduct of the office.

Luther writes: "Every preacher should prove these two things: first, a blameless life so that he can be firm and no one will have cause to blaspheme his doctrine; second, irreproachable doctrine so that he will mislead none of those who follow him; and so he may correctly stand on both sides: with the good life against the enemies who look much more at life than at doctrine and despise the doctrine because of the life; with the doctrine toward the friends, who pay much more attention to the doctrine than to the life and bear also the life for the sake of the doctrine" (XI, 776).

The same: "Where the life is not good, it is also rare that one preaches correctly; he must always preach against himself, which he can hardly do without additions and peripheral doctrines" (XI, 111).

Johann Gerhard: "Although the effectiveness of the Word and the Sacraments is by no means dependent on the worthiness or unworthiness of the minister of the church, it is still clear from the matter itself that the course of the heavenly doctrine and the fruitfulness of the Word meet with no small restraint and hindrance through the godlessness of the ministers of the church. Respect for doctrine is lost when the voice is not supported by the deed. Those who teach correctly and live godlessly tear down again through bad morals what they build through pure doctrine. By voice they build toward heaven; but with the life, toward hell. They dedicate the tongue toward God; the soul, to the devil. They are like signposts that show others the way which they themselves do not take. They are like the carpenters who were helpful to Noah in building the ark in which some were preserved from the flood, but they themselves perished in the flood" (*Loc. de ministerio ecclesiast.*, Sec. 275; see Sec. 276-284).

**Comment 3.**

A preacher must consider that, as a person in public view, because of offenses which so easily arise, he should guard with special care not only against all actual sins but also against anything that could give an appearance of evil. We may here specifically mention the appearance of world-love, love for a

**Fig 17: The church Walther pastored in St. Louis, MO.**
Courtesy of Concordia Historical Institute.

comfortable life, laziness, immoderate, irresponsibility, untruthfulness, pride, a tendency to be suspicious, failure to keep confidences, listening to gossip, impatience, murmuring under the cross, and the like.

From consideration for his office and love for souls, especially the weak, a preacher must limit the use of his Christian freedom more than other Christians. So he should totally avoid some things which he cannot absolutely forbid to others. [Examples include ostentation in the clothing and furnishings and worldliness in reading material and entertainment.]

## Comment 4.

A preacher should recognize it as his holy duty not only to remember daily his whole congregation, especially those who are in spiritual or physical misery, in fervent intercession before God (Acts 6:4; Phil. 1:3-11), but also to be seriously concerned that the congregation see in his own family a faithful zeal for family devotions [*Hausgottesdienst*, worship in the home].

## Comment 5.

Continued study is a major aspect of a preacher's life. If all Christians should grow in knowledge and not remain children in understanding (Col. 1:11; 2 Pet. 3:18; 1 Cor. 14:20), that is without doubt much more necessary for a servant of the Word. Therefore the Apostle calls to the young Timothy with great earnestness: "Give attendance to reading" (1 Tim. 4:13). It is tragic if the practical preacher loses interest in theology. Luther says in the marginal gloss on Sirach 39:1: "A pastor or preacher should study and exercise himself in all kinds of books. In that way God gives him understanding. But He leaves belly servants alone" (see Sirach 38:25-39:15).

# 49

## The Pastor's Synodical Membership

It is the duty of every Christian to be diligent in preserving the unity of the spirit in the bond of peace (Eph. 4:3). This duty certainly obligates a minister of the church in twice as high a degree. He should zealously promote brotherly fellowship with his colleagues and neighboring pastors, also toward his school teacher; attend the local and district conferences available to him; join a synod as soon as he has opportunity; never miss its meetings without the most urgent necessity; and help it to be fruitful insofar as God gives him grace for it. He should in general, with all his powers, further the purposes of the synodical association which he has joined and also awaken in his congregation a sense and a zeal for the common well-being of the church, for example: to found and preserve institutions of higher education and seminaries for preachers and school teachers, to recruit students, to support poor pupils and students, to distribute the Bible, to support home and foreign missions, to provide for hospitals and orphanages and the like. The preacher should also, if God gives him the gifts for it, work with the periodicals of his synod, or as much as possible further interest in them and their circulation among his congregational members, and also bring good books into every family.

**Comment 1.**
Basil is certainly correct in writing: "The left hand does not need the right as much as the church needs harmony" [*Non tam sinistrae opus est dextera, quam ecclesiae opus est concordia*]. This harmony of the church requires above all the harmony of the ministers. We read in Luther's Table Talk: "In Jenner in the fortieth year Dr. Martin Luther received a supplication from a pastor who complained about the disobedience of his chaplain. Then

## The Pastor's Synodical Membership

Dr. Martin Luther said: Oh, dear God, how hostile the devil is to us! He causes disunity even among the servants of the Word so that one hates the other! Accept it that we are not the same in life and walk, and one who has a different way and is amazing to the other: one must let that go and happen (for it has its limit). For one cannot make everything as straight as an arrow and all along the same lines when it comes to morals and life. As long as we are united in the correct, pure doctrine—there not even the least bit may be impure and false; rather everything must be pure and choice, as from a dove. There no tolerance nor overlooking nor love avails; for a little leaven leavens the whole lump, as St. Paul says in 1 Cor. 5:6" (XXII, 820f.).

Luther said: "I know of no greater *donum* [gift] that we have

**Fig. 18: Organization of English MO Synod. Walther preaching at Gravelton, MO 1881.**
Courtesy of Concordia Historical Institute.

than *concordiam docentium* (the harmony of the teachers), that here and there in the principalities and imperial cities the teaching is uniform with ours. . . . I would not take the Turkish empire in exchange for this consensus" (XXII, 1005). As dear as a preacher holds the glory of Christ, the furthering of His Gospel, and his own salvation, so ready he should be to bear the burdens of his colleagues in the office (Gal. 6:2) and rather suffer everything than to let a bitter root grow up between them and him, which would destroy peace.

**Comment 2.**
Harmonious cooperation between the preacher and his school teacher is as important for the building of God's kingdom as is a cordial relationship among the preachers. It is a very heavy cross for a preacher, and the work of God is necessarily hindered, if his school teacher opposes him. He has just as glorious a support in him [the teacher] if he works together with him [literally: "pulls at the same yoke," like a team of oxen] in true unity of spirit. The preacher should never forget that the school teacher is also a servant of the church and administers an auxiliary office branched off from his [the pastor's] office, and in this relationship is also his colleague. So the preacher should do everything he can to stand in a cordial, fraternal, and collegial relationship with his Christian school teacher.

**Comment 3.**
Pastoral conferences are not a modern or specifically American institution. In the Lutheran church also in earlier times, there were such assemblies of pastors for mutual advancement in knowledge and faithfulness. [Walther gives a lengthy quotation about educationally very thorough pastoral conferences that were held in Hamburg in the sixteenth century.]

**Comment 4.**
[Walther shows with many quotations that every local congregation has full church authority; associations such as synods may be formed in Christian freedom; but they are human, not divine, institutions.]
Luther writes in his 1545 writing against the Papacy founded

by the devil: "We know that in Christendom it is done that all churches are equal, and there is no more than one single Church of Christ in the world for if there is a church wherever it can be in the whole world, then it has no other Gospel or holy Scripture, no other Baptism and Sacrament [of the Altar], no other faith and prayer, no other hope of eternal life, than we have here in our church at Wittenberg; and its bishops or pastors and preachers; none is lord nor servant of the other; they have the same mind and heart; and everything that pertains to the church is all the same; except that, as it says in 1 Cor. 12:8ff. and Rom. 12:6, one preacher or even one Christian may be of stronger faith, have different or more gifts, than the other; such as one can interpret Scripture better; this one can rule better; this one can discern spirits better; this one can comfort better; this one has more languages; and so forth; but such gifts make no inequality nor lordship in the church; indeed, they do not make any Christians (Matt. 7:22-23); rather they must be Christians first" (XVII, 1398).

Nevertheless a preacher who, insisting on his freedom, wanted to remain independent with his congregation, although he was offered the opportunity to join an orthodox synod, would thereby act contrary to the purpose of his office, the well-being of his congregation, and his duty toward the Church as a whole [the invisible Church] and would reveal himself as a separatist.

## Comment 5.

The preacher should work toward the goal that his congregation also join a synod, but great care should be taken first to instruct the congregation about the meaning of a synod and to take time so that the impression is not given that burdens are being imposed upon them, that their freedom is being limited, that their church property is being taken away, nor that the yoke of a spiritual government is being laid upon them. Rather it should be shown that it is only a matter of their own well-being and of the duty of caring for their children, their posterity, and the kingdom of God in general—and finally that a correct synod wants to be only an advisory, auxiliary body, not one that will dominate individual congregations.

# 50

## The Decision About a Call

The decision whether a preacher should accept another position which has been offered to him, depends on the consideration of the following five rules: 1. the preacher should wait calmly for a call that may be extended to him and should never seek to get away on his own, least of all to secure a higher salary or a more pleasant or easier position (Jer. 23:21); 2. he should never leave because of the wicked in his congregation who make his life bitter (Rom. 12:21), unless it were merely a matter of his personal weakness so that another orthodox preacher could carry out what would not be possible for him because of personal tensions with the majority of congregational members (2 Cor. 13:10); 3. it must be clear before human eyes not only that the new office offered to him is a more important one but also that he could use his gifts for the greater benefit of the church in it than if he would remain (1 Cor. 12:7); 4. he should not easily decide for himself but should consult for the decision both his present congregation and the one that is calling him away as well as learned theologians (Prov. 12:15); 5. he should not leave his congregation without its explicit agreement unless it would be obvious to everyone that it was absolutely denying its consent out of pure stubbornness, without considering the well-being of the church.

**Comment 1.**
[With quotations, Walther shows that two extremes are to be avoided. The pastor is not always bound to his first regular call, but he should also not accept any and every call away from his present congregation. No call should be accepted because of earthly, carnal, or financial considerations nor from ambition, a misplaced desire to please the pastor's wife, or a desire to escape difficulties. Nor should a call be sought by the pastor himself or by his friends

## The Decision About a Call

or relatives on his behalf. Ex. 4:11; 1 Kings 13:24; Prov. 22:13; Is. 30:20-21; Jer. 1:17; Jonah 1:4; Matt. 7:12; 25:30; Acts 5:9; 17:15; 18:5; 20:7; Rom. 12:4-8; 1 Cor. 4:17; 9:17; Eph. 4:10-12; 1 Thess. 2:2; 1 Tim. 1:3; 3:13.]

**Comment 2.**
[A preacher may not leave his congregation because of wicked persons in it. Walther gives several testimonies which refer to the following Bible passages: Matt. 2:13; 10:16, 22; 12:15; 14:13; Luke 4:28ff.; John 8:59; 15:19; Acts 8:1; 9:25; 13:51; 2 Cor. 11:33.]

To the question of two preachers, "Whether they should leave their church and yield to the enemies of the Gospel," Luther answers as follows in 1530: "I have read your letter to me, dear gentlemen, in which you desire my advice, whether you should yield and give place to the enemies of the Gospel among you, who nevertheless present themselves as friends. To that my answer and opinion is briefly that you should by no means yield yet at this time so that it does not have the appearance that you are leaving your sheep like hirelings. So you should both continue in your office, which has been committed to you by your church. Suffer everything that you have to suffer until they depose you with force or the government orders you away; otherwise you should by no means yield to the grim raging of Satan.

"You are not alone in suffering such. The private persecution that is done by false brothers strikes and oppresses us all under our pious rulers, not under the tyrants and enemies of the Word. Because we are not now, praise God! persecuted by outward, manifest enemies of the Word, yet it is the nature of the Gospel that it cannot be, much less grow and spread, without persecution. So we may suffer this private persecution, provided by those who are at home with us. But it will and must be suffered, whether it comes from enemies or friends. So be strong and accept this your cross, and follow Christ the Lord. Then you will find rest for your souls. Christ, Who is the Leader and Comforter of all the godly who bear the cross, preserve and strengthen you with His joyous Spirit" (X, 1890.f.).

To the question: "Whether a servant of the church is permitted to flee at the time of persecution," J. Gerhard answers: "Tertullian disapproves it absolutely, but Christ's advice shows the opposite in Matt. 10:23: 'But when they persecute you in this city, flee ye into another.' Further there is the example of Christ in Matt. 2:13; 12:15; John 8:59; Luke 4:30; and of the Apostle Paul in Acts 9:25; 2 Cor. 11:33; of Polycarp and Athanasius. So a distinction is to be made between particular persecutions, which are directed only to the person of the servant of the church, and general persecutions of the whole church; in the latter we declare flight to be permitted, in the former only in a certain respect. For there is further to be a distinction between the conditions of the church. For sometimes the servant of the church flees with the agreement, indeed, with the advice of his listeners, so that sometimes the church over which he has been placed has no shortage of other capable teachers, which we consider allowed; but sometimes he flees so that the listeners, who neither advise nor approve of his flight, are given an offense, and enemies are given occasion for blasphemies and an opportunity to attack the sheep, which we consider not to be permitted" (*Loc. theol. de minister. eccl.*, Sec 291)

## Comment 3

A preacher should yield if it is obvious that not his doctrine but rather his frail person constitutes offense and that his remaining would hinder the progress of God's work while there is a prospect that another would further it in his place.

Martin Chemnitz writes: "If it is intended only toward the pastor, against whom the enemies of the truth are especially embittered for certain reasons which they have, and so peace and rest could be restored to the church if he would step down, then the servant of the Word is certainly sinning against the rule of love if he notices that it is mainly intended against his person, that the church could enjoy peace, and that others are available who could serve the edification of the church in his absence, but he certainly did not want to yield only so that he would not have to bear the troubles of exile" (*Evangelische Harmonie*, Cap. 72, on Matt. 10:23).

## Comment 4.

A preacher already in office should never deliver a trial sermon. If he does so and comes to the [other] office in this way and so has pursued it, he is putting himself in danger of being uncertain about the legitimacy of his call. In any case, he gives the evil appearance of having the attitude of an hireling and makes himself despicable to his own congregation, which must retain him if he does not

## The Decision About a Call

receive the promotion he has desired.

**Comment 5.**
A preacher should also not accept the position of one who has been unjustly driven away; it still belongs to the latter in the sight of God [Matt. 5:40; Luke 6:29].

When a preacher in Zwickau was driven out in 1531, Luther wrote to Pastor Nikol. Hausmann there: "You know you are the true, called pastor and curate [*Seelsorger*] of the church at Zwickau, accepted by both the council and the congregation; that you will therefore have to give account on that day for the same church which has been entrusted to you, and are obligated, as long as you live, to provide it with pure doctrine, to pray earnestly for it, to care, to watch, to risk and give your life in all need and danger that may occur, such as plague or other diseases, whatever they may be, and to take the foremost position against the gates of hell, and to suffer and endure everything which a pious, faithful pastor and curate [*Seelsorger*] ought to do according to his office.

"Truly, those are all hard, great, indeed, divine works; as you have until now, praise God! done diligently and faithfully. But now your council, driven by the evil spirit, rejects the preacher at St. Catharina, who has been neither accused nor convicted of any misdeed by any judge. Rather they are undertaking that in their own power and sacrilege as mad people and real church robbers (not of physical goods, but of the office and honor of the Holy Spirit) and want to be party and judge at the same time in the same case. In no way is it to be tolerated that you should be quiet about that or approve of it, so that you do not participate in this church robbery by others nor become guilty of the improper and disgraceful violence committed against the rejected brother.

"But if he had been liable to punishment and had made himself guilty, so that there had been a cause for deposing him from office, that should have been undertaken lawfully with your knowledge and advice as the pastor [*Pfarrherr*]. But it is even worse that they are putting another into the place of the one who has been rejected without your permission, indeed, against your will, and are therefore pushing him in from this same power and wrongfulness of their own, now committed also against you.

"Here, dear Sir and Friend, be warned for Christ's sake that you take great care (for it is not a simple, little thing) that you do not make yourself guilty with the church robbers, so that part of the curse does not also come upon you. Now you ask what you should do here. Indeed, I do not know much to advise, but I consider it good and advise you faithfully that you do in this matter what I would do in it. First you should summon the uncalled and shoved-in preacher before yourself in the presence of others of your assistants and present to him kindly but earnestly the sacrilege and arrogance of the council; and further inform him that he has not been called through you (to whom the church has been entrusted) and is therefore teaching and ruling as a thief and a murderer, and that in the same church of yours, for which you must give account. Therefore he should know that he is pushing in with force and robbing your pastoral office without your knowledge and consent. Therefore you are admonishing him to abstain from such robbery."

[Luther advises Hausmann then to confront the town council. If they will not abstain from their sacrilege, he should appeal to the people with a clear explanation of the sacrilege. He cannot accept as a colleague the pastor who has been wrongly brought in.]

("Admonition to a Pastor That He Should Not Be Silent About the Improper Deposing of a Pastor," 1531, X, 1892-97).

To the question: "Whether one who has been called to the place of an innocent pastor who has been deposed and accepts it *rebus sic stantibus* (under such circumstances), has a Christian call?" Moerlin answers: "1. If the former has been incorrectly deposed, the choice of the one who has forced his way in is to be disapproved. 2. Since he has no honorable, divine title and call, having been installed in stollen, robbed goods, from which a poor, innocent man has been forced out contrary to right, therefore the one who has pushed his way in has no true call until it is rightly carried out that the predecessor has been rightly deposed.

"Objection: There is a distinction between a house father, who is the hereditary lord of his goods, and a called preacher, who is only an employed servant in the office. Answer: 1. Sometimes town councillors are used to speaking in that way, that the preacher has his office from them, for they pay him and have the right and power to depose him (as any lord with his servant); and such people also see the call of the preacher as nothing other than one makes with someone to herd cows or pigs. 2. God is much rather the natural hereditary Lord of His preaching office, as a house father with his goods. For He has installed His servants and does not want them to be forced out, and one who wants to force out such a preacher is interfering in God's jurisdiction and property. 3. Dr. Luther says that not even a small-time house father will suffer it that one depose one of his innocent, deserving servants against his will nor let someone else arrange his household in his place. So how does it come about that the poor Christ alone must suffer it? If that does not mean *os ponere in coelum* (fighting against God), then I do not know what it would mean" (*Decisiones mille et sex casum*, by L. Dunte, pp. 667f.).

**Comment 6.**

According to God's Word, a preacher is not a lord of his congregation but rather its minister and is responsible to it (2 Cor. 1:24; 4:5; 1 Cor. 3:5; Col. 4:17). So he has no right (either from anger or for recreation) unnecessarily [that is, except in an emergency] to omit a worship service, to miss or to leave meetings of officers or of the congregation, or to refuse a Baptism, a funeral, etc. If he does so, he is forfeiting his office [Rom. 12:7; 1 Cor. 3:22-23; 9:16].

Dunte presents the following opinion of the ministerium at Riga: "If a preacher has received his appointment and call, he should not imagine that he can act in the church according to his pleasure and deny the office to the church [refuse to serve in some way that pertains to his office] when he wants to. Rather he must elevate the congregation of God, as St. Paul says beautifully with these words: 'Whether Paul, or Apollos, or Cephas, or the world, or life, or death, or things present, or things to come; all are your's; and ye are Christ's; and Christ is God's (1 Cor. 3:22-23)" (*op. cit.*, pp. 666f.).

The preacher should also not let someone else preach for him too often and unnecessarily, remembering the apostolic word in Rom. 12:7: "Or ministry, let us wait on our ministering." Naturally the preacher is even less allowed to open his pulpit to persons whom the congregation does not want to hear.

**Comment 7.**

[A preacher might give up the ministry to become a school teacher if he did not have the gifts for the ministry but were better suited for teaching school or if his health required it. A preacher must not leave the ministry in order to have more leisure or a greater income.]

**Comment 8.**

To the question: "Whether one who has been legitimately installed as a servant of the church, faithfully administers his office, and is still sufficiently equipped to carry it out, and continues to be wanted by his congregation, can lay down his office with a good conscience, either because he has become sick and tired of the work and effort, or because he has in abundance what he and his family need for their support, or because he is moved by fleshly considerations to lay down his office voluntarily"; Christian Kortholt answers: "The orthodox theologians answer this question in the negative and establish their negation: 1. with the testimonies of Scripture (1 Cor. 7:20; Matt. 10:22; Luke 9:62); 2. with examples taken from the same source, where we read that the apostles and prophets did not leave their office until they had finished their course, as the Apostle confesses of himself (2 Tim. 4:7); 3. reason teaches that, since it is an unpermitted and forbidden matter to call oneself and to push into the office, it is also not open to a servant of the church arbitrarily to leave and lay down the office he has once taken over" (*Pastor fidelis*, p. 62.s.).

Deyling speaks similarly and then adds: "But a proper exception is the case of loss of memory or an incurable disease, when a servant of the church thereby becomes incapable of administering the office: also laying down the office because of irreconcilable hatred on the part of the listeners or other persecutors and because of continual denial of support so that the poor servant of the church finds no way to nourish himself and his family" (*Institution. prud. pastoral.*, p. 762).

It is self-understood that going astray from the correct doctrine, which the preacher has made a holy vow to present, is a necessary reason to lay down the office, unless it is only a passing temptation. Luther writes: "So all preachers should also be certain that they can say: God says it, that is God's Word, it is the same as if I am taking an oath. Now one who is not certain of it and cannot say: God says it!, he may well give up preaching, for he will not accomplish anything good" (VI, 1404).

# Index

## A

Absolution  22, 42, 113, 120, 122, 123, 126, 129, 134, 137, 145, 184, 212, 213, 237, 245
absolve  38, 42, 113, 116, 127, 137, 138, 150, 202, 232, 233, 244, 252
action  144
adiaphora  90, 101, 259
Adiaphorists  137
adiaphoron  35, 37, 47, 130, 162, 185
adiaphorous  103
admonition  31
adulterers  167
adultery  161, 163, 167, 168, 174, 175, 176, 177, 179, 181, 182, 208, 237, 238, 248
advisory  273
affliction  70
agenda  212
alleged marriage  183
almoner  219, 222
alms  41
altar  32
Ambrose  255
amends  150, 254
Amsdorf  145
Anabaptists  42, 90, 96, 105, 237
Andreae, J. Valent.  237
angels  30, 143
announce  39, 191
Announcement  107, 192
anointing  185, 187
Anselm of Canterbury  224
Anti-Christian  35, 175
Antichrist  14, 263
Antinomians  73, 74
antiphon  212
Antitrinitarian  93, 94
Apollos  279
Apology  116, 120, 187
Apology of the Augsburg Confession  60, 237, 246
apostate  98
Apostle  10, 23, 27, 32, 44, 64, 65, 71, 76, 97, 100, 101, 110, 113, 132, 137, 148, 177, 178, 180, 187, 198, 215, 218, 220, 231, 241, 255, 257, 258, 266, 269, 280
Apostle Paul  13, 35, 71, 196, 276
Apostles' Creed  34, 37, 100
apostolic  154, 177, 219, 231, 252, 254, 279
apostolic age  254
apostolic Word  112
application  52
Aquinas  15
archdemons  32
Arcularius  261
Arians  94, 95
Athanasian  33
Athanasius  94, 276
atheism  82
audit  256
Augsburg Confession  16, 38, 49, 116, 120, 137, 139, 234
Augustine  125, 136, 223, 234, 240, 241
Augustinian  92
auxiliary  254
auxiliary body  273
auxiliary office  254, 258, 272

## B

Baier, J. W.  183, 214

Balduin  40, 42, 93, 149, 165, 217, 236, 260
banns  156, 169, 170
Batism  22, 35, 68, 86, 87, 88, 89, 90, 92, 93, 94, 95, 96, 97, 98, 99, 100, 101, 102, 103, 104, 105, 109, 114, 134, 135, 137, 145, 146, 166, 185, 190, 228, 229, 235, 273, 279
Baptismal  102, 105, 185, 245
Baptismal customs  100
Baptismal font  104
Baptismal formula  86, 87, 95
Baptismal gowns  189
Baptismal grace  185
Baptismal hymn  105
Baptismal water  88, 89
Baptist  14, 105, 148
baptistry  102
baptize  17, 34, 86, 87, 88, 89, 90, 91, 92, 93, 94, 95, 96, 97, 98, 102, 103, 105, 109, 137, 138, 146, 185, 189, 228
Basch, Siegmund  53
Basil  58, 270
believe  62, 69, 72, 102
believers  109
Bellarmine  135, 166
betrothal  72, 158, 160, 161, 162, 163, 168, 169, 179, 182
Beza  14
Bible  39, 56, 93, 208, 270
Bible passages  207, 254
Biblical  47
Bidembach, Felix  203, 205, 207, 210, 212, 225
binding key  233, 240
blasphemous  164, 214, 215, 217, 276
Blasphemy  215
Bohemian Hussites  146
Bohemians  146
book  99
Book of Concord  208
Brenz  13, 14, 86
bribery  230
Brochmand  46
Bucer  132
Bugenhagen  13, 84, 89, 187, 235
Bunyan, John  14
burial  113, 226, 227, 228, 229, 230
burying  227, 253
business  251

## C

call  16, 17, 18, 19, 20, 21, 23, 24, 25, 26, 27, 28, 29, 30, 31, 35, 37, 38, 39, 40, 44, 45, 47, 51, 52, 53, 134, 136, 232, 274, 276, 278, 279, 280
Calvin  14, 130, 132
Calvinists  48, 94, 137, 139, 140, 165 229
candidate  31, 35, 37, 44, 48, 50
capital crime  229
capital punishment  165
Carlstadt  24, 36, 121, 142
carnal security  205, 215
casuistry  13, 15
catechetical  59
catechetics  10
Catechism  45, 49, 78, 118, 171, 187, 188, 191, 208, 261
catechist  193, 194
catechizing  193, 194
catechumens  188, 190, 191, 193, 194
cemetery  229, 230
Cephas  279
ceremonial law  158
Ceremonies  37
ceremony  35, 37, 100, 103
chastity  163
cheirothesia  185
Chemnitz, Martin  19, 103, 124, 135, 186, 187, 225, 252, 254, 276
children  78
chrisma  185
Christ  12, 20, 22, 23, 24, 27, 28, 32, 33, 36, 38, 39, 42, 48, 62, 66, 67, 69, 70, 71, 72, 73, 74, 75, 78, 87, 88, 89, 90, 91, 94, 95, 100, 101, 102, 103, 108, 110, 111, 113, 115, 116, 118, 122, 127, 129, 130, 131, 133, 134, 137, 139, 140, 141, 144, 145, 148, 149, 154, 165, 177, 181, 186, 191, 194, 196, 198, 199, 206, 208, 213, 215, 219, 221, 223, 224, 227, 230, 231, 232, 233, 236, 239, 240, 242, 243, 246, 249, 267, 272, 273, 275, 276, 277, 279
Christendom  13, 267, 273
Christian freedom  36, 37, 73, 77, 90, 130, 254, 269, 272
Christ's institution  92, 96

# Index

Christ's Supper 138
Christ's Word 90
Christ's Words of Institution 212
Chrysostom, John 107, 133, 196
church 8, 10, 14, 16, 18, 19, 22, 23, 26, 27, 29, 31, 32, 33, 34, 37, 38, 39, 40, 42, 44, 47, 48, 49, 50, 51, 56, 58, 59, 65, 67, 68, 70, 72, 75, 78, 82, 85, 86, 94, 95, 96, 98, 99, 100, 101, 102, 104, 105, 108, 110, 113, 116, 120, 121, 122, 123, 127, 129, 131, 132, 133, 135, 136, 137, 138, 140, 141, 143, 144, 148, 150, 152, 153, 154, 162, 163, 166, 169, 170, 171, 186, 187, 189, 191, 192, 195, 196, 197, 198, 199, 200, 201, 202, 203, 204, 205, 212, 213, 214, 218, 219, 221, 226, 227, 233, 234, 236, 237, 240, 241, 242, 244, 245, 249, 252, 254, 255, 259, 260, 262, 266, 268, 270, 272, 273, 274, 275, 276, 277, 278, 279, 280
church and state 219
church assembly 258
church book 59
church customs 221
church discipline 72, 126, 163, 232, 234, 235, 236, 237, 238, 239, 240, 248, 249, 250, 251, 254, 255, 259
church fellowship 110
church officer 254
Church Order of Electoral Saxony 228
church orders 122, 201
church property 254, 256, 264, 273
church schism 233
church treasury 58
church visitation 199
church year 72
churches 66, 172, 208, 273
churchly confession 34
churchly offices 222
Chytraeus 180
circumcision 91, 101, 109, 146, 229
circuses 191
civil 169
civil government 252
Civil Laws 155, 157, 179
civil marriage 152
clothing 193

coarse sins 208
colleague 270, 272
collect 212
comfort 17, 31, 42, 62, 63, 65, 70, 71, 76, 80, 81, 86, 115, 121, 122, 123, 138, 200, 201, 203, 207, 213, 223
comfort-rich doctrine 75
Comforter 64, 115, 275, 208
commandments 80
commune 110, 122, 142, 145, 146, 151, 244, 263
communicant 32, 104, 107, 111, 125, 131, 134, 140, 141, 142, 143, 144, 145, 146, 148, 151, 212, 252
communing the sick 212
Communion 110, 117, 125, 130, 132, 143, 144, 188, 213, 235, 252
conditionally 87
conferences 270
confess 92, 107, 110, 123, 126, 127, 128, 131, 164, 129, 132, 143, 148, 187, 224, 244, 150, 209, 261, 267
confession 31, 33, 37, 49, 50, 53, 66, 78, 105, 107, 110, 119, 120, 121, 122, 123, 124, 126, 127, 128, 129, 138, 139, 140, 141, 143, 145, 164, 186, 190, 191, 192, 212, 238, 259, 261, 262, 263, 264, 265
Confessional announcement 107, 116, 117, 235
confessional ceremonies 31, 37
confessional chair 127
confessional seal 128
confessional writings 39, 116
Confessions 238, 261
confessions 50, 107
confessors 138
confirm 188, 190, 191, 192
confirmand 188, 190
confirmation 185, 186, 187, 188, 189, 190, 191, 192
confirmation instruction 188, 193
congregation 19, 21, 26, 27, 28, 29, 31, 32, 34, 35, 37, 38, 39, 40, 44, 45, 47, 48, 51, 52, 55, 56, 58, 61, 64, 75, 76, 77, 79, 80, 94, 104, 105, 106, 108, 114, 117, 120, 122, 125, 126, 138, 139, 143, 149, 151, 158, 169, 170, 171, 183, 190, 191, 192, 196, 199, 201, 202, 214, 218, 219, 220, 221, 222,

283

226, 230, 233, 234, 235, 236, 238, 240, 242, 244, 245, 246, 247, 248, 250, 251, 252, 254, 256, 257, 258, 261, 262, 263, 264, 269, 270, 272, 273, 274, 276, 277, 279, 280
congregational 251, 259
congregational assembly 246, 250, 257
congregational constitution 262, 264
congregational meeting 256, 259, 263
congregational members 262, 270, 274
congregational officers 254
congregational poor chest 222
congregational resolution 250, 258 218, 231, 232, 265
conscience 17, 19, 25, 29, 31, 36, 37, 38, 49, 50, 59, 62, 70, 77, 79. 80, 85, 114, 123, 126, 128, 129, 148, 154, 162, 166, 167, 178, 180, 192, 193, 209, 212, 221, 246, 249, 259, 266, 280
consciences 49, 62, 79, 80, 123, 166
conscientious 108, 191, 193, 254, 256
consecrate 130, 131, 132, 133, 134, 140, 142, 142, 145, 151, 152, 155, 157
consecrated wafers 130, 141, 144, 152, 212
consistory 161, 236
constitution 264, 265
consummated marriage 162
contagious 201
contagious disease 202
Continued study 269
conversion 64, 198, 230, 251
convert 26, 92, 98, 109, 164, 201, 205, 261, 262
Cordatus, Conrad 27
correct books 39
Corvinus, Johannes 136
created 223
Creator 94
Creed 78, 105, 116, 118, 217
cremate 227
crime 162, 167, 225, 242, 245
criminals 229
cross 70, 100, 102, 181, 269, 272, 275
Crusius Christian August 157
curate 277
custom 47, 79, 90, 96, 100, 101, 104, 107, 116, 117, 120, 129, 130, 144, 169, 170, 171, 185, 186, 187, 189, 249
customary 90, 91, 95, 102, 142, 143, 212, 226, 227
Customs 100
Cyrus 196

# D

damnation 111, 112, 198, 200, 224
dances 191
dancing 79
Daniel 24
Danksagung 131
Dannhauer 128, 150, 169, 171, 175, 236, 248
David 11, 71, 246
Davidic 102
deacon 44, 53, 200, 222, 235, 255
dead 230
deaf-mutes 147
death penalty 167
deceased 230
Dedekennus 94, 123, 143, 147, 149, 162, 165, 182, 249
degree 157
degree of relationship 156, 157, 158
degrees that are forbidden 183
depose 127, 202, 278, 279
Deposing 202, 278
desert 177, 178, 179, 180, 183
despisers 229
Deuteronomy 180
devil 12, 14, 16, 17, 18, 20, 23, 30, 32, 34, 35, 37, 66, 68, 73, 113, 114, 135, 181, 185, 201, 214, 215, 216, 217, 221, 223, 268, 271, 273
devout 214, 232, 234
Deyling 15, 87, 88, 90, 95, 98, 101, 126, 128, 140, 143, 144, 147, 179, 185, 195, 226, 229, 280
diaconate 254
Dietelmair, J. A. 53
diploma of vocation 40
discipline 114, 232, 233, 234, 236, 237, 240, 246, 248, 252
disease 161, 162, 182, 187, 277, 280
distribution formula 140, 141
district synod 188, 191
divine institution 162
divine Word 46

# Index

divorce 154, 156, 166, 174, 175, 176, 177, 179, 180, 181, 182, 183, 248
divorced spouse 178
doctrine 8, 9, 10, 14, 17, 18, 20, 24, 27, 28, 31, 34, 36, 37, 42, 45, 47, 50, 53, 62, 63, 64, 65, 66, 70, 71, 72, 76, 77, 78, 79, 80, 81, 83, 101, 103, 110, 116, 127, 135, 136, 138, 149, 153, 154, 186, 188, 202, 231, 237, 239, 254, 255, 257, 259, 261, 266, 267, 268, 276, 280
donkey's burial 229
drunk 161
drunkenness 246, 266
Drusilla 197
dueling 248
Dunte 279
duress 161
Dying 223
dying 199, 200, 210, 225
dying person 223, 224

## E

early church 88
Easter 74, 189
ecclesiola in ecclesia 56
elder 44, 56, 67, 145, 234, 255, 262
election 72, 77
election of officers 255
Elisha 42
embalm 227
emergency 150, 231
emergency Baptism 105
engagement 156, 161
Enlightenment 93
enmity 56
epidemic diseases 202
epilepsy 161, 162
Epiphanius 130
episcopalian 254
epitaphs 230
Erasmus 14, 15
erring 188
erring key 126
Error 122
errorists 164, 198
eternal life 11, 213, 273
eternity 52
Eucharist 131, 132, 144
Eutychian 74

Evangelical 53, 54, 148
Eve 171
everlasting life 102
evil 216
evil spirits 216
ex opere operato 132
examine 44, 45, 46, 55, 108, 111, 116, 117, 118, 119, 146, 147, 188, 190, 191, 192, 193, 205, 262
exclude 232, 234, 250
excommunicate 57, 96, 98, 104, 125, 126, 150, 214, 229, 231, 232, 234, 235, 237, 238, 239, 244, 245, 247, 248, 249, 250, 251, 252, 253, 261
execution 225, 229
Exile 181
exorcism 35, 103
exorcists 216

## F

faith 9, 17, 22, 26, 27, 30, 33, 36, 45, 46, 49, 64, 65, 66, 68, 69, 70, 72, 73, 75, 77, 78, 79, 86, 92, 93, 97, 101, 103, 108, 109, 110, 111, 114, 115, 116, 121, 122, 126, 132, 135, 139, 140, 141, 143, 144, 147, 148, 149, 153, 186, 187, 188, 190, 204, 205, 206, 215, 216, 219, 223, 224, 234, 240, 261, 262, 263, 273, 277, 278, 280
faith fellowship 114
false 149
false churches 262
false confession 32, 34
false doctrine 37, 45, 63, 79, 85, 89, 165
false holiness 80
false religion 214
false teacher 34, 39
family devotions 269
fanatic 16, 66, 70
fanatical spirit 36, 121
fanaticism 108
fanatics 17
fasting 82
Father 22, 86, 87, 93, 94, 100, 103
Fecht, G. H. 59
Fecht, Johannes 47, 58, 94, 127, 128,

138, 195, 201, 217, 236, 237
feeble-minded 247
Felix 197
fellowship 110, 122, 138, 141, 148, 165, 169, 229, 237, 240, 248, 250, 251, 252, 262, 263, 270
Flacius 198
flattery 230
flesh 68, 69, 183, 198
flesh of his flesh 157
Foertsch Mich. 197
forbidden degree 154
foreknowledge 203
forgive 22, 42, 110, 116, 122, 130, 141, 150, 174, 175, 213, 237, 245, 252
forgiveness of sins 53, 61, 62, 68, 72, 74, 108, 120, 213, 246
form of Baptism 87
formula 86, 87, 93, 95
Formula of Concord 34, 37, 50, 133, 134, 234
fornication 163, 237
Fortunatus 136
Foundlings 96
freedom 36, 37, 38, 50, 81, 83, 101, 117, 273
Freedom of conscience 50
Fresenius, J. Ph. 54
Friedrich 142
fruit of faith 69
fruits 69
funeral 226, 227, 279
funeral procession 226, 227
funeral sermon 229, 230

# G

Galatians 35
Gallus, Joh. 137
general Absolution 122, 123
general confession 120, 122
gentleness 200
Gerhard, Johann 10, 15, 88, 90, 100, 102, 103, 104, 131, 134, 135, 136, 147, 148, 153, 158, 160, 161, 162, 163, 164, 166, 175, 177, 178, 180, 181, 182, 183, 221, 237, 254, 257, 268, 275
gifts 270, 273, 274
gifts of the Holy Spirit 187

Gnostic Enkratites 130
God 11
godfather 105
godliness 45
godmother 91
godparents 104, 190
God's field 229
God's Law 158
God's own Word 20
God's Word 9, 12, 16, 22, 24, 25, 27, 29, 30, 31, 34, 38, 39, 45, 50, 60, 61, 63, 64, 65, 66, 67, 68, 70, 76, 79, 80, 81, 82, 83, 89, 93, 101, 108, 109, 114, 116, 120, 121, 129, 137, 138, 139, 141, 146, 153, 154, 156, 157, 160, 161, 165, 177, 181, 183, 190, 196, 200, 206, 215, 219, 229, 233, 234, 240, 244, 248, 249, 250, 257, 259, 261, 262, 264, 279, 280
God's wrath 29, 198, 252
Goeze, J. Melch. 53
good works 36, 62, 68, 69, 71, 73
Gospel 14, 20, 21, 28, 35, 36, 42, 53, 54, 63, 65, 71, 73, 75, 79, 80, 97, 109, 115, 117, 120, 122, 123, 137, 152, 221, 224, 235, 239, 246, 249, 266, 272, 273, 275
gossip 127, 239, 269
government 163, 167, 168, 231, 236, 255
grace 10, 18, 19, 26, 36, 45, 62, 67, 72, 73, 74, 75, 80, 83, 102, 108, 109, 110, 112, 114, 135, 183, 185, 204, 206, 208, 224, 233, 267, 270
grace-preacher 70
Grapius, Zach 138
graveyard 229
greed 248
Greek and Roman churches 130
Greek church 146
Greeks 227
Guericke 190
Guerike 10
gymnastic 19

# Index

## H

Hanneken 151
Hartmann 10, 15, 28, 44, 97, 119, 201, 221, 225, 232, 234, 241, 245
Hausmann 67, 147, 278
Hausmann, Pastor Nikol 277
Hausmann, Valentin 28
heathen 97, 165, 166, 171
heaven 22, 43, 91, 112, 182, 268
Hedinger 219
hell 43, 80, 112, 202, 223, 268, 277
heresy 94, 97, 164, 248
heretical pastor 232
heretics 92, 93, 94, 97, 147, 164, 229, 237
Heshusius, Tilemann 21, 137, 246
heterodox 104, 232
hidden sins 240, 241, 242
higher education 270
hireling 40, 59, 66, 112, 202, 275, 276
holiness 10, 45, 73, 128
Hollaz 89
holy Baptism 37
Holy Ghost 93
holy Sacrament 125
Holy Scripture 13, 14
Holy Spirit 10, 11, 22, 29, 63, 74, 83, 85, 86, 87, 89, 91, 93, 95, 100, 103, 147, 185, 209, 223, 277
holy Supper 31, 32, 36, 37, 38, 39, 48, 125, 126, 129, 130, 131, 134, 135, 136, 137, 139, 146, 147, 148, 149, 150, 151, 186, 187, 189, 191, 192, 212, 217, 223, 235
home and foreign missions 270
home devotions 72
home visits 195, 196, 197, 198
homiletics 10, 60, 85
homosexuality 248
hospitals 270
hosts 130, 145, 147
house father 278, 279
humanism 82
humility 11, 20
Hunnius, Aegidius 181
hymn 144, 188, 207, 208, 223, 226
hymnals 56
Hyperius 143
hypocrisy 52, 66, 73, 79

## I

ill 214, 215
illness 145, 150, 162, 187, 199, 200, 201, 202, 204, 205, 207, 206, 208, 210, 222
illuminate 10, 11
image of God 68
Immersion 90
immorality 238
impenitent 62, 111, 112, 125, 201, 204, 208, 229
impenitent sinner 124, 233
impotence 162
imprisonment 181
impure spirit 216
Inability to consummate 161
inaugural sermon 52, 55
incest 162, 183, 184, 208, 248
infant Baptism 104
infirm 218
inheritance 154
initial or inaugural sermon 51
innovations 52
inquisition 123
insane 147, 161, 162, 182, 247
inspiration 71, 72
installed 49, 255, 278, 280
instruct 59, 63, 67, 73, 76, 98, 113, 114, 116, 120, 127, 144, 186, 188, 195, 196, 199, 206, 249, 262,
intention 92
involuntary divorce 178
irregenerate 62
Israel 33, 111, 164

## J

Jeremiah 61
Jerome 136
Jewish 98
Jews 32, 97, 141, 165, 227, 229
job description 255, 256
John the Baptist 16, 73
Jonas 13, 123, 235
Joseph 175
Judas 148
judgement 73, 80, 110, 112, 148, 153, 154, 175, 197, 224, 204
judgement seat 75

justification 72, 75, 80, 262
justifying faith 10

# K

keys 22, 23, 120
Kortholt, Christian 240, 280
Kromayer 96

# L

Large Catechism 238
Lassenius 214
last will 227
Law 53, 63, 65, 71, 74, 75, 80, 81, 117, 144, 152, 154, 163, 166, 180, 181, 208, 224, 241, 245, 249
Law and Gospel 53, 62, 63
law-driver 70
laws of marriage 154
laws of the state 155
lawsuits 56
lawyers 97
lay elders 254
lay hands 47
laying on of hands 44, 100, 185, 212, 217, 255
legal impediment 156
legalistic 80, 192
Lenaeus 261
leprosy 161
Lessing 53
levirate marriage 184
license 47
Liturgical 100
liturgy 10, 35, 60, 226
Loescher Val. Ernst 187, 240
loosing key 129
Lord's Day 189
Lord's Supper 136, 139
Lord's Table 108, 114, 115, 143 125, 141, 146, 147, 190
Lower Saxon Church Order 150
Luciferians 136
Luther 12, 11, 13, 14, 15, 16, 18, 19, 20, 21, 22, 23, 24, 25, 26, 28, 29, 30, 32, 33, 34, 36, 42, 43, 49, 61, 62, 66, 67, 68, 69, 71, 73, 74, 77, 78, 80, 81, 82, 84, 86, 89, 90, 96, 105, 106, 109, 111, 112, 114, 116, 117, 119, 121, 122, 123, 124,
126, 127, 129, 133, 134, 135, 136, 139, 140, 142, 143, 145, 146, 147, 152, 153, 166, 167, 168, 171, 175, 176, 178, 179, 180, 181, 182, 184, 187, 192, 202, 208, 215, 217, 219, 221, 222, 225, 231, 232, 235, 237, 238, 239, 264, 266, 271, 272, 275, 277, 278, 279, 280
Lutheran Church 33
Lutherans 33
Luther's Catechism 31, 34, 39, 116, 261
Luther's Table Talk 270

# M

Macedonians 94
magic 87, 94, 132, 133
magicians 132
major 103
major excommunication 237
major exorcism 100
Majorists 137
malicious deserter 162, 175, 177, 178, 179, 180, 181,
Manicheans 94
manifest sin 114, 204, 240, 241, 244, 246, 249
Mansfeld Agenda 187
marital 152, 153, 154, 171, 179, 181, 183
marital bond 152, 161
marriage 72, 97, 152, 153, 15 4, 155, 156, 157, 158, 159, 160, 161, 162, 163, 164, 165, 166, 167, 168, 169, 171, 172, 174, 175, 176, 177, 179, 181, 182, 183, 184, 251
marriage laws 152
marriage license 156
marry 152, 160, 164, 165, 166, 167, 168, 176, 178, 180, 181, 183
Martial 184
martyr 225
Masius, Andreas 15
materialism 82
Mathesius 223
means 8, 10, 125, 129, 131, 133, 134
means of grace 62, 108, 233, 234
meeting 192, 258, 260, 262, 270, 279,
Meisner Balthaser 123
Melanchthon Philip 13, 15, 85, 117,

# Index

123, 235
membership 32
membership list 262
Menzer 163, 171
mercy 70, 216
Methodist 14, 34, 107, 111, 148
mid-wives 105
Mine 62
minister 8, 10, 19, 22, 27, 28, 39, 40, 41, 42, 43, 48, 49, 94, 95, 97, 101, 1 08, 114, 118, 127, 131, 132, 138, 139, 144, 148, 152, 153, 154, 163, 196, 197, 198, 199, 200, 201, 203, 205, 212, 213, 214, 221, 227, 237, 234, 241, 249, 260, 266, 268, 270, 279
ministry 9, 52, 72, 104, 167, 279
minor 103, 156, 235
minor excommunication 237
minor exorcism 100
minutes 251
miracles 42
miscarriages 98
Misler, Joh. Nikolaus 28, 182
Missouri Synod 188, 190, 191
Moerlin 278
monasticism 82
monks 192
moral law 157, 158
Moravians 14
Mormons 165
mortal sin 123, 125
Moses 24, 29, 30
Mueling Mich 148
murder 208, 228
murderer 232, 278
Musaeus 236
musical clubs 191
Muslims 165

# N

Nathan 246
natural law 157, 166, 183
near of kin 157
Nestorian 35, 74
new man 70
Nic. Haas 214
Nicea 23
Noah 268

novels 191
nurseries 58

# O

oath 160, 280
Obscenity 215
offend 142, 149, 163, 175, 240, 244, 245
offense 37, 101, 104, 125, 143, 145, 193, 198, 219, 233, 234, 238, 240, 241, 244, 245, 246, 258, 261, 266, 268, 276
offensive sin 247
office 16, 17, 18, 19, 20, 21, 22, 23, 24, 26, 27, 28, 29, 30, 31, 34, 35, 39, 40, 41, 43, 44, 45, 46, 47, 48, 49, 50, 51, 52, 53, 55, 60, 61, 62, 65, 66, 68, 70, 76, 79, 82, 84, 108, 113, 114, 123, 125, 127, 129, 134, 135, 136, 153, 163, 195, 198, 201, 202, 222, 232, 233, 246, 254, 255, 256, 264, 266, 267, 269, 272, 273, 274, 275, 276, 277, 278, 279, 280
officers 222, 255, 256, 264, 279
official duties 218
old Adam 68, 74
old man 70, 102
Olearius 204, 206, 211, 214
ongregation 22
open 247
open and manifest sins 245
ordain 22, 45, 46, 47, 48, 49 134, 156, 212, 255
order 204
order of salvation 75
ordination 44, 47, 50, 53, 136
organizations 192
original sin 100, 103
orphanages 270
orphans 218, 221
orthodox 8, 13, 21, 31, 32, 33, 34, 35, 36, 45, 47, 53, 75, 93, 94, 108, 122, 126, 135, 136, 164, 171, 183, 231, 233, 234, 262, 265, 274, 280
orthodox agenda 171, 188
orthodox church 79, 90, 148, 234
orthodox congregation 33
orthodox judgment 153

289

orthodox pastor 32
orthodox synod 50, 273
orthodoxy 47, 79
Osiander 198
Osiander, Lukas 66
Our Father 61, 78, 100, 116, 118, 212, 217, 223

## P

pagan spouse 178
Pagans 229
Palm Sunday 189
Papacy 23, 115, 137, 216, 246, 263, 272
Papist 12, 15, 34, 48, 63, 78, 94, 95, 132, 136, 152, 174, 185, 186, 229, 232
Papistic monks 216
Papistic superstition 187
Papocaesarism 152
paralysis 162
parent 160, 161, 163, 168, 192
parental authority 96, 97
parental permission 156
parish 55, 92, 98, 231, 232, 233
parishioner 124, 124, 199, 231
parsonage 56
partiality 230
particular church 248
Passover 146
Pastor 51, 202, 266, 270
pastor 9, 12, 13, 20, 25, 28, 31, 32, 37, 38, 43, 46, 47, 55, 56, 58, 59, 60, 66, 73, 104, 105, 111, 112, 113, 114, 115, 117, 118, 123, 124, 125, 126, 137, 138, 140, 144, 150, 170, 175, 179, 188, 192, 195, 196, 199, 200, 201, 208, 217, 221, 227, 231, 232, 233, 235, 238, 239, 253, 255, 256, 259, 261, 262, 263, 274, 276, 277, 278
Pastoral Care 214, 223
pastoral care 58, 60, 108, 192, 204
Pastoral conferences 272
pastoral epistles 13
Pastoral Office 16, 59, 278,
pastoral sick calls 201, 203
pastorally 127
pastor's sermon 76
pastor's wife 274
patient 199, 203, 204, 205, 206, 207, 208, 209, 210
Paul 14, 44, 46, 69, 97, 110, 111, 113, 124, 154, 165, 177, 178, 219, 221, 240, 245, 266, 279
penance 82
penitent 52, 62, 79, 125, 126, 129, 137, 138, 175, 245
penitent confession 249
penitential psalms 208
Pentecost 74, 190
pericope 51, 53, 72
periodicals 270
persecute 221, 275, 276, 280
personal announcement 38
Peter 23, 112, 240
Petronius 127
Pfeiffer J. Glob. 195, 198
Pharisaical 219
Pharisees 73, 154
Photinians 94, 95
physical welfare 218
Pietists 57
pilgrimage 217
pious 40, 62, 70, 137, 154, 267, 277
plague 202, 277
Polycarp 276
polygamy 154, 165, 166
Pomeranus 13
Pommer 84
poor 56, 151, 199, 218, 219, 220, 221, 222, 227, 280
poor chest 221
poor-houses 219
Pope 15, 49, 73, 81, 82, 109, 121, 123, 152, 175, 237
Porta, Conrad 15, 90, 225
possessed 214, 215, 216, 217, 247
possessed by Satan 214
possessed person 217
posterity 273
poverty 227
practice 53
pray 11, 12, 85, 207, 251, 277
prayer 22, 51, 52, 60, 62, 72, 85, 100, 101, 102, 186, 187, 202, 212, 216, 217, 221, 223, 256, 260, 273
praying 220
preacher 12, 16, 72, 77, 225
preaching 42, 48, 60, 61, 66, 75, 76,

# Index

79, 80, 81, 84, 126, 195, 220, 221, 222, 236, 243, 260
preaching office 81, 254, 258, 260, 278
predecessor 57, 58
Premature children 98
presbyters 257, 258
presbytery 254, 255
president 258
priesthood 22, 135
priests 216
prison 144, 225, 229
private 60
private Absolution 120, 123
private Communion 134, 213
private Communion of the sick 35
private confession 35, 115, 116, 123 118, 120, 121, 124
private confession and Absolution 38, 122
private pastoral care 195, 197, 198
private sins 239
Privatseelsorge 195, 198
procuring a divorce 177
property 264
prophecy 255
Prophet Ezekiel 111
prophets 10, 11, 18, 24, 25, 61, 64, 65, 71, 187, 215, 280
prostitution 248
Protestants 107, 187
providence 52
Pruckner 144
psalms 208
pseudo-Lutherans 141
public confession 249
public offense 163, 245, 249
Public repentance 246
public sins 242, 244
public worship 195, 201, 208, 226, 252, 254
pulpit 85, 198, 246, 263, 279
pulpit orator 61
pure 34, 237
pure books 37
pure doctrine 33, 35, 79, 236, 262, 268, 271, 277

## Q

Quasimodogeniti 189, 190

Quenstedt, J. A. 61, 134, 215, 225
Quistorp Dr. J. 187
quorum 259

## R

Rambach, F. E. 49, 52, 56, 91, 225
Rambach, Joh. Jak. 63
rationalism 82
re-baptism 96
Reason 82
rebellion 248
Rebhahn Nicholas 245
reconciled 54, 56, 146, 149, 150, 167, 175, 180, 181, 232, 244, 245, 252
record 260
redeemed 122, 223
redemption 73, 74, 122
Reformation 236, 237
Reformed 14, 34, 35, 98, 111, 130, 131, 132, 142, 148, 229
Reformed Beza 130
regenerate 10, 91, 109, 146, 261
Regensburg Colloquy 187
relief funds 219
remarry 166, 167, 179, 180
repentance 26, 64, 72, 75, 77, 80, 109, 112, 113, 125, 126, 132, 148, 167, 174, 206, 215, 223, 224, 225, 229, 230, 233, 242, 244, 245, 246, 252
repentant confession 252
repentant sinner 245
reputation 242
resolution 259, 260, 264
restitution 146, 151
restored 150
resurrection 102
Rhegius 14
righteousness 45, 67, 76, 215, 240
robbery 278
Roman 50, 148, 227
Roman Catholics 229
Roman Church 47, 135, 169
Rudelbach 10, 12, 102, 105, 141
Rudelbach, Dr. 9

## S

Sabellians 95
Sacrament 17, 22, 32, 34, 36, 38, 39,

291

47, 48, 66, 87, 88, 96, 97, 101, 103, 108, 109, 110, 111, 112, 113, 115, 116, 118, 124, 130, 131, 132, 133, 134, 135, 137, 138, 139, 140, 142, 143, 144, 145, 146, 147, 148, 149, 151, 152, 154, 186 185, 187, 195, 199, 200, 201, 221, 229, 235, 237, 245, 248, 268, 273
Sacrament of the Altar 139
sacramental action 90, 131, 144
sacramental union 134
Sacramentarians 140, 237
sacrilege 277, 278
sacristy 145
salary 40, 42, 43, 274
salvation 9, 20, 36, 44, 46, 48, 52, 53, 54, 66, 71, 72, 75, 80, 82, 83, 92, 96, 109, 110, 114, 116, 195, 196, 199, 204, 208, 215, 225, 228, 229, 235, 238, 240, 241, 272
sanctification 71, 73, 75, 204, 206
sanctified 223
Satan 71, 103, 115, 198, 201, 214, 215, 217, 275
Saul 266
Saxon General Articles 123, 199, 252
Scherzer, J. A. 87
schismatic 44, 50
Scholastics 136
school 31, 39, 55, 58, 59, 66, 121, 254, 279
school books 37
school teacher 58, 270, 272
schoolmaster 56, 59, 192, 227
Schulze 217
Schwaermer 17, 130
Schwaermerei 108
Schwaermergeist 16, 36, 116
schwaermerisch 70
Schwenkfeldians 137, 234
Scriptural 154, 158
Scripture 11, 13, 14, 31, 39, 45, 46, 47, 49, 63, 64, 71, 73, 74, 79, 83, 88, 93, 103, 113, 120, 154, 157, 175, 188, 206, 207, 208, 227, 245, 261, 262, 273
seal 185
seal of confession 127, 128
second marriage 183
secret 129

secret and hidden sins 123
secret betrothals 160
secret sins 117, 123
secret societies 82, 218, 219
secretary 260
sect 25, 34, 72, 75, 188
sectarian 17, 20, 108
securely 208
Seelsorge 195
Seelsorger 32, 37, 108, 111, 112, 137, 140, 192, 202
seelsorgerisch 127
Seidel 48, 49, 51, 54, 55, 56, 58, 91, 102, 142, 141, 143, 145, 174, 193, 204, 210, 223, 225, 230
self-denial 194
self-examination 147
self-excluded 250
self-righteousness 80, 208
seminaries 58, 270
separated 180, 219
separatism 50
Separatist 148, 273, 50
sermon 52, 61, 62, 63, 64, 65, 67, 70, 75, 79, 80, 81, 82, 83, 84, 109, 110, 121, 131, 144, 198, 208, 225, 230
sexual immorality 161, 162, 174, 177, 266
Sexual unfaithfulness 160
sick 55, 56, 145, 182, 183, 196, 199, 200, 203, 212, 218, 221, 222, 225
sick bed 204, 208
sick call 208
sick communicants 142
sick person 183, 199, 200, 203, 205, 207, 208, 212, 213
sigillum confessionis 127
sign of the cross 102, 141, 185
Simon Magus 261
sin 17, 36, 42, 47, 63, 66, 68, 70, 73, 74, 79, 81, 82, 109, 110, 111, 112, 113, 114, 117, 118, 122, 123, 124, 125, 126, 128, 129, 131, 137, 138, 140, 141, 148, 150, 163, 174, 208, 215, 223, 224, 232, 233, 237, 239, 240, 241, 242, 243, 244, 245, 246, 247, 248, 249, 252, 266, 268, 276
sin against the Holy Spirit 72

# Index

sin-inventing 175
sinful custom 211
sinful flesh 68
sinner 108, 198, 223, 240, 246, 249
sinners 208, 237, 247, 266, 267
sinners to repentance 198
sins of weakness 245, 266
slander 239
Smalcald 123
Smalcald Articles 21, 49, 151, 237
Small Catechism 188
Socinian 95, 229
Solomon 24, 192
Son 11, 86, 87, 93, 94, 100, 103, 111
Sonntag, Christoph 15
sorcery 248
soul 8, 28, 47, 48, 54, 55, 59, 65, 75, 80, 83, 85, 96, 110, 112, 113, 117, 178, 185, 193, 196, 198, 199, 201, 219, 220, 221, 224, 231, 268, 269, 275,
soul-carers 202
sound doctrine 45, 236
Spangenberg's 12
Spener 54, 83, 187
sphragis 185
Spirit 16, 19, 22, 69, 216, 275
Spirit of God 14, 46
spiritual priesthood 135
sponsors 35, 98, 99, 100, 102, 104, 235
spouse 157, 162, 163, 166, 169, 174, 175, 176, 177, 178, 179, 180, 181, 182, 183, 266
St. Paul 13, 17, 18, 22, 25, 36, 40, 42, 61, 65, 67, 68, 74, 76, 136, 180, 181, 231, 267, 271, 279
St. Peter 232
state 219, 242, 244, 254
state church 219, 236, 257
state poor institutions 219
steward 113, 114, 123, 195
Struensee, Adam 52
study 60
subscription 49
suffering a divorce 177
suicidal thoughts 214
suicide 227, 228, 229
superstition 101, 102, 186, 217, 248
superstitious ritual 186
supervision 188, 192, 195, 254

Supper 35, 88, 107, 108, 109, 110, 111, 115, 116, 117, 118, 119, 125, 132, 133, 137, 140, 141, 143, 144, 145, 146, 213
suspend 125, 126, 149, 150, 235, 245, 246
Swedenborgians 95
symbolical books 49
symbolical writings 31, 34
synagogue 263
syncretism 248
synod 38, 50, 156, 188, 235, 270, 273
synodical association 270
Synodical Membership 270
synods 272

## T

Tarnov, Paul 45, 94
teacher 10, 279
temperance fanatics 130
temptation 11, 12, 69, 77, 200, 204, 214, 280
Ten Commandments 78, 116, 118
Tertullian 10, 102, 104, 185, 275
testament 131
thanksgiving 145, 171
The Apology 246
the laying on of hands 223
theater 191
thief 125, 232, 266, 278
Thirty Year's War 187
Thomas 15
timely preaching 81
Timothy 35, 241, 269
transfers 49
trial sermon 276
trials 214
tribulation 70
Trinity 86, 87, 93, 94
Triune God 105
Turks 32, 137, 229, 272

## U

unalterable 264
Unaltered Augsburg Confession 31, 34, 39, 261
unbelief 67, 68, 82, 122, 136, 139, 164, 166, 218, 219
unconsecrated 145
Union-Evangelical 34, 111

Unionist 141, 148
Unitarians 95
unjustly 233
unrepentant sinner 248
unworthy communicants 111
unworthy reception 111, 125
usurer 72, 74, 112, 113, 115, 248

## V

vacancy 56
Valentinians 94
vestments 35, 213
viaticum 213
violence 215
visible 248
visible church 248
visit 198, 201, 203, 208, 210, 214, 225
visiting the sick 43, 201, 202, 210, 221, 222
visitor 43
voluntary divorce 177
vote 257, 258, 259, 260, 262, 264
voting member 258, 262
vow 190, 280

## W

war 164
weakness 122, 138, 241, 247, 274
wedding 152, 156, 161, 163, 169, 170, 171, 172
Weimar Bible 261
Welfare 218
Weller, Hieronymus 71
Wesley, John 14
widow 163, 166, 168, 218, 221
widowed adulterer 166
widowed father 161
widower 166
Wigand 167
witnesses 96, 156, 160
Wolferinus, Simon 145
Word 10, 11, 16, 17,19, 22, 23, 28, 30, 33, 34, 40, 41, 42, 44, 45, 46, 56, 61, 63, 65, 66, 70, 72, 73, 76, 87, 88, 89, 92, 97, 108, 109, 111, 112, 135,136, 138, 139, 140, 164, 175, 195, 196, 201, 205, 221, 222, 236, 248, 255, 256, 268, 269, 271, 275, 276
Word of God 17, 23, 24, 46, 82, 83, 141, 201, 218
Words of Institution 90, 94, 95, 131, 132, 133, 134, 139, 140
works 17, 65
worldly government 219
worship 55, 110, 191, 226
worship service 191, 192, 279
wrath 62, 112, 117, 150, 204, 224, 242, 245
wrath and judgment 18
written Word 81
Wuertemberg Church Order 200

## Y

young people 78, 192
youth 58, 59, 118, 191, 192

## Z

Zwinglian 32, 133, 139, 145
Zwinglian Doctrine 121

# *Bible Passages*

## A

Act. 2:41; 8:27-39  92
Acts 1:15, 23-26  257
Acts 13:1  26
Acts 13:2  255
Acts 14:22  70
Acts 15:22  255, 257
Acts 15:6  258
Acts 16:3  35
Acts 17:15-34  76
Acts 18:27  262
Acts 19:16  215
Acts 2:38; 10:48  88
Acts 2:38; 10:48; 19:5  87
Acts 2:38ff.; 8:37ff.  101
Acts 2:39  92
Acts 20:20  55
Acts 20:20, 26-27  60
Acts 20:20, 31  196
Acts 20:20-21, 26-27  72
Acts 20:28  26, 196, 231, 266
Acts 21-23  76
Acts 22:16  89, 90
Acts 24:24-25  197
Acts 26:22  60
Acts 26:22-29  53
Acts 5:9  275
Acts 6:1  220
Acts 6:1ff.  220, 222
Acts 6:1ff.; 11:30; 12:25; 24:17; Rom. 12:8, 13  218
Acts 6:2  257
Acts 6:3  255
Acts 6:4  269
Acts 8:1; 9:25; 13:51  275
Acts 8:13ff.  261
Acts 8:18-24  246
Acts 8:2  226
Acts 8:36; 10:49  88
Acts 9:25  276

## C

Col. 1:11  269
Col. 3:21  192
Col. 4:17  257, 279
1 Cor. 1:10  32
1 Cor. 1:10-13  57
1 Cor. 1:10-13; 11:18-19  50
1 Cor. 1:13  88
1 Cor. 1:21-25; 2:1-5; 4:1-2  53
1 Cor. 1:27-28  221
1 Cor. 1[:11]  124
1 Cor. 10:16  132
1 Cor. 10:17  110
1 Cor. 10:2  89
1 Cor. 10:21  110
1 Cor. 10:31  10
1 Cor. 11:16  258
1 Cor. 11:26  110
1 Cor. 11:27  111
1 Cor. 11:27, 29  110
1 Cor. 11:28  188, 190
1 Cor. 11:28-29  146
1 Cor. 11:29  148
1 Cor. 11[:18]  124
1 Cor. 12:13  261
1 Cor. 12:28  26, 254, 255, 258
1 Cor. 12:7  274
1 Cor. 12:7 ff.; 14:32  13
1 Cor. 12:8ff.  273
1 Cor. 14  18
1 Cor. 14:20  269
1 Cor. 14:30  258
1 Cor. 14:34-35  257

1 Cor. 14:40  23, 144
1 Cor. 15  20
1 Cor. 15:12ff  65
1 Cor. 15:58  19
1 Cor. 15:8-10  20
1 Cor. 16:15-16  27
1 Cor. 16:3  40
1 Cor. 16:9  19
1 Cor. 3:1-2  60, 77
1 Cor. 3:22-23  279
1 Cor. 3:22-23; 9:16  279
1 Cor. 3:5  279
1 Cor. 3:9  196
1 Cor. 4:1  38, 72, 107, 113, 134
1 Cor. 4:15  70, 192
1 Cor. 4:17; 9:17  275
1 Cor. 4:1ff  27
1 Cor. 4:2  46
1 Cor. 5  249
1 Cor. 5:1  157
1 Cor. 5:1-13  249
1 Cor. 5:1-2, 13  240
1 Cor. 5:1-5  247
1 Cor. 5:1-5, 9-13  234
1 Cor. 5:11  247, 248
1 Cor. 5:11, 13  113
1 Cor. 5:13  247
1 Cor. 5:2, 4, 13  250
1 Cor. 5:2; 6:2; 10:15; 12:7  257
1 Cor. 5:4  257
1 Cor. 5:5  214
1 Cor. 5:6  271
1 Cor. 5:9-13;
1 Cor. 5[:1]  124
1 Cor. 6:1-8  249
1 Cor. 7  180
1 Cor. 7:10-11  180
1 Cor. 7:10ff  154
1 Cor. 7:13-14  165
1 Cor. 7:14  96, 97
1 Cor. 7:15  177, 178
1 Cor. 7:16  165
1 Cor. 7:20  280
1 Cor. 7:36-38  160
1 Cor. 7:39  164
1 Cor. 7:4-5  180
1 Cor. 9:1-14  40
1 Cor. 9:19-23  55
1 Cor. 9:7  40
1 Cor. 9:7-15  43

2 Chron. 18-22  165
2 Cor. 1:24  72
2 Cor. 1:24; 4:5  279
2 Cor. 1:24; 4:5-6; 5:17-21  53
2 Cor. 1:3-7  71
2 Cor. 10:15-16  231
2 Cor. 11:33  275, 276
2 Cor. 13:10  274
2 Cor. 13:3  19
2 Cor. 2:12  19
2 Cor. 2:16  29
2 Cor. 2:16; 3:5-6  10
2 Cor. 2:6  257
2 Cor. 2:6 [sic, 7]  245
2 Cor. 2:6-11  234, 252
2 Cor. 2:6-8  257
2 Cor. 3:2  19
2 Cor. 3:5  9
2 Cor. 3:6  75
2 Cor. 5:19-21  54
2 Cor. 5:20  19
2 Cor. 6:14 ff.  32
2 Cor. 6:14-18  113, 261
2 Cor. 6:3  266
2 Cor. 8:21  198
2 Cor. 8:8  257

# D

Deut. 13:1-4  24
Deut. 15:4  219
Deut. 17:6; 19:5  104
Deut. 21:11  164
Deut. 21:18-21  247
Deut. 25:5  184
Deut. 27:20-23  157
Deut. 4:2  73
Deut. 7:3  160
Deut. 7:3-4  164

# E

Eph 4:11  55
Eph. 4:10-12  275
Eph. 4:11  26, 107, 196
Eph. 4:13-14  77
Eph. 4:22-28  68
Eph. 4:3  50, 270
Eph. 4:3-6  261
Eph. 4[:8]  22
Eph. 5:25-26  261

# Bible Passages

Eph. 5:26  88
Eph. 6:4  247
Ex. 12:48  146
Ex. 12:48  110
Ex. 22:17  160
Ex. 24:8  89
Ex. 3:1  24
Ex. 34:16  164
Ex. 4:10-14  29
Ex. 4:11  275
Ezek. 18:20  98
Ezek. 18:4  248
Ezek. 3:17-21  107
Ezek. 3:17; 33:7-8  196
Ezek. 3:17ff.  80
Ezek. 33:1ff  47
Ezek. 34  198
Ezek. 34:1-16  199
Ezek. 34:16  55
Ezek. 34:4  221

## G

Gal. 1:1  20
Gal. 1:1-2  17
Gal. 1:2  247
Gal. 1:8-9  65
Gal. 2:10  221
Gal. 2:13-14  240
Gal. 2:3-5  35, 130
Gal. 2:4-5  90, 261
Gal. 2:9-10  218, 220, 221
Gal. 4:10-12  65
Gal. 5:1  36
Gal. 5:10  65
Gal. 5:17  69
Gal. 5:6  45
Gal. 5:9  65
Gal. 6:2  115, 247, 272
Gal. 6:6  41, 42, 43
Gen. 17:7  228
Gen. 2:22  171
Gen. 2:24  157, 159
Gen. 29:21  160, 161
Gen. 3:19  227
Gen. 37:27  159
Gen. 38:1; 41, 45  164
Gen. 39:5-6  43
Gen. 6:2; 26:34f  165

## H

Heb. 1:1  19
Heb. 10:22  89
Heb. 13:17  27, 107, 112, 196
Heb. 13:4  171
Heb. 13:7, 17, 24  255
Heb. 5:11-6:2  60, 77
Heb. 5:4  134
Heb. 5:4-5  16
Heb. 9:19  89
Hos. 4:6  26

## I

Is. 30:20-21  275
Is. 38:1  199
Is. 38:1-22  208
Is. 38:1ff  210
Is. 40:1-2  71
Is. 40:2  54
Is. 41:27  26
Is. 49:2; 51:16  19
Is. 52:8  196
Is. 53:9  226
Is. 56:10  112
Is. 57:1  14
Is. 59:21  19
Is. 6:8  25
Is. 66:13  70
Is. 8:20  259
Isaiah 49:22-23  42

## J

James 1:27  218
James 2:1-9  55
James 3:1  16
James 3:2  115, 247
James 5:14  55
James 5:14-15  199
Jer. 1:17  275
Jer. 1:4-8  29
Jer. 15:19  26
Jer. 22:18-19  226, 229
Jer. 23:21  16, 274
Jer. 23:28  60
Jer. 48:10  61
Jer. 6:17  196
Job 33:15-30  208

John 1:16-17   74
John 1:25   19
John 1:47   33
John 10:1   24
John 10:10   17
John 10:3   19, 55
John 10:8   232
John 12:42-43; 9:34-37   231
John 13:21ff.   247
John 14:23   23
John 15:27   75
John 16:2-3   231
John 16:23   216
John 17:20-21   53
John 19:19-22   141
John 19:30   142
John 21:15   55
John 3:5   88
John 5:1-16   208
John 6:37   231
John 6:53   146
John 8:47   84
John 8:59   276
John 8:59; 15:19   275
Jonah 1:4   275
Joshua 23:12   164
Judges 3:5-7   165
1 John 2:13   55
1 John 2:19   247, 250
1 John 4:1   65
2 John 10-11   32, 113, 261
2 John 9-11   247
3 John 10   231
3 John 8-10   262

## K

1 Kings 11:2-4   164
1 Kings 13:24   275
1 Kings 16:31   165
2 Kings 23:18   230
2 Kings 5:20ff   42

## L

Lev. 18   158
Lev. 18:1-30; 20:10-23   157
Lev. 18:14; 20:20   157
Lev. 18:16; 20:21   184
Lev. 18:18   158
Lev. 18:20-23   158
Lev. 18:6   158
Lev. 18:9   158
Luke 1:2   72
Luke 1:3   60
Luke 1:70   19
Luke 1:76   19
Luke 10:16   19, 27
Luke 10:4-8   43
Luke 11:26   73
Luke 12:14   154
Luke 12:42   60
Luke 15:11-32   208
Luke 15:4   198
Luke 16:1-2   114
Luke 16[:1]   123
Luke 17:3   125
Luke 17:3-4   244
Luke 17:4   243
Luke 17;3-4   245
Luke 18:13   224
Luke 2:41-42   188
Luke 22:12   131
Luke 22:20-23   148
Luke 23   223
Luke 23:38   141
Luke 24:27   72
Luke 3:2   17
Luke 3:8   72
Luke 4:28ff.   275
Luke 4:30   276
Luke 6:29   277
Luke 9:62   280

## M

Mal. 2:14   171
Mal. 2:7   46
Matt, 18:15   240
Matt, 19:3   154
Matt. 5:23-25   149
Matt. 1:18-20   161
Matt. 1:19   175
Matt. 10:10   42
Matt. 10:11   198
Matt. 10:22   26, 280
Matt. 10:23   275, 276
Matt. 10:30   203
Matt. 10:32-33   261
Matt. 10:8   42
Matt. 11:28   200, 231

# Bible Passages

Matt. 11:5  221
Matt. 12:45  73
Matt. 13:52  46
Matt. 14:12  226
Matt. 14:3-4  157
Matt. 16:18-19  95
Matt. 16:19  112
Matt. 16:3  60
Matt. 16:6  65
Matt. 18  240, 243
Matt. 18:15  246
Matt. 18:15-17  238, 247, 255
Matt. 18:15-17; 7:6  234
Matt. 18:15-20  67, 126
Matt. 18:15; 5:23-24  244
Matt. 18:15ff  241
Matt. 18:17  113, 247, 250, 257, 264
Matt. 18:17-18  231, 257, 261
Matt. 18:19-20  23
Matt. 18:20  22
Matt. 18[:15]  239
Matt. 19:5  159
Matt. 19:8  152
Matt. 19:9  175, 177
Matt. 2:13; 10:16, 22; 12:15; 14:13  275
Matt. 2:13; 12:15  276
Matt. 20:25-26  257
Matt. 22:11-14  115
Matt. 23:24  73
Matt. 23:8  27
Matt. 24:5  86
Matt. 25:36  55
Matt. 25:36ff  199
Matt. 26  132
Matt. 26:12  227
Matt. 26:12-13  226
Matt. 26:29  130
Matt. 28:19  87, 88, 94, 100
Matt. 28:19; 3:11  86
Matt. 4:4  71
Matt. 5  150
Matt. 5:13  83
Matt. 5:23  213
Matt. 5:23-25; 18:28ff.  125
Matt. 5:31-32  154
Matt. 5:40  277
Matt. 7:12; 25:30  275
Matt. 7:22-23  273
Matt. 7:6  38, 107, 113
Matt. 8:22  230

Matt. 8:26; 17:15  215

# N

Neh. 13:23ff  164
Num. 30:4-6  160
Num. 35:30  104, 248

# P

Phil. 1:3-11  269
Phil. 3:1  75
Phil. 3:2  65
Phil. 4:3  101
Prov. 11:13  129
Prov. 12:15  274
Prov. 18:1  50
Prov. 22:13  275
Prov. 7:13  191
Ps. 101:6-7  266
Ps. 119:32  71
Ps. 121[:8]  102
Ps. 34:9  54
Ps. 66:18  116
Ps. 68:12  26
Ps. 8:3  26
Psalm 119  11
Psalm 23  213
Psalm 32:3-5  209
Psalm 82  232
1 Pet. 2:2  190
1 Pet. 2:9  22
1 Pet. 3:21  89
1 Pet. 4:11  60
1 Pet. 4:15  232
1 Pet. 5:1-  266
1 Pet. 5:1-3  257
1 Pet. 5:1-4  27
1 Pet. 5:2  196
1 Pet. 5:2-3  46
1 Pet. 5:2; 4:15  231
1 Pet. 5:3  231
1 Pet. 5:5  257
2 Pet. 1:5-7  45
2 Pet. 3:18  269

# R

Rev. 2 and 3  208
Rev. 2:15  65

Rev. 2:2, 14-15, 20   234
Rom. 1:16-17; 15:29-33   53
Rom. 1:5   86
Rom. 10:15   16, 134, 231
Rom. 12:1   69
Rom. 12:1-5   70
Rom. 12:10   258
Rom. 12:21   274
Rom. 12:4-8   275
Rom. 12:6   273
Rom. 12:7   60, 279
Rom. 12:8   254, 255, 258
Rom. 14:1ff.   247
Rom. 15:4   45, 63, 70, 71
Rom. 16:17   32, 113, 247
Rom. 16:25-26   64
Rom. 2:16   240
Rom. 4:11   32, 110
Rom. 5:20   208
Rom. 6:2ff   74
Rom. 6:3-4   89
Rom. 6:6   102
Rom. 7:1-3   177

## S

Sirach 38:25-39:15   269
Sirach 39:1   269
Sirach 39ff   40
Sirach 7:39   199
1 Sam. 2   266

## T

Titus 1:6   45
Titus 1:6-9; 2:7-   266
Titus 1:7   266
Titus 1:9   45, 46
Titus 1:9-11   65
Titus 3:10-11   113, 247
Titus 3:5-6   89
Tobit 1:19-21   226
1 Thess. 2:10[-11]   55, 196
1 Thess. 2:13   53
1 Thess. 2:2   275
1 Thess. 2:7   70, 192
1 Thess. 4:11-12   218, 219
1 Thess. 5:12-13   27
1 Thess. 5:22   198

1 Tim. 1:20   214
1 Tim. 1:20; 3:5; 5:20   234
1 Tim. 1:3; 3:13   275
1 Tim. 1:7   45
1 Tim. 2:8-15   257
1 Tim. 3:1   25, 46, 107
1 Tim. 3:1-10   266
1 Tim. 3:10   44
1 Tim. 3:2   45, 65, 266
1 Tim. 3:4-5   266
1 Tim. 3:8-12   255
1 Tim. 4:12-13   12, 46, 269
1 Tim. 4:14   19, 255
1 Tim. 4:16   10, 19, 27, 266
1 Tim. 4:4   171
1 Tim. 5   255
1 Tim. 5:1   67
1 Tim. 5:1-2   198
1 Tim. 5:1-3   55
1 Tim. 5:10   218
1 Tim. 5:17   27, 42, 43, 254, 255, 258
1 Tim. 5:20   240, 241, 245, 249, 257
1 Tim. 5:22   44, 47, 111, 125
1 Tim. 5[:22]   124
1 Tim. 6:3-5   113
1 Timothy   13
2 Thess. 2:3   175
2 Thess. 3:14   113
2 Thess. 3:14-15   234, 247
2 Thess. 3:15   257
2 Thess. 3:6   113
2 Tim. 1:13; 3:14-15, 17   46
2 Tim. 1:6   46
2 Tim. 1:8   33, 261
2 Tim. 2:1   46
2 Tim. 2:15   46, 60, 62
2 Tim. 2:15, 25-26   112
2 Tim. 2:17   65
2 Tim. 2:2   44, 45
2 Tim. 2:24   55, 65
2 Tim. 3:1-5   113
2 Tim. 3:16   45, 65, 71
2 Tim. 3:16-17   9, 60, 63
2 Tim. 3:17   9
2 Tim. 3:6   198
2 Tim. 4:14-15   261
2 Tim. 4:2-3   27, 76
2 Tim. 4:3   44
2 Tim. 4:5   75
2 Tim. 4:7   280

## Translator

John M. Drickamer, a lifelong Lutheran, was raised in the suburbs of Cleveland, Ohio. He was educated at Lutheran parochial schools through the eighth grade. In 1971 he received the B.A. degree from Capital University, with majors in philosophy, history, and ancient languages. His seminary education was at Concordia Theological Seminary, Springfield, Illinois (now located at Fort Wayne, Indiana), from which he received the M. Div. degree in 1975. His vicarage was at Zion Lutheran Church, Chamberlain, South Dakota, in 1973 and 1974.

In 1978 Drickamer received the Th.D. degree from Concordia Seminary, St. Louis, majoring in historical theology. From 1977 to 1980 he taught courses in theology and religious history at Concordia College, Ann Arbor, Michigan. From 1980 to 1986 he was pastor of Immanuel Lutheran Church, Georgetown, Ontario, Canada, and also taught theology at Concordia Lutheran Theological Seminary in St. Catharines, Ontario. Since returning to the United States he has served churches in Illinois, Kansas and Oregon.

Drickamer has published over nine hundred items, including books, poems, hymns, translations, scripts, sermons and short stories.

# Additional Items Available

### Pewter Statue of C.F.W. Walther
Stands 2 and one half inches tall and is hand painted.
**$12.95**


### Law and Gospel
by CFW Walther
Selected writings of CFW Walther as translated by Herber J.A. Bouman and edited by Aug. R. Suelflow.
192 pages (hardcover)
**$15.50**


### The Proper Distinction between Law and Gospel
by CFW Walther
A translation of the German edition of 1897 by WHT Dau with a foreword by Jaroslav Pelikan.
426 pages (hardcover)
**$16.00**


### Christian News Encyclopedia
*by Herman Otten*
This five volume set includes some of today's best and most up-to-date articles by leading scholars on such subjects as the pastoral ministry, death, confirmation, marriage, divorce, the call of the pastor, sermons, etc. It also includes such subjects as abortion, alcoholism, Baptists, Bible, birth control, capital punishment, church growth, communion, evolution, drugs, gambling, homosexuals, Jews, music, pornagraphy, racism, sports, war, women, worship and more.
Over 4000 pages (five volumes)
**$75.95**
(please call for individual volume pricing)

## Prefer to use your credit card?
## 1-573-237-3110

**Fax:** (573)237-3858
**E-MAIL:** cnmail@fidnet.com
Or Return To: Lutheran News, 3277 Boeuf Lutheran Rd, New Haven, MO 63068

☐ My check, money order or cash is enclosed.

☐ Please charge $ _____ to my:

MasterCard ☐   Visa ☐

Card #   \_\_\_\_ - \_\_\_\_ - \_\_\_\_ - \_\_\_\_

Exp. Date   \_\_\_\_ / \_\_\_\_

Signature ————————————————

Daytime Phone (\_\_\_) ————————————

| Quantity | Description | Price | Total |
|---|---|---|---|
|  | Pastoral Theology | $ 7.99 |  |
|  |  |  |  |
|  |  |  |  |
|  |  |  |  |

Items Total  _____

Shipping (10% of Items Total)  _____

Grand Total  _____

## Prefer to use your credit card?
## 1-573-237-3110

**Fax:** (573)237-3858
**E-MAIL:** cnmail@fidnet.com
Or Return To: Lutheran News, 3277 Boeuf Lutheran Rd, New Haven, MO 63068

☐ My check, money order or cash is enclosed.

☐ Please charge $ _____ to my:

MasterCard ☐   Visa ☐

Card #  ____ - ____ - ____ - ____

Exp. Date  ____ / ____

Signature _____

Daytime Phone (____) _____

| Quantity | Description | Price | Total |
|----------|-------------|-------|-------|
|          | Pastoral Theology | $ 7.99 |  |
|          |             |       |       |
|          |             |       |       |
|          |             |       |       |
|          |             | Items Total | _____ |
|          | Shipping (10% of Items Total) | | _____ |
|          |             | Grand Total | _____ |

**Prefer to use your credit card?**
**1-573-237-3110**
**Fax:** (573)237-3858
**E-MAIL:** cnmail@fidnet.com
Or Return To: Lutheran News, 3277 Boeuf Lutheran Rd, New Haven, MO 63068

☐ My check, money order or cash is enclosed.

☐ Please charge $ _____ to my:

MasterCard ☐    Visa ☐

Card #   ____ - ____ - ____ - ____

Exp. Date   ____ / ____

Signature _____

Daytime Phone (____) _____

| Quantity | Description | Price | Total |
|---|---|---|---|
| | Pastoral Theology | $ 7.99 | |
| | | | |
| | | | |
| | | | |

Items Total  _____

Shipping (10% of Items Total)  _____

Grand Total  _____

## Prefer to use your credit card?
## 1-573-237-3110

**Fax:** (573)237-3858
**E-MAIL:** cnmail@fidnet.com
Or Return To: Lutheran News, 3277 Boeuf Lutheran Rd,
New Haven, MO 63068

☐ My check, money order or cash is enclosed.

☐ Please charge $ _____ to my:

MasterCard ☐    Visa ☐

Card #  ____ - ____ - ____ - ____

Exp. Date  ____ /____

Signature  _____

Daytime Phone (____) _____

| Quantity | Description | Price | Total |
|---|---|---|---|
|  | Pastoral Theology | $ 7.99 |  |
|  |  |  |  |
|  |  |  |  |
|  |  |  |  |

Items Total  _____

Shipping (10% of Items Total)  _____

Grand Total  _____